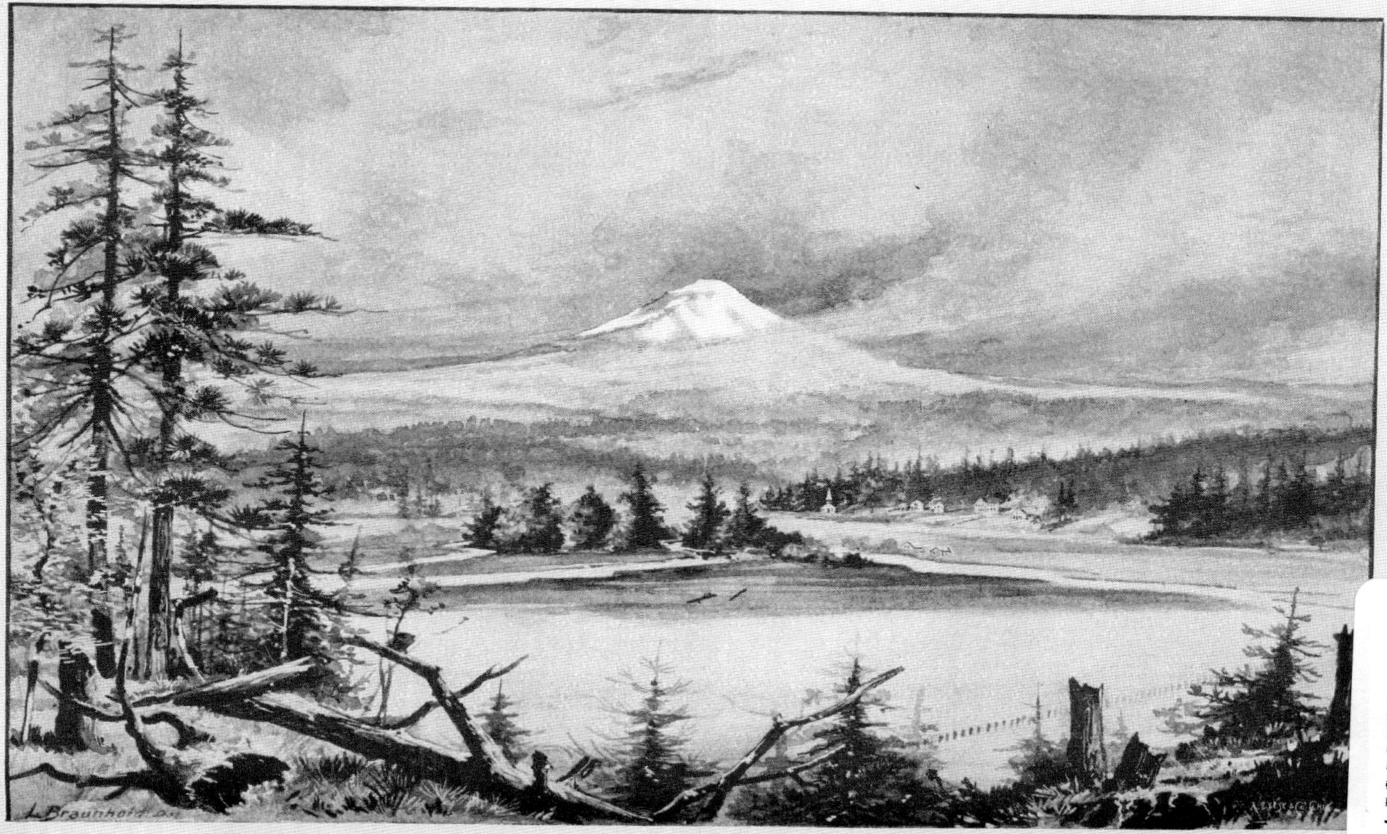

THE TIDE FLATS, THE INDIAN RESERVATION, THE FOOT HILLS AND MOUNT TACOMA. (14,444 FEET HIGH.)

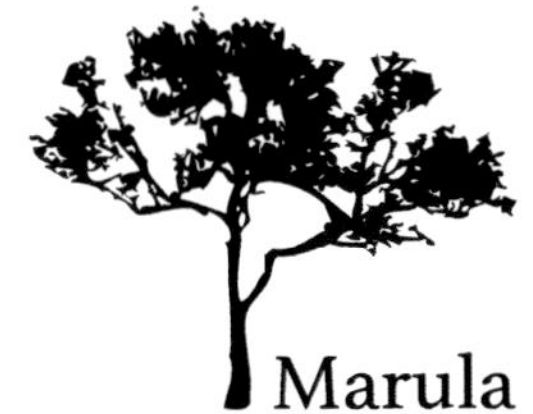

An imprint of Arcadia Publishing

Tacoma Illustrated
A Careful Compilation of the Resources, Terminal Advantages, Institutions, Climate, Business, and Manufacturing Industries of the "City of Destiny"

Published under the Auspices of the Tacoma Chamber of Commerce

A Marula Historical Reprint
Originally published in 1889

Published by Arcadia Publishing
Charleston SC

ISBN 978-0-7385-9488-0

Printed in the United States of America

For all general information contact Arcadia Publishing at:
Telephone 843-853-2070
Fax 843-853-0044
E-mail sales@arcadiapublishing.com
For customer service and orders:
Toll-Free 1-888-313-2665

Visit us on the Internet at www.arcadiapublishing.com

TACOMA ILLUSTRATED

PUBLISHED UNDER THE AUSPICES OF THE

TACOMA CHAMBER OF COMMERCE

A CAREFUL COMPILATION OF THE RESOURCES, TERMINAL ADVANTAGES, INSTITUTIONS, CLIMATE, BUSINESS, AND MANUFACTURING INDUSTRIES OF THE "CITY OF DESTINY."

FINELY ILLUSTRATED THROUGHOUT BY PROMINENT ARTISTS.

PUBLISHERS:
BALDWIN, CALCUTT & CO.
184 AND 186 MONROE ST., CHICAGO.

SOLE AGENT:
CHAS. H. HERALD,
TACOMA, WASH.

PRESS OF THE BLAKELY PRINTING CO., CHICAGO.

. . . Tacoma · Illustrated . . .

THE work herewith presented needs little introduction to the citizens of Tacoma, but to the public at large, whose hands it is destined to reach, some explanation may not be out of place.

The object of the publication is the embodiment, in concise and correct form, of the rise and progress of a city whose growth in population, trade, manufactures, and whose surrounding resources are almost without parallel.

The resources of the State of Washington are first given a space in our columns; then a cursory history of Tacoma and her important interests, followed by full descriptions of these interests, and concluding with histories of her leading business houses. The familiar features of some of our prominent and enterprising citizens will also be recognized in its pages; many others are equally deserving of a place in our limited gallery, but further space could not be afforded.

It is proper to say that the principle upon which this book has been published is quite contrary to that ordinarily prevailing. Not an illustration, a plate, an advertisement or a portrait, has been paid for. Dependence has been placed solely upon the sale and circulation of the work to compensate for its cost and attain the objects of its publication, and its further success must rest upon a generous appreciation of its merits. These we trust are apparent, since no expense has been spared to have the data as carefully and conservatively compiled as possible, and to make the work one of the finest specimens of the typographic art.

With this brief introduction, "TACOMA ILLUSTRATED" is submitted to the favor of a city whose generosity and enterprise are not less remarkable than its progress and prosperity.

Respectfully,

Baldwin Calcutt & Co

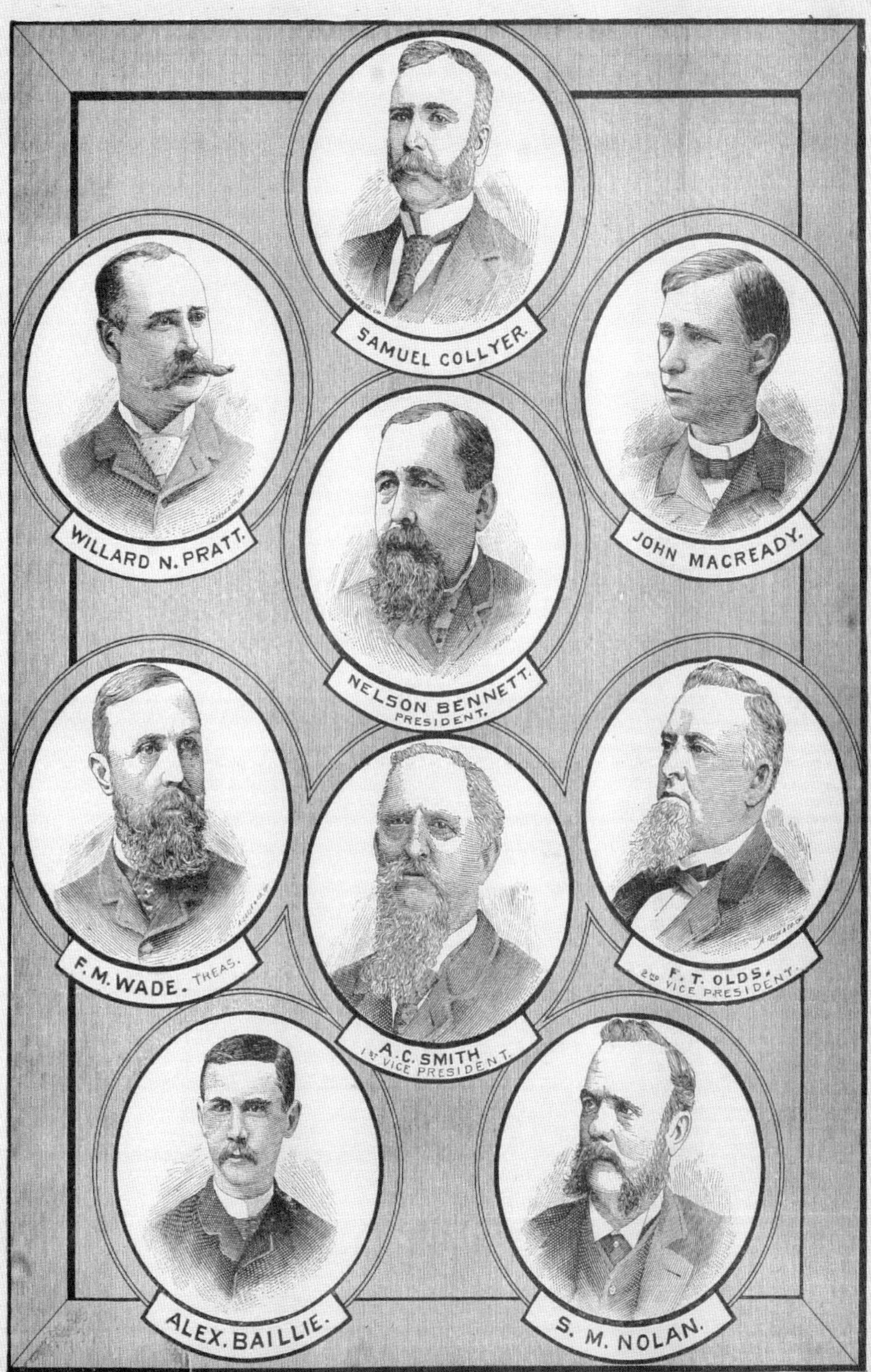

EXECUTIVE COMMITTEE OF THE CHAMBER OF COMMERCE.

STATE OF WASHINGTON.

A General Review of her Situation, Climate, and Unbounded Resources.

NATURALLY the publication of this work is in the interests of Tacoma, but as the resources of the surrounding country are always the great factor in building up cities, so it is our object to show the immense resources of the State of Washington, and tributary to the "City of Destiny."

Washington Territory has at last been admitted an acceptable sister in statehood, and she heralds her advent with such wonderful display of vigor, prosperity and wealth, that it will be safe to predict for her a grand future. For years Washington has been so far removed from the great centers of trade and population, debarred from the privileges obtainable from direct railroad communication, that her progress was very much retarded.

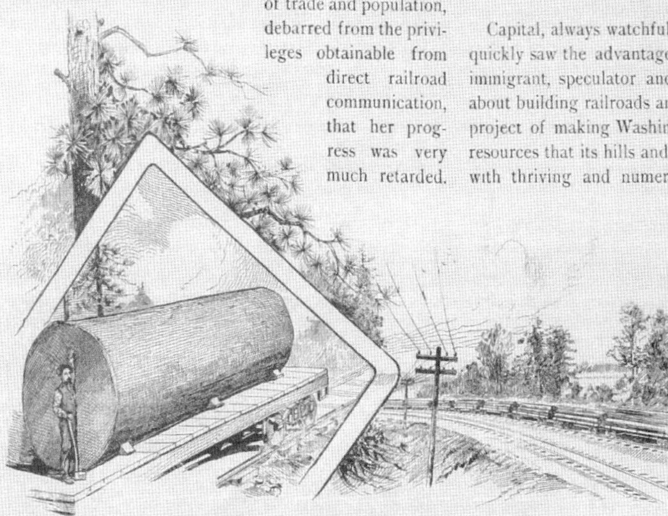

The situation is now all changed, and its railway and water transportation facilities are complete in every sense of the word. The development of the States of Kansas, Nebraska, Minnesota and Colorado, Dakota and other Territories, naturally preceded Washington, but now on a footing with these predecessors, the natural resources of the wonderland will soon place it in the front rank of prosperous States.

Washington is destined to be, like the Empire State of the Union, a State with many cities, and in this respect has numerous advantages over other Territories recently admitted into statehood. It is only a question of a very few years when at least a dozen cities in this State will each have a population of over 50,000.

Washington is naturally divided by the Cascade Mountains into two great parts, commonly known as Eastern and Western Washington. These in turn are subdivided into lesser parts known as "Countries." These include the Puget Sound, the Chehalis, the Lower Columbia, the Walla Walla, the Palouse, the Big Bend, the Yakima, the Okanogan, the Spokane and Colville Countries.

The State is 360 miles from east to west, and 249 miles north and south, and contains 69,994 square miles, or about 20,000 square miles more than England.

Eastern Washington—that portion of territory lying east of the mountains—is a vast farm and stock range with but little timber. It is well watered, and very productive of fruits, vegetables and cereals natural to the temperate zone. Western Washington is a country of hills and valleys, covered nearly in its entirety with heavy timber and hiding in its womb immense deposits of precious ores.

The Cascade Mountains give birth to many streams which empty into Puget Sound, several of which are navigable nearly to the foothills of the mountains, and flow to the sound through narrow valleys of exceeding fertility.

THE PROMISED LAND.

Capital, always watchful of the chance to increase itself, quickly saw the advantages offered by Washington to the immigrant, speculator and manufacturer, and at once set about building railroads and steamship lines to facilitate the project of making Washington a State so attractive in its resources that its hills and valleys would rapidly be covered with thriving and numerous settlements, and settled on

THE PUGET SOUND COUNTRY,

as that part of the State which presented the most natural advantages. Puget Sound has been fitly styled the "Mediterranean of America," and its shores "Wonderland." From its bosom one views in wonderment the cloud piercing peaks of Mounts Baker aud Tacoma clothed in eternal robes of white, tokens of grand sublimity.

While the area of land at present used for agriculture around Puget Sound is not large, its productive capacity is so great that with propriety it may be called a fine agricultural country.

Puget Sound is the great central feature of Western Washington, extending south from its northern line and reaching into every valley in the hills for 150 miles, and presenting a shore line of 1594 miles. It divides Western Washington again fairly in the middle, from Commencement Bay south to the Columbia River. For thirty miles before reaching Kalama, the point of crossing into Oregon, the Pacific Division of the Northern Pacific Railroad follows the Cowlitz River, which empties into the Columbia. All west of Puget Sound is an immense timber section, broken in like manner by the rich valleys of streams flowing into the Pacific Ocean at Gray's Harbor. Of these the Chehalis River is chief, and of this whole coast region Gray's Harbor is the notable feature. A large lumbering industry is carried on there. The whole of the Chehalis valley forms one of the richest agricultural districts in the State. From all these districts, Gray's Harbor on the southwest, the rich valley of the Nesqually on the southeast, and skirting the east shore of the Sound to the Canadian line on the north, railroads are being projected, to concentrate at Tacoma. The climate of Western Washington and the soil of its valleys, is especially adapted to the growing of hops, grasses and hay, and therefore for stock raising and dairy products, it is destined to become famous. The uplands yield wonderfully of fruits, and well repay the labor and expense of clearing them; these lands are now regarded more valuable, as a rule, for agriculture than for timber. Then there are, besides, about 200,000 acres of tide lands, susceptible of cultivation, on which enormous crops of oats and hay are raised. About 30,000 acres of these lands have been reclaimed, and 100 bushels of oats, or from three to four tons of hay to the acre, are the average yield. Apples, pears, cherries, plums, prunes, berries and vegetables of various kinds, are grown in unrivaled excellence and quantity.

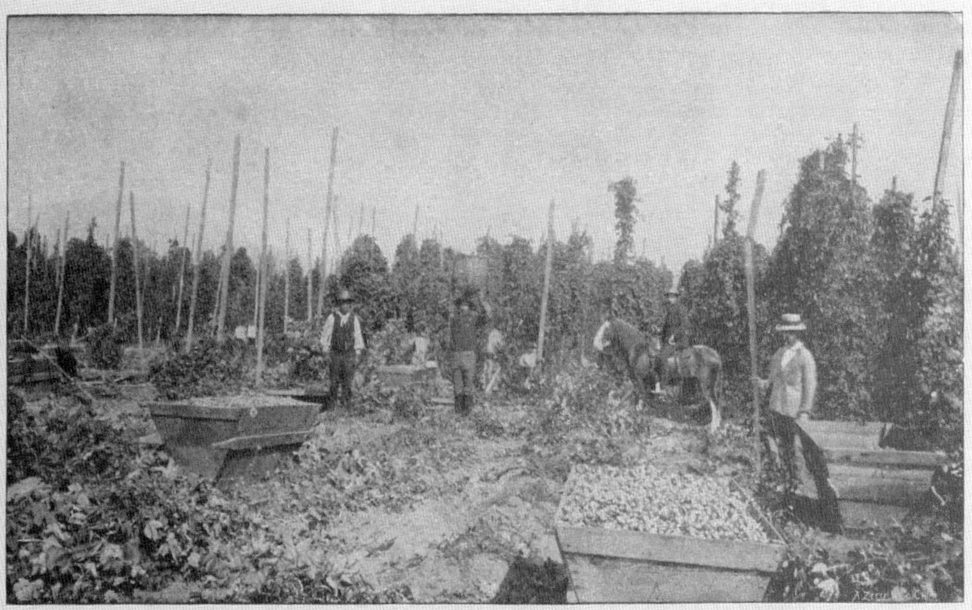

INDIANS PICKING HOPS.

THE TIMBER BELT

of Washington includes the whole extent of land from the Cascade Mountains to the ocean, and from Columbia River on the south to the British line on the north, an area equal to that of the State of Iowa. It is estimated to contain one hundred and seventy-five billion feet. Most of this timber will cut from twenty-five thousand to as high as sixty thousand feet to the acre. It is composed chiefly of fir and cedar, the former growing to a height of two hundred and fifty feet, with a body in proportion. Cedar grows to a height of one hundred and fifty feet, with an average diameter of four feet. These magnificent timbers are shipped to all parts of the world, while sawed lumber from this region is sent to California, South America, Europe and Asia, and its famous cedar shingles are encroaching upon the markets of the East. The cut of Washington's mills now covers about two million feet per day, yet it will be over one hundred years before this vast timber country will perceptibly feel this immense consumption of its supplies.

ITS IMMENSE COAL FIELDS.

Thirty miles east of Tacoma, in the foothills of the Cascades, and on the line of the Cascade division of the Northern Pacific, are vast beds of coal. The principal mines are now being worked at South Prairie, Wilkeson and Carbonado. From all accounts of mining engineers and experts in coal measures, Western Washington, the Cascade Mountains and their foothills, form a vast coal field, the deposits of which are as varied in character as those of any coal bearing region in the world. Nearly all of the coal mines proper have been found in and near Puget Sound basin. There are lignite mines at Renton and Newcastle, and the bituminous and semi-bituminous adjacent to the Puyallup River. Two other important coal fields are those of Cedar and Green Rivers and the Nesqually, which are believed to be a continuation of the Puyallup veins; they are of bituminous character.

The lignites mined at several points on the Sound country are of a fair quality for domestic purposes, and are used to some extent for steam making, but the bituminous products of the Puyallup fields tributary to Tacoma take the lead of all coals mined on the Pacific coast for coking, blacksmith work, gas, steam making and domestic use. All of these mines are tributary to Tacoma by the Cascade division alone, and are, therefore, not to be reached by any other than this most beautiful and popular route.

COKE AND IRON.

The Tacoma Coal Company have erected furnaces for the manufacture of coke on an extensive scale at Wilkeson, and are at present shipping largely to San Francisco, Victoria, Montana, and other points, which have heretofore been supplied with coke from Pennsylvania. From the Wilkeson mine is also taken in large quantities a blacksmith coal of superior quality. The cheap production of coking coal means the establishment of gigantic iron works, of smelting and reduction works, and various manufacturing industries and all the concomitant results, which inevitably accompany the production of cheap iron. The value of these products will be in the near future a source of great wealth to the "City of Destiny."

There are also vast deposits of iron on the line of the Cascade division and the Pacific Investment Company of this city are taking steps to develop and manufacture on a large scale.

HOPS.

A seaport already possessing every facility for rail and water transportation, and seated in the heart of a country where its resources are in their infancy of development, and yet of such magnitude that they attract the attention of the world, may well be called the "City of Destiny."

The rise, progress, present status and future prospects of the hop industry of Washington Territory, have been a fruitful theme for study among statisticians and communities elsewhere, as well as among our own people, whom it would, at first thought, seem were almost the only interested parties. The establishing of this business here upon a firm basis has wrought far reaching results and changes not dreamed of as probable, or even possible. From a struggling industry upon an uncertain basis this industry has constantly forged ahead to a solid position upon the fixed principles that insure success; from the humble beginning of the little plantation that yielded a first crop of one bale in the crop year of 1864, to that of 40,000 bales in that of 1888; from a crop of 184 pounds the first year to that of from 10 to 12 million pounds the present year; from the value of a first crop of less than $100 to that of over $1,500,000; from the position in the early years of its history of humbly begging for a market rated as seconds to its competitors to that of moving straight up to the front, as in the recent sale in one day of over a quarter of a million pounds upon the London market in direct competition with not ouly the boasted New York State hop, but also with the product of the world, attaining a price yielding a profit, while its competitors were selling at a loss, thus another industry opens its possibilities. No wonder, with such results, that we hear of the destruction of thousands of acres of hops in the older districts of the United States, England and Germany, and yet see the acreage gaining in our midst and the interest expanding year by year to the utmost possible limits of their ability of procuring the necessary labor to secure the crop in harvest time.

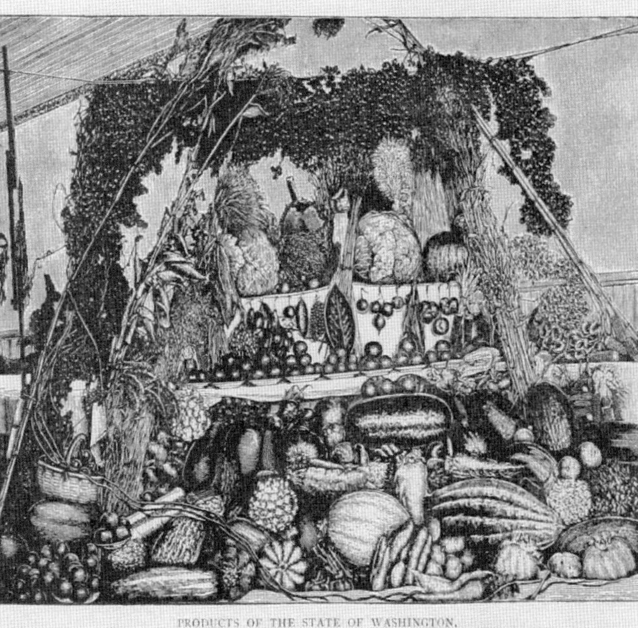
PRODUCTS OF THE STATE OF WASHINGTON.

The prolific way in which hops are grown in the Puyallup valley is something phenomenal. Two tons to the acre is not an uncommon yield, and several cases have been cited where growers have harvested as much as ninety tons off sixty acres. Nor is the question of yield all that can be said of the Washington hops. Grown, as they are, principally upon the deep, rich, fertile soil of the valleys adjacent to Puget Sound, the roots strike deep into the alluvial deposits of which the soil is composed, so that the plant never suffers from want of moisture, hence it is always matured and never lacking in strength and fragrance when properly managed after picking. The cool, long seasons for growth, coupled with the sufficient rainfall and stimulating dews, brings a perfection to the hop for flavor and keeping quality, which is essential to the enhancement of its market value.

A regular traffic for this crop has been established between Tacoma and London, England, and special train loads of hops have been dispatched direct to New York, to be thence transferred to ocean steamers sailing direct to London, which is an extremely profitable market, being capable of receiving all the produce of this kind we send.

FRUIT AND VEGETABLES.

Western Washington and the Puget Sound basin has advantages over Middle and Eastern Washington in the matter of growing fruit and vegetables, owing to its moisture and equable climate, produced by the proximity of the ocean and the tempering breezes that bring with them the warm breath of the Japan current. This mild and even climate, together with a soil adapted to fruit culture, make Washington as fine a fruit country as can be found in the United States. This remark only applies to such fruits as apples, pears, plums, prunes, cherries, and all kinds of berries and small fruits. Peaches are grown to advantage in Eastern Washington where the summers are hotter than in the Puget Sound basin. They are also grown successfully in favored spots east of the mountains. No element or constituent is wanting in either the soil or climate of Washington to produce any vegetable that can be raised in the temperate zone. This new State is destined to play no small part in supplying this country and a great many others with vegetable as well as various other products.

FISHERIES.

The fisheries is another source of great wealth to this fortunate State. To give an idea of the value of this industry, we will here give some figures which pertained to last year's catch. The salmon catch on the Columbia River during the year 1888 was three hundred and sixty thousand cases, giving Washington credit for one-half, or one hundred and eighty thousand cases. Twenty-five thousand cases were put up on Puget Sound, or about double the best previous year's record. About twenty thousand cases were put up at Gray's Harbor and other places. These figures aggregate two hundred and twenty-five thousand cases of salmon. The trade employs for several months each year, three thousand men, the capital invested being one million dollars, and the product is valued at a much greater sum. A few thousand barrels of salmon are usually put up each year, and during the season of 1888 the business was inaugurated of sending to Eastern markets in refrigerator cars. The fisheries were further extended. Three large schooners came from the coast of Massachusetts, which were employed in catching halibut and preparing them for the market. Their operations extended from the mouth of the Columbia River to Alaska, and they included many cargoes of fine fish. These were partially disposed of in the local markets, but the great bulk was sent to the East by rail. Much more in this line has been done this year, and the fish are not only sent fresh to the market, but are thus preserved by local drying establishments. The fur seal fisheries also made advances last season. Something will, it is more than likely, be done in the way of fishing for cod, and possibly also in whaling. There can be no question that Puget Sound and the Gulf of Georgia are most admirably adapted for the general fisheries. This fact is being seen and acknowledged more and more each succeeding year, and it is a matter of a short time only until our fisheries rival in extent those of the New England coast, Newfoundland and Norway.

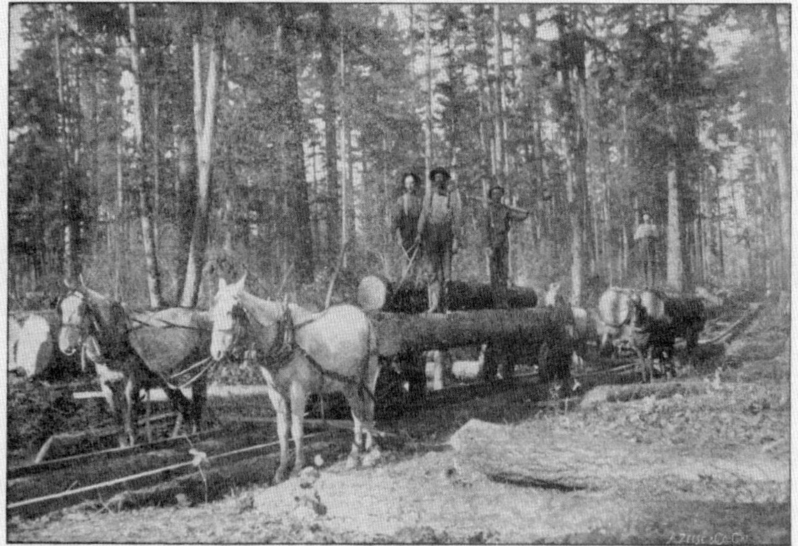

HAULING LOGS.

WASHINGTON'S RAILROAD LINES.

In 1885 the railroads of Washington aggregated an extreme length of 566 miles; in 1886, 954 miles; in 1887, 1,061 miles; in 1888, 1,410 miles; and by the end of the present year it is estimated not less than 2,000 miles of road will be in operation, and as a result of this impulse given the population and business of Washington by the extended railroad facilities, most of the towns have increased their number of inhabitants at least twenty-five per cent., while the "City of Destiny" proudly claims not less than three hundred per cent. of this increase.

MINERALS.

The mineral resources are too large and of too much importance to be touched upon to any considerable length in an article that is written simply to give the reader, unfamiliar with this young but prosperous State, a general idea of what lies within the borders of Washington, so that in order to do them justice, the compilers of this work have decided to produce articles on these industries separately.

CLIMATE OF WESTERN WASHINGTON.

Those who have gone no farther in studying the character of Washington than its situation on the map, will be surprised at nothing in its long list of surprises, more than its climate. When the reader is here informed, therefore, that the weather experienced throughout Washington west of the Cascade Mountains, is as mild, uniform and equable as anywhere in the United States, he may accept it as stated with the utmost conscientiousness, and as being true. The words "mild" and "equable" must be accepted for what they mean. Here an excessive heat or cold is unknown. The thermometer rarely registers 90 degrees, and it has not been known to reach zero but one day in six years. Our location on the map is wholly misleading in this regard, for we are on a line with Montreal, where the ice palace is the one great boast. But the relative positions with regard to north and south do not by any means wholly govern temperatures. For if the same line is carried on past Montreal it will be found running through the vineyards of France. Why Washington is so favored in its climate, is easily explained. The warm Japan current, of which every schoolboy knows, strikes the coast below the mouth of the Columbia River, and follows the line north into the very home of winter. It meets and tempers its cold winds, and changes its snows to rain. Then the high sentinel range of Cascade Mountains, 125 miles inland, stands forward, beckoning the clouds, and draining the fountains of rain and snow. These conditions make winter. A curtain of low clouds is drawn over the country from the sea to the mountain tops, much of the time during the winter months, and frequent light rains form the distinguishing feature of the season. The mountains attract the clouds to themselves, and the sky of Eastern Washington is thus kept clear nearly the year round. The winds blow from the south during the winter months, but from the north during the summer. For when the Southern summer grows hot the north winds are hurried to its relief by a law of nature. The great glaciers of Alaska standing as the outposts of winter's stronghold, are but a day's good blow from the north, and while its cold winds (just off the ice, so to speak) hurry on their kindly mission toward the equator, (where they will probably form a tornado), the summers of Washington Territory are found delicious. This is not mere fancy. Probably nowhere in the world is the weather so even the year round. Great and sudden changes so trying and so common in the East, are unknown. Twilight in midsummer extends to ten o'clock, and on summer nights the snowy summit of Mount Tacoma, sixty miles distant, can be plainly seen from the streets of Tacoma.

Of the season only the word "perfect" is necessary in description. In winter many people do not consider an overcoat necessary, while in summer most people find a blanket for a bed covering quite comfortable.

With these conditions it will be readily seen the seasons of the year are not as strongly marked as elsewhere. They merge into each other almost imperceptibly. September is characterized by an occasional shower. These become more frequent as the season advances – light, soft rains from low clouds most resembling a Scotch mist, and that do not interrupt the regular current of life. Men, and women as well, go about in them undisturbed, stop and exchange words or talk business, as they meet on the street without shelter. During November and December this weather is the rule. It is wholly unattended by that searching cold that enters the marrow of men and makes them wholly wretched, and such as characterizes the winter rains of the eastern middle States. It is quiet and even tempered, with no high winds. In January the thermometer usually drops another peg or two, and the rain turns to snow for a season of from three days to three weeks. Then comes the warm "chinook" wind, and winter disappears before it. The rains continue frequent through the early spring months, growing rarer as summer approaches, until it settles down again to a period of perfect days and nights of summer. In other words, every year casts up a fair average of fair days. But the reader should note this: Heavy storms, high winds and cyclones are absolutely unknown. Thunder and lightning are the most novel of nature's phenomena. On the other hand there are many who believe that Washington Territory is deluged with rain from six to eight months in the year. This too is as untrue as the common belief as to the cold. The gradual merging of winter into summer and summer into winter again, as indicated in the greater or less frequency of rain, characterizes the spring and fall, and winter means that rain is the order of things, while summer means the contrary. It may be remarked that we have devoted considerable space to a description of the climate; we have done so with the purpose in view of undeceiving the many people who have an idea that there is nothing in the winter months but rain.

In concluding this brief review of Washington's resources it would be well to say that we have merely touched on some of them; it has been necessary for the time being to do this, but as we proceed with the work we will endeavor to give a detailed description of these resources in their proper places and show the bearing they have on Tacoma, and how, by her natural location at the head of Puget Sound and as the terminus of the Northern Pacific, together with her smelters, warehouses, coal bunkers, manufacturing and shipping industries, she is better adapted to handle these resources than any other city in Washington, or in fact, any city on the Pacific Coast.

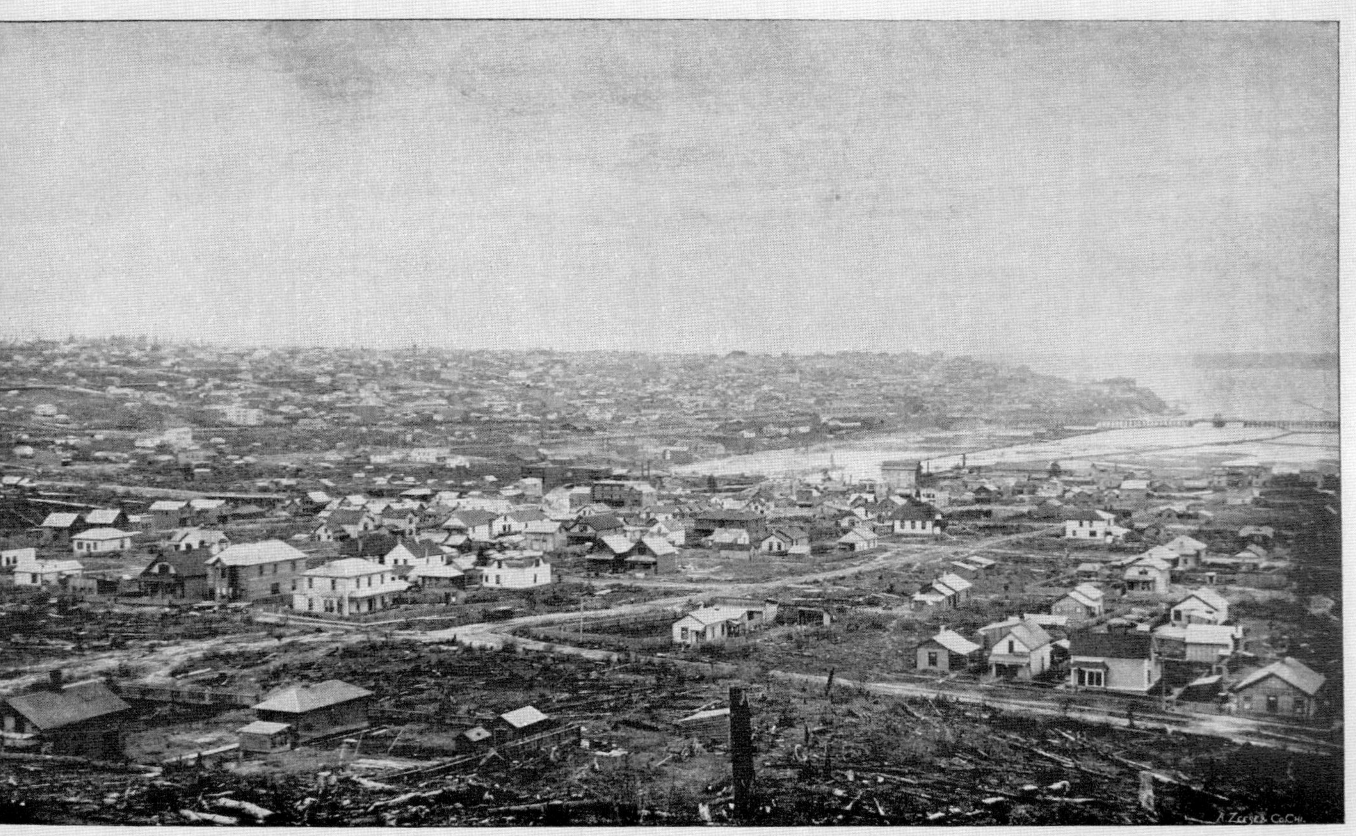

BIRDS' EYE VIEW OF TACOMA (FROM THE HILL NEAR THE RESERVATION).

TACOMA.

HER HISTORY, GROWTH AND RESOURCES—A COMPREHENSIVE REVIEW OF THE CITY OF DESTINY.

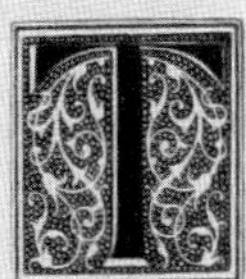

TACOMA ILLUSTRATED, as the title of this work implies, is published to illustrate or set forth as clearly as possible the innumerable advantages that the "City of Destiny" possesses. Its rapid growth in the past few years from an insignificant hamlet of a few hundred people to a bustling metropolitan city of over 30,000 inhabitants; its unequaled transportation facilities as the western terminus of the great Northern Pacific Railroad, which joins the Puget Sound country with the Eastern States; its railroad facilities to the southward, and its point of vantage at the head of navigation of one of the grandest inlets of the sea in the world; its wealth, as the center of vast and magnificent forests, mines of precious and baser minerals, and its fisheries; its ever-increasing commerce, that is reaching out to all parts of the habitable globe; and finally, its climate, which by reason of the slight changes during the different seasons of the year, makes Tacoma one of the most desirable places to reside in on the face of the earth.

Thus, the compilers of this work wish to give as clear and comprehensive an idea of Tacoma as possible. It will be advisable for us to go back to the year 1873, just before the directors of the Northern Pacific Railroad unanimously decided that the most advantageous point on the North Pacific Coast for the terminus of the road they were then constructing across the northern part of the United States, was the western shore of Commencement Bay, an inlet at the head of Puget Sound, a location admirably adapted for the building of an immense city, with unequaled harbor facilities. What a difference between Tacoma then and now! That part of the city now known as the First Ward, is the site of old Tacoma, which in 1873 consisted of a straggling village of about 300 souls, and its buildings of no greater extent than a sawmill and a few houses, homes of the men employed in the mill, while the present portion of the city was a mass of stumps and underbrush.

We produce herewith a sketch of the only house now standing which was on the present site of New Tacoma when the Northern Pacific terminus was located.

Having determined upon this site, the railroad company purchased 3,000 acres, and 13,000 acres of additional and neighboring lands.

The Tacoma Land Company, on the other hand, laid out the city directly south of the old town site, toward the head of the bay, and shortly afterward commenced the erection of the finest hotel on the coast north of San Francisco, and the president of the company, Charles B. Wright of Philadelphia, built a beautiful church structure, and liberally endowed the Annie Wright Seminary, for girls, and the Washington College, for boys. These substantial and imposing looking buildings at once gave Tacoma a foundation showing permanency and future greatness. It was then that investors and home seekers turned their faces in the direction of Tacoma, and there has since been a continual stream of them, ever increasing in volume.

The land company has pursued a conservative policy in the sale of its lands to new comers, avoiding any semblance of "booming" or inflating values. It has simply aided or kept pace with the steady march of progress, held its prices on a par with general values, and has not altered its original method of easy terms.

The publication of the resolution of the railroad company to make Tacoma the western terminus, through the newspapers, gave notice to the world that a new and great city was to be built in the West. Many intelligent people, being aware of the opportunities such a project involved, made preparations to come here. They knew that at the terminus of a great trunk line stretching across the continent, especially if that terminus was a seaport where ship and rail would meet for the transfer of cargoes, there must come shippers and money changers, and that the business incident to such a place would be sufficient in itself to insure the building of a city. They had seen Chicago grow, and were anxious to be in at such another birth. But at that time the end of the railroad track had only reached Bismarck, Dak., 1,400 miles distant from the site of the proposed city. The rails were being laid at the rate of 250 miles per year across the plains, and in the path toward Puget Sound lay two high mountain ranges—the Rockies, in Montana, and the Cascades, in Washington. The Rockies, when reached long afterward, were readily overcome with a 3,600 foot tunnel, but to overcome the Cascades was a more difficult undertaking. The Stampede Pass presented the least difficulties of several passes that were discovered, and yet it required nearly three miles of tunneling, including a tunnel under the summit of nearly two miles in length. The road through these mountains to Tacoma would cost eight millions of dollars.

The construction of a hundred miles of railroad from Tacoma to the Columbia River, was the quickest and least expensive way of reaching Puget Sound from the east and south. The Northern Pacific directors therefore decided to connect with the Sound, first, by the Columbia River route, and accordingly they located what is now known as the Pacific Division and secured control of the navigation of the Columbia from Kalama to Portland, and Walla Walla. For several years this was the only route between the eastern and western parts of Washington. The original plan for a direct line to Puget Sound, though held temporarily in check, and still further retarded by the financial crisis of 1872 and '73, was never abandoned. The terminus of the main line had been definitely established at Tacoma where the lines of traffic from the south and east converge, and the ground was laid out for a large city. The causes which delayed the completion of the railroad hindered the settlement and development of the entire western part of the Territory, and of course prevented the city of Tacoma from

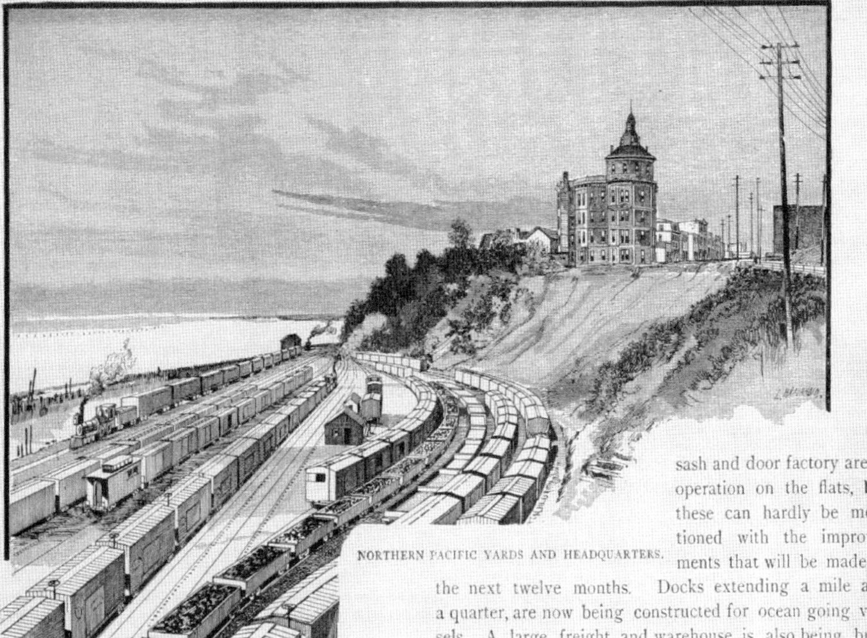

NORTHERN PACIFIC YARDS AND HEADQUARTERS.

realizing at once the hopes of its founders. But notwithstanding these adverse circumstances, its growth for the first few years was relatively greater than that of the country tributary to it, and far in excess of rival towns. But as soon as direct communication was made across the Cascade Mountains, the growth of Tacoma was phenomenal.

THE CITY AS IT IS.

The peninsular promontory upon which Tacoma is built, runs out to a point forming a triangle. Taking Twenty-First Street at the head of Commencement Bay, and traveling in its direction west for five miles, we come to the waters of Puget Sound again at the Narrows. From Twenty-first streeet to Point Defiance northward, is a distance of five miles. To the line of the Puyallup Indian reservation is four miles. The highest point of the promontory is in its center, a moderately high ridge extending its whole length until at its extreme northern point it ends in an abrupt bold precipice, presenting that appearance, as approached from the north by the Sound, which suggested the name of "Defiance." The main land at the head of the bay, slopes gradually down to the water from the south, and an area of three and a-half square miles lies so low that the high tides cover a large portion of it. This tract is known as the "tide flats." Those when dyked, will afford the very best locations for mills and factories which have business equally with ships and cars.

Already a mammoth sawmill as well as an equally large sash and door factory are in operation on the flats, but these can hardly be mentioned with the improvements that will be made in the next twelve months. Docks extending a mile and a quarter, are now being constructed for ocean going vessels. A large freight and warehouse is also being built upon the wharf. Another proposed improvement is the building of an immense suspension bridge across the broad arm of Puyallup River, from either Ninth or Tenth streets to the flats. The importance as well as the expenditure of such an undertaking as this can only be appreciated by one familiar with the site.

From here the land rises gradually in natural terraces back from the water, as well as along its front. No more perfect natural location for a great city could be conceived. When the railroad company determined upon this as a terminal point, it instructed its engineers to lay this land out for the building of a city; to forget the wilderness that crowded it; to forget that it was on the extreme frontier; to bear in mind only its future greatness, and to have a care that its streets and avenues should have noble proportions in keeping with that idea, that when they should be lined with stately buildings there should be nothing to regret. They entered into the full spirit of their work, and to-day, friends, jealous rivals and indifferent strangers alike agree that no city on the continent is so splendidly planned. The engineer declared when he entered upon the work that the streets should have such easy grades that a horse with buggy and driver might go from any one point to another in a lively trot, and he carried his point. The east and west streets climb the hills at gentle grades, and easy stages, the main avenues (north and south) stretch along natural benches of the side hills, forming the most magnificent of drives. The streets are all eighty feet wide, the avenues one hundred, and the alleys forty feet. The top of the hill is reached at a half a mile back from the water and the land, thence spreads away on a level plateau until within a short distance of the Narrows, when it again slopes in the same way to the water.

HOW TACOMA IS GROWING.

Previous to November, 1880, the little town of Steilacoom was the county seat of Pierce County, but as Tacoma grew and the principal interests of the county became centered here, it was decided that at the general elections held in November, the question of the permanent location of the headquarters of the county officers should be left to the vote of the people, and on the tenth day of November, 1880, the county commissioners formally declared Tacoma the choice of the public by an overwhelming vote. At the opening of the year 1887, the most enthusiastic champions of Tacoma did not estimate its population above 9,000, and this had been the result of a gradual, steady growth since the little sawmill settlement was electrified by the news that it had been chosen as the site for the terminus of the railroad. While the most enthusiastic citizen of 1887 did not rate the population over 9,000, the most conservative citizen of 1889 does not place it under 30,000. The city has spread over miles of additional territory, and what was a suburb a few years ago, is now comparatively the center of the city. The hilly situation of the city and the numerous stumps made the grading of streets an expensive undertaking, but notwithstanding this, Tacoma now has fifty-two miles of admirably graded streets, and ninety-eight miles of sidewalks. Since May 1, 1889, over eighteen miles of streets and twenty-six miles of sidewalks have been graded, and it is the intention of the city surveyor to grade twenty-two miles more of street, and put down thirty miles more of sidewalk before the beginning of the year. With regard to the sewerage system of Tacoma the same energy has been displayed by the city government. The city now possesses a system that is second to none on the Pacific coast. Since last May fifteen miles of sewers have been constructed, and before the end of the year fifteen miles more will be finished. The expenses of the city for street improvements for the fiscal year ending June 30, 1889, are as follows: For grading and sidewalks, $150,564.78; for sewers, $70,609.66; for condemnation of property for streets, $10,127.75; for repairing of sidewalks, streets, sewers and wharves, this together with the general expenses, including salaries and light and water bills, etc., makes the total expenses $353,718.96. The question of paving the streets with some suitable material that will facilitate traffic and enable the cleansing of the streets, has been discussed by the city council and as the winter season prevents the introduction of a permanent pavement, the principal streets and avenues are being planked. It is also proposed next year to put down cedar blocks or asphalt.

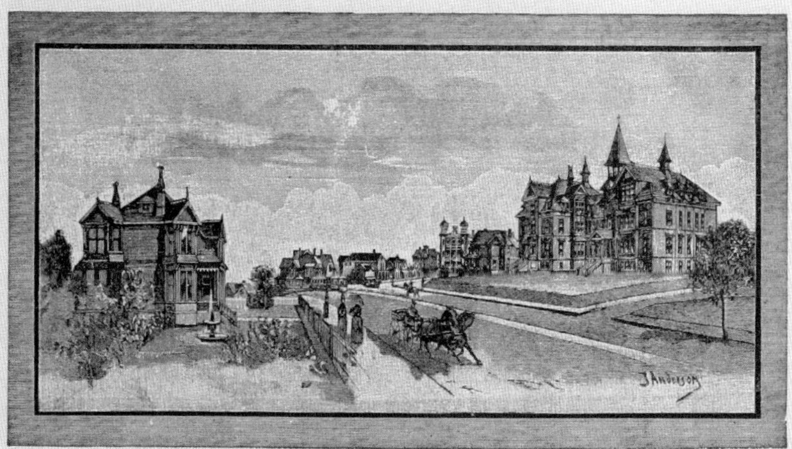

VIEW OF TACOMA AVENUE.

THE BUSINESS PORTION.

The business portion of the city extends principally from the head of the bay along the water front for the distance of several miles. On the even, low lying ground at the head of the bay are grouped mills, factories, machine shops and foundries. The railroad coming west down the valley of the Puyallup River sweeps round in this direction (with convenient sidetracks), and extends along the water front to the Point Defiance Park. The ocean freight wharf and shipping docks are at a point about one-fourth of this distance north, where the tide flats end and the deep water begins. Here commences a series of coal bunkers and wheat warehouses, and further along, the great Tacoma mill, fish cannery, the Pacific mill and the smelting and reduction works, with smaller industries interspersed. From the ocean freight docks a street (now being remodeled at great cost into a splendid thoroughfare) has been cut out of the side hill extending at a grade sufficiently easy to accommodate the heaviest traffic, up to the top of the first bench, where it leads in a straight line and on a natural grade, down to the passenger depot and manufacturing and wholesale section at the head of the bay again, and on for a mile beyond. This is Pacific avenue, the main business thoroughfare, at the highest point of which, as it rises from the wharf and docks and commanding a perfect view of the shipping and railroad yards, stands the new Western office building of the Northern Pacific Railroad Company. From this point to the passenger station at Seventeenth street, this thoroughfare is built up with costly brick blocks from three to seven stories high. At the foot of Fifteenth street, the city is now constructing expensive and commodious docks for the numerous Sound steamers that make Tacoma their headquarters to receive and discharge freight.

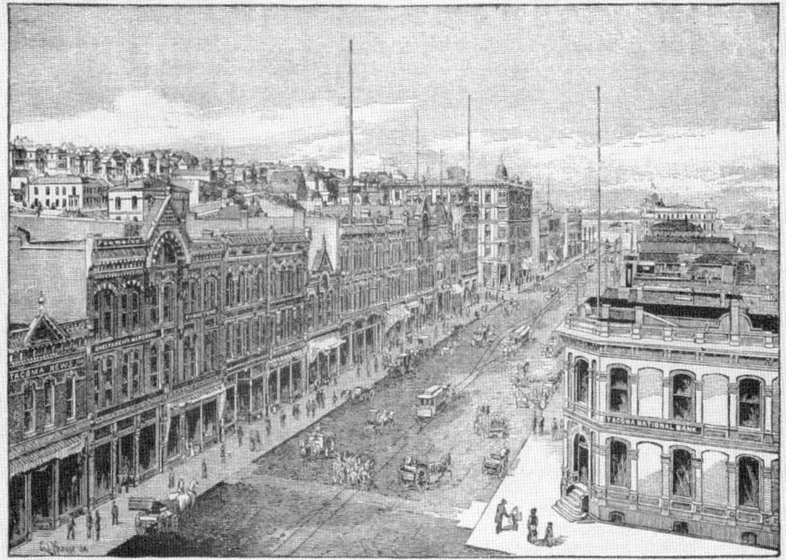

VIEW OF PACIFIC AVENUE.

THE RESIDENT PORTION.

The resident portion of Tacoma is situated upon the higher ground, and is thus lifted above the stir and noise of the business portion; the citizen continually enjoys the purest of air, the best of drainage, and the most delightful of views. Such is the gradual slope of the hillside that, like raised chairs in a theater, the windows of nearly every house upon it command the incomparable view spread before it.

The bay, with its quiet waters and green islands, is given a spirit of life by a multitude of water craft, from the tiny canoe, pleasure boat and noisy tug, to the dignified ocean steamer and full-rigged ship, moving hither and thither, or lying quietly at anchor in the bay or moored to the docks. Across the bay the eye follows the meanderings of the Puyallup River—a thread of silver winding through the meadows of the valley, fringed with changing verdure, on through the Indian reservation, past the church and school and little settlement, on until it is lost in the dark pine woods of the foothills. Then, above this dark green girdle the imposing majesty of great Tacoma lifts its mighty head far into the clouds. Be the soul of the observer ever so unimpressible it must be stirred with sudden wonder and awe. From the quiet pastoral beauty of the valley of the Puyallup to this great white robed monarch of all the mountains is a contrast that, travelers tell us, has no parallel in the world's panorama. There are higher mountains than Tacoma, but not one other known peak that rises so grandly alone from the level of the sea to such a height. It is covered with a complete robe of snow from the line of green foothills in which its base is lost to the distant observer, to the top where the steam of a slumbering volcano hovers over its crown forming what is called the "liberty cap."

Looking to the west from these same windows there are the jagged peaks and white snow caps of the Olympic or Coast Range, forming another beautiful and distant horizon. Look at this picture as often as you will, it is ever the same. The play of light and shade and changing cloud effects, the sunrise and sunset, the rising moon and every breeze touch it with an artistic hand to add new beauties. This view—"a view of the mountain"—is the first consideration

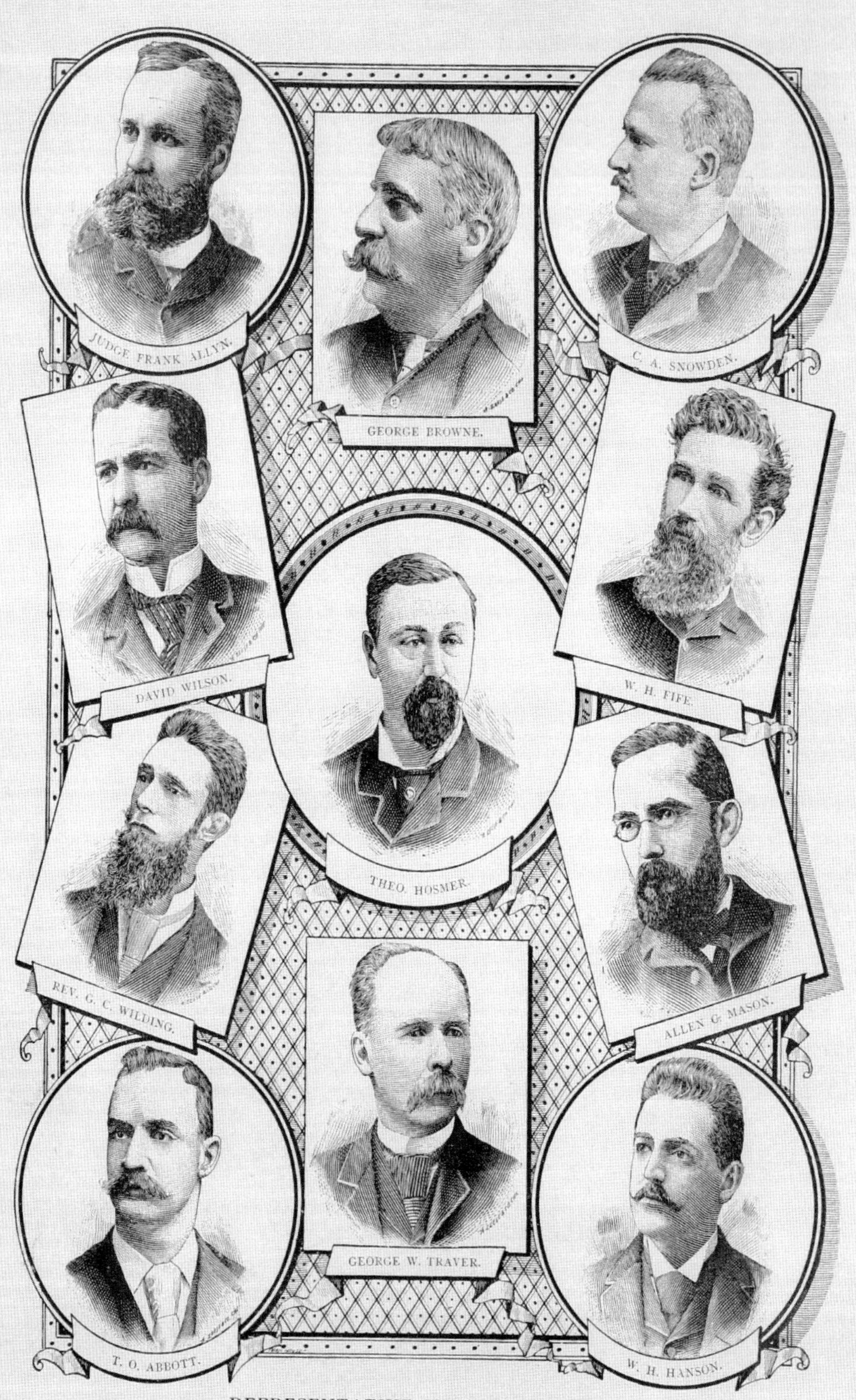

REPRESENTATIVE MEN OF TACOMA.

with the purchaser of residence property in the city and whether it is good or imperfect has a very great influence on the price which he is asked.

MANUFACTURING.

Tacoma is rapidly taking position as a great manufacturing center. Heretofore it has imported the bulk of the products consumed by its people. While it bought of distant cities flour and feed, furniture, boots and shoes and other articles of daily use, it shipped away lumber, coal, wheat, and hides of which these things are made. But the course of trade has already in a great measure changed, and is still changing. With abundant coal and coke, several varieties of iron ore and limestone for flux necessary to the making of iron and steel, abundant wood and water, unequaled transportation facilities and a great market, at hand. Tacoma must necessarily come to the front of all rival towns on the Pacific coast as a great manufacturing center. The railroad company established machine shops here as early as 1877, and other works followed until the list of paid operatives and the amount of money paid workmen here is greater than any place north of Portland, Oregon. There are now numerous iron and brass foundries, stove works, machine shops, car and locomotive shops, flour mills, furniture factories, sewer pipe, tile and potters' works, brickyards, a number of shingle mills, sash and door factories, in fact, every industry of importance is represented in the City of Destiny. As to the sawmills, the aggregate daily output is 1,500,000 feet per day. Tacoma is the lumber center of the North Pacific coast. The Ryan Smelter and Reduction works with a capacity of 15,000 tons of ore, will be in full operation by June 1, 1889. It would not be doing the City of Destiny justice to attempt to show forth the industries that are within her gates, in a general article on the city, and in order to expatiate upon them, the compilers of this work have decided to take up each branch in a systematic manner.

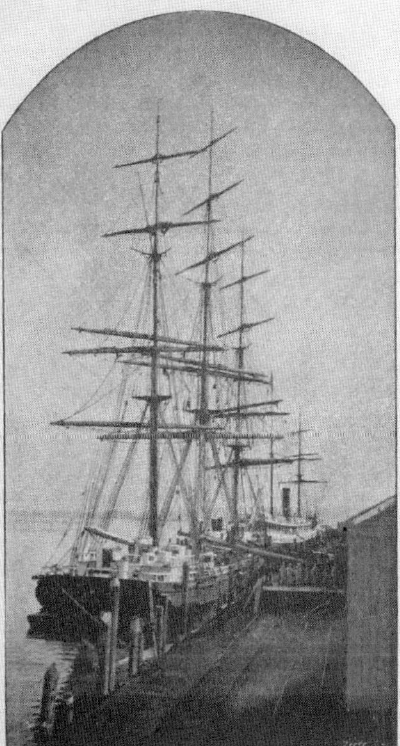

UNLOADING TEA FROM CHINA AND JAPAN.

THE PUBLIC PARKS.

The City Council have taken steps to secure for the city the grandest system of public parks of any city in the country. As is well known, the United States Government reserved from the public lands thrown open to settlement Sections 16 and 36 in every township. A section of land is a square mile, and these, as surveyed in tracts of 36 square miles and numbered from 1 to 36, form a township. All the rest, except the even hundred sections for fifty miles along the railroad, which form the land grant to the company, are open to settlement, as is well known. The sections 16 and 36 are reserved, to be sold when the Territory shall become a State, the proceeds to form a public school fund. Under a recent act of Congress, the county commissioners are authorized to lease these lands in order that they shall draw a revenue pending this time. The City Council of Tacoma at once negotiated the lease of one-half of 16 and all of 36 from the county commissioners. Section 16 of township 21, in which Tacoma is located, adjoins the present city limits on the south, and section 36 adjoins it on the northwest. It is contemplated that the city will purchase the lands as soon as statehood makes that possible. In the heart of the present city a reservation of thirty acres was left by the Land Company for park purposes, and this has already been improved by the city. The National Congress at its last session passed an act dedicating the United States military reserve, comprising over 600 acres at Point Defiance, for the use of the city of Tacoma as a public park. These, with several smaller tracts in different sections of the city, connected by broad and beautiful drives, complete a system of parks that will forever be a public pride. Indeed, the country for a distance of twenty miles south of Tacoma, and including Section 16, is a perfect natural park, as level in many places as a floor, free of underbrush, but rendered beautiful by groves of fir, evergreen and small oak, and here and there a lake bordered with pine and hazel brush. Around and through this one may drive winter and summer in any direction. It is covered with a thin grass, and in early summer with myriads of beautiful flowers. In the most northerly portion of this natural park is located the only race track near Tacoma. The land was recently purchased for this use by a company organized in Tacoma, and here it is intended to hold the races and fairs. At a distance of about twelve miles and in the open prairie are found what are known as Gravelly and American Lakes, a region of great beauty, adding much to the attractiveness of the country which immediately surrounds this beautiful "City of Destiny."

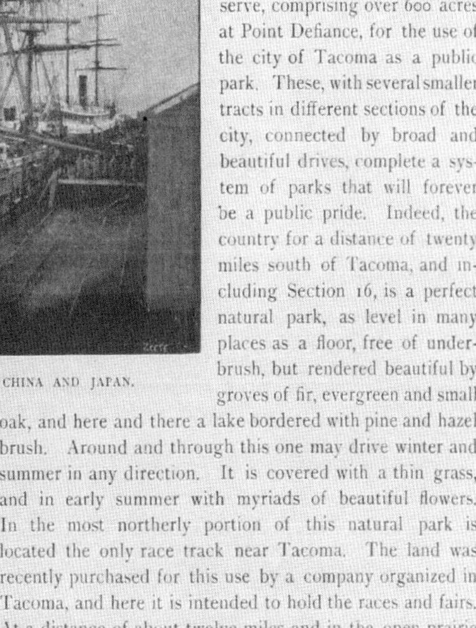

IMPORTS OF TEA AND GENERAL SHIPPING.

The port of Port Townsend, through which all vessels coming into or going out from Puget Sound, pass, has become the fifth port in importance in the United States. The value of incoming and outgoing cargoes at four ports in the country, only, exceed the value of those passing through Port Townsend, and more cargoes go out from or are bound to Tacoma, than any other city on Puget Sound. Tacoma has one of the finest harbors in the world. It is several miles in length, and the water is from 40 to 75 fathoms deep. The distance to Port Townsend is about 75 miles, and the cost of towing vessels in from the sea and back again is very small comparatively.

For the year 1888, the total lumber exports of Tacoma amounted to 94 cargoes, or 73,454,905 feet of lumber, valued at $873,707.75, as against 63,371,141 feet, valued at $760,453.70 for the year 1887. The lumber exports for the year 1889 will be still larger. There are several large mills now in operation that were not yet completed last year. The lumber is shipped to San Francisco and other coast cities, and to Europe, South America and ports on the Atlantic coast. Large quantities of lath, spars and pickets are also exported from Tacoma. It is likely that the value of lumber exports from Tacoma for the year 1889 will exceed $1,000,000. The coal shipped from Tacoma during 1888 aggregated 111 cargoes; amounting to 272,529 tons, valued at $1,426,012.25. The amount of coal shipped from this port during 1889 will be considerably greater than that shipped in 1888. Less than half of the coal taken out of the mines tributary to Tacoma is shipped. Some of the largest mines are owned by the Northern Pacific railroad company, and is all used by the railroad itself. The exportation of wheat from Tacoma has also been touched upon at length in another article.

Tacoma is connected with San Francisco by a line of steamers, one of which arrives and departs from Tacoma every five days. These returning steamers transport to San Francisco from Tacoma large quantities of flaxseed, hides, and other commodities. These steamers bring up from San Francisco large quantities of manufactured goods, besides fruit and vegetables during the summer season, before those grown around Tacoma are fully matured.

Tacoma is also becoming a great importing city. She imports tea by the shipload from Japan and China, and many cargoes yearly of different commodities from Great Britain.

During the year 1888 the value of the tea imported to Tacoma was $438,089, on which duties amounting to $23,280.25 were paid. Most of the tea thus imported consisted of five cargoes brought over in the ship by W. J. Rotch, St. Francis, Republic, and the barks George S. Homer and Spartan. Two cargoes of tea were imported to Tacoma in 1887, and three during 1889. The three cargoes imported this year were brought over from Japan by the ships Lucy A. Nickels, Frank Pendleton and Wildwood. In all about 25,000,000 pounds of tea have been imported to Tacoma. The tea was shipped east over the Northern Pacific railroad and was destined to Eastern cities and London.

A number of British iron ships arrive in Tacoma each year with general cargoes from Great Britain. Already this year, nine British vessels have arrived in Tacoma. These were the Lady Cairns, Francis Thorpe, Nith, Keir, La Escocesa, Edinburshire, Madeira, Dumbartonshire and Ullock. These vessels were loaded with cement, fire brick, steel nails, and other English products. There are now four other vessels on the way to Tacoma from England, and several others have been chartered. The vessels coming from England load wheat or lumber for export. This is one reason why vessel owners like to send their ships to Tacoma; they are always sure of securing a charter for their vessel to load wheat or lumber at this port.

THE STREET RAILWAYS.

Tacoma is a city built upon a hill, and does not seek to hide her light under a bushel. The fact however, that she has steep grades makes the subject of this article, street railway facilities, an all important one, both for present and future consideration. The astonishing growth of Tacoma, and the rapid sale and settling of suburban property are forcing the subject imperatively upon the consideration of her inhabitants as one that must be promptly dealt with.

With their usual energy the capitalists of Tacoma have grappled with this problem; accordingly a number of lines have been projected, and a list of franchises applied for that will gridiron the city with tracks, bringing the outskirts of the town into closer connection with the business portions and increasing the value of every foot of property past which they are laid.

It is impossible to give in the allotted space, a complete enumeration of every already constructed or projected street railway. Among the principal ones which may be mentioned, is the Tacoma Railway & Motor Company, whose franchises, as ascertained, cover about all of the principal streets in the business and residence portions of the city.

The Tacoma Central railway is controlled by Messrs. Manning, Bogle and Hays. It will extend south on Sixth street, to Division avenue, Prescott avenue, Pine street, and to the city limits. Another franchise covers Eleventh street from Pacific avenue to K and from there to Thirteenth and along Thirteenth to Pacific avenue again. R. F. Radebaugh owns a franchise to run along Delin street from Pacific to Wright avenue, to the southerly limits of the city on G street, and on South Twenty-ninth from Pacific avenue to Delin street. The North End road, mainly controlled by Allen C. Mason, will, as its name indicates, pass through the northern suburbs, and have a branch which will reach to the smelter. The westerly limits of the city will be reached by a line running along Eleventh street from K to the limits.

At the time of writing miles of street railway tracks are being graded and laid in various portions of the city, and there is no question that shortly the whole town will be furnished with a thoroughly equipped street car system, the peer of any similar system in the United States.

JOURNALS AND JOURNALISTS.

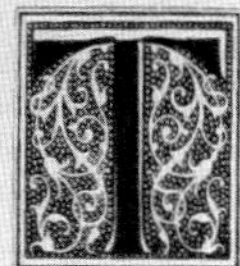

HERE are more newspapers published in Tacoma than in any other city in Washington. Besides three dailies publishing full telegraphic reports and employing a large force of editors, reporters and special writers, there are nine weeklies published in various languages, and devoted to various interests.

The *Morning Globe* and *Daily Ledger* are issued every morning, and the *Evening News*, as its name implies, dishes up every evening in an entertaining manner, all events of interest that occur during the day. The weeklies are, the *Sunday Times*, a bright and entertaining society paper, the *West Coast Trade*, devoted to the wholesale and jobbing interests; *Every Sunday*, giving a resume of occurrences at the end of each week; the *Globe*, *Ledger* and *News*, weekly editions; the *Real Estate Journal*, devoted to real estate; the *Northwest Horticulturist and Stock Journal*, the *Baptist* and the *Watch am Sunde*, a German paper. The *Real Estate and Industrial Journal* and the *Bulletin* (the latter published by the Y. M. C. A.) are monthlies.

THE TACOMA LEDGER.

THE TACOMA LEDGER is the oldest established paper in Tacoma, and Pierce County. It was established as a weekly eight column four page folio paper, by R. F. Radebaugh of San Francisco and H. C. Patrick of the Santa Cruz (Cal.) *Courier*, making its first appearance on Wednesday, April 21, 1880, and thereafter every Friday. At the head of the columns on the first page, under its title, there appeared, and still appears in the weekly, the following terse declaration outlining its policy: "An independent journal, devoted to the development of the resources of Washington Territory." This policy has been adhered to. Its political leanings have been toward Republicanism. It was uphill work publishing a paper in the early days of New Tacoma, with its population of less than 800, but as the town prospered the LEDGER prospered with it. In May, 1882, R. F. Radebaugh became the sole proprietor of the LEDGER, and still retains ownership. On Saturday, April 7, 1883, the first issue of the DAILY LEDGER was published, in six column four page folio form, carrying the dispatches of the Western Associated Press. It is still the only paper in Tacoma that receives them. Increasing business necessitated an enlargement of the LEDGER, a few months later, to an eight column paper. On March 1, 1885, it was enlarged to a six column eight page paper, which form it retained until April 2c, 1888, when it was enlarged to a seven column paper, its present size.

Up to Monday, February 25, 1889, the DAILY LEDGER was issued only six days a week, from Tuesday to Sunday inclusive, but on the above date the Monday paper was first issued, and a seven day journal established, the Sunday paper appearing as the SUNDAY LEDGER. While advocating the interests of Tacoma, the LEDGER never lost sight of the Territory, and there is not a paper in Washington which has done more to attract immigration and capital by hard missionary work in repeatedly calling the attention of the world to the boundless resources of this great commonwealth.

THE TACOMA MORNING GLOBE.

The *Tacoma Morning Globe* was started in October, 1888, by the Globe Publishing Company, and has made a record unparalleled in the history of newspapers. From the first it has been a live local paper, largely due to Chas. E. Race, who had charge of the local department for the first six months, and with Frank J. Millard, business manager, did all the editorial work, including the telegraph and proofreading. January 1 it was enlarged to its present size. In February Col. Will L. Visscher became editor in chief, and the paper soon took its place as one of the leading dailies of the metropolis of Washington. Upon the retirement of Mr. Race, the local department fell to Chas. Woodworth who had been on the staff for some time. The telegraph service of the paper is unsurpassed by any in the State, and is under the supervision of C. E. Crittenden. A perfecting press has been ordered, and is now on the way from Chicago, and the *Globe*, in one year, from a small folio, is now a handsome newspaper, known and read in every hamlet in the State.

THE TACOMA EVENING NEWS.

This sheet was first published as the *Pierce County News*, whose first number appeared in the then small village of Tacoma, on Aug. 10, 1881. George W. Mattice was its publisher. The *Pierce County News* was enlarged Oct. 26, 1881, and again on Jan. 25, 1882. H. C. Patrick, now a Justice of the Peace in Tacoma, made a daily evening paper of it Sept. 25, 1883, and called it *The Tacoma News*. He sold his interest to George R. Epperron & Co. (the silent interest being held by Allen C. Mason, W. A. Berry, James Wickersham and William McIntyre). The *News* Publishing Company was organized March 1, 1886, with Richard Roediger, William McIntyre, Allen C. Mason, W. A. Berry and James Wickersham, as incorporators. The latter three subsequently retired, and the property was then owned by Messrs. Roediger and McIntyre. Thomas E. Scantlin bought an interest in the establishment in the fall of 1888, and the owners and officers of the paper now are: President, William McIntyre; vice-president, T. E. Scantlin; secretary, Richard Roediger. The *Evening News* has since been enlarged to an eight column folio, is a prosperous and enterprising Democratic journal, and the only evening paper in Tacoma. Mr. Scantlin is the editor-in-chief; city editor, H. Hal Hoffman; telegraph editor, George P. Jacobs; assistant city editor, Edward H. Miller.

The company also operates a large job printing department. The excavations for a new four story brick and stone building, which *The Evening News* will erect between Railroad and C streets, south of Eleventh street, are now under way, and a new Perfection press for the daily is now on the way.

THE WEST COAST TRADE.

This excellent paper is published and edited by Mr. Orno Strong, late of Michigan.

The *Trade* is an independent journal, devoted to the mercantile interests of the North Pacific country. It contains quotations on the leading articles of merchandise, a weekly review of the markets in general, a record of the events of trade and business, editorial essays and notes, industrial, financial, manufacturing and shipping news.

The aim of the *Trade* is to represent, fully and fairly, Washington's mercantile interests, and to prove a careful, faithful friend to the retail merchant—in brief, to serve those engaged in the business of buying and selling.

To Mr. Strong the compilers of "TACOMA ILLUSTRATED" are indebted for valuable information concerning Tacoma's rapidly increasing jobbing trade.

THE JOURNAL.

THE JOURNAL was first established as a real estate journal in Tacoma by Mr. A. W. Berry as publisher, and Col. C. W. Hobart, an able and prominent newspaper man formerly connected with the principal newspapers of Chicago, as editor and manager. May 1, 1888, it was just a four column quarto, devoted exclusively to the real estate of Tacoma, and issued weekly. It met with favor and financial success from the first month, and 5,000 copies were issued each week, and largely circulated throughout the Eastern States.

At the end of the first year and volume, its name was changed to "THE JOURNAL, devoted to the Real Estate and Industrial Interests of Washington," and its form changed to a six column folio, in which shape it is now published.

In August, 1889, Boothroyd & Co. succeeded A. W. Berry as publisher, the editorial management still remaining in the hands of Col. C. W. Hobart. The change in name and scope extended its field to the entire Territory, in which it meets with success as a worker in the upbuilding of the grand future State of Washington.

EVERY SUNDAY.

Mr. Edward N. Fuller arrived in Tacoma on the 26th of July, 1882, and at once enlisted as editor of the *Weekly News*, which was purchased by Mr. H. C. Patrick a few weeks previous. He continued to edit that paper until September, 1883, when the daily edition was commenced. Early in the year 1885, he resigned the editorship of the *News* to become secretary of the Tacoma Chamber of Commerce, which position he held for two years, in the meantime (May, 1886) starting a weekly paper called *Commerce*. In May, 1887, he removed this paper to Puyallup, W. T., it being the first newspaper ever printed in the great scope of country between the cities of Tacoma and Seattle. In August, 1888, Mr. Fuller sold the *Commerce* to Col. J. W. Redington, and made an engagement as editorial writer on the staff of the Tacoma *Daily Ledger*, which terminated on the 1st of January, 1889. On March 3, 1889, he started *Every Sunday*, in the first ward of Tacoma, known as "Old Tacoma," which paper has made good progress, and promises to become a successful journal. Mr. Fuller began his newspaper career in February, 1842, in a Dover (N. H.) printing office, and proposes to celebrate his fiftieth anniversary in 1892. His son Robert, and daughter Fay Ed. Fuller, are associated with him in the conduct of *Every Sunday*.

HARBOR AND RAILROAD ENTERPRISES.

Tacoma harbor may be divided into three sections: The old ocean docks, extending from the railroad wharf down the west shore to the smelter; the head of the bay, extending from the ocean wharf one mile south of Twenty-third street; and the new and proposed ocean docks on the tide flats.

The Commencement Bay Co. is now building a wharf one mile long in the latter section, at a cost of $100,000. The Hart mill now under contract and the St. Paul mill built last spring, and the Wheeler sash and door factory recently completed, are also in this section. A bridge costing $100,000 will be built over the channel to this section this year.

Along the west side of the channel to the head of the bay from Fifteenth to Twenty-third streets has been built nearly half a mile of wharves, warehouses and factories.

The balance of the improvements have been made by the N. P. R. R. Co. which appropriated for this year's improvements $1,000,000; $750,000 will be spent this year. An appropriation of $500,000 will be made next year to build machine and car shops.

Last year 11 miles of track were laid in the yard, extending from the smelter to the Reservation. This year 10 miles will be laid, 4 in the half moon, 4 at the head of the Bay, and 2 miles private sidings. The bluff along Pacific avenue leading to the old docks has been cut down, and the dirt filled in the half moon by hydraulic works, making about 8 acres additional yard room, and 3,000 feet of dock front. The work on the avenue will make a 100 foot street of a 20 foot road. Beyond the ocean dock the new coal bunkers, with room for two ships to load, were built this season, and further down the N. P. elevator, the Kershaw wheat house, the mill of the Puget Mill Co., and at the end of the track the Ryan smelter.

At the head of the bay the greatest work has been done; 120 acres of tide flats have been filled in by the great rotary dredger, from earth taken from the channel to the head of the bay, making a channel 35 feet deep and 600 feet wide. A hill of about 40 acres in extent, averaging 20 or 30 feet high, has been dug away, and the earth used in filling in the flats, by two steam shovels, the factories, stores and dwellings located on the tract being moved out upon skidways and then lowered to the new level.

This tract will be the main yard of the N. P. R. R.; five miles of track have already been laid and a freight house built, costing $22,000; and next year the engine and car shops will be built, costing $500,000.

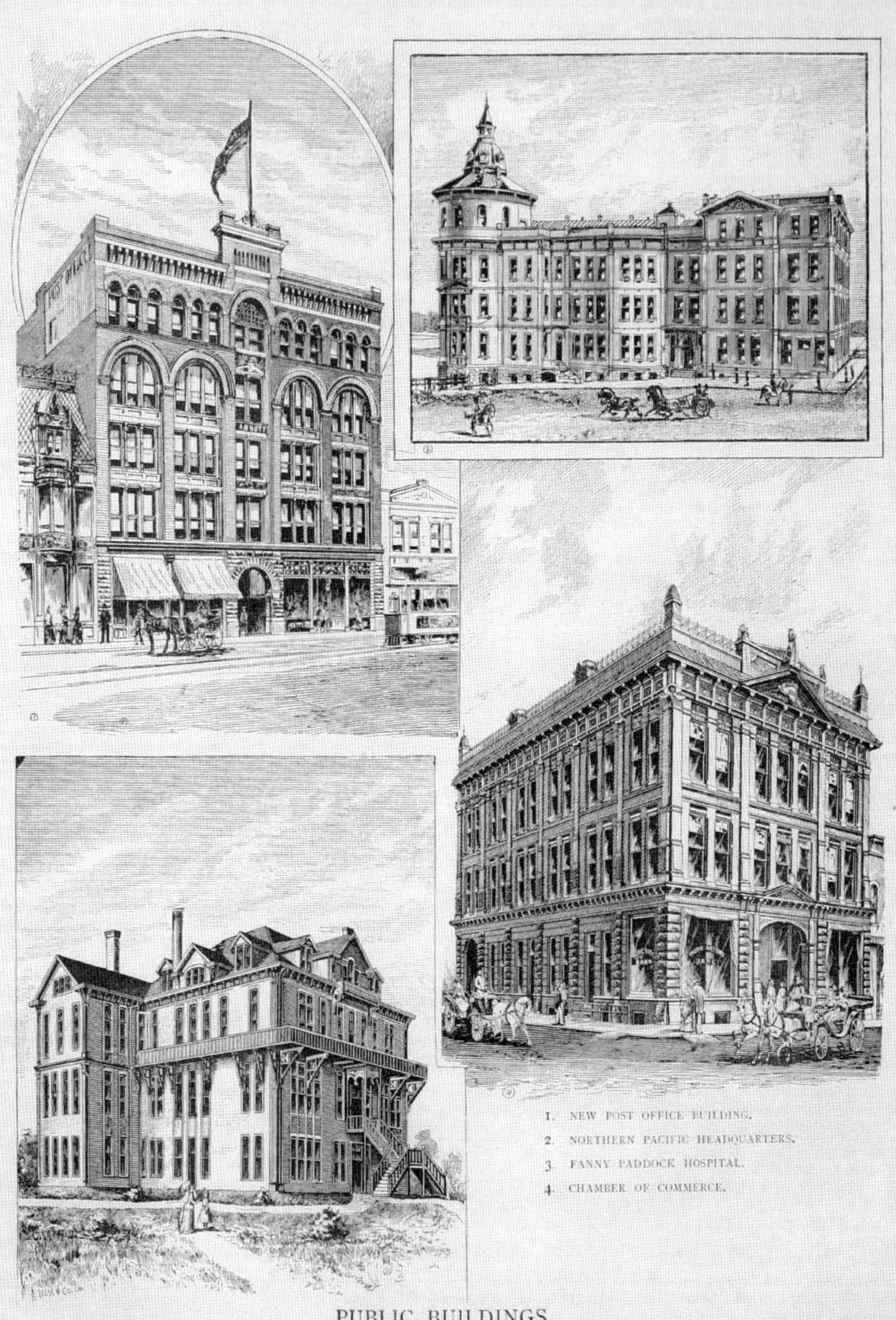

1. NEW POST OFFICE BUILDING.
2. NORTHERN PACIFIC HEADQUARTERS.
3. FANNY PADDOCK HOSPITAL.
4. CHAMBER OF COMMERCE.

PUBLIC BUILDINGS.

THE GREAT RYAN SMELTER.

How it will Help Tacoma's Industries, and Make her a Great Financial Center.

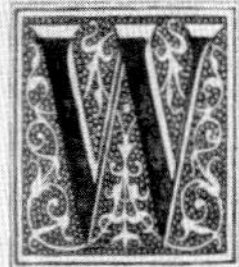

WE have the largest smelter on the Pacific coast nearly completed, and ready to start up for actual work some time this fall. Over $200,000 have been expended already, and if all the buildings contained in the plans are completed, the cost will probably be as much more. The smelter is being built by the Dennis Ryan Syndicate of St. Paul—a syndicate wealthy enough to put up such a plant as ought to be in operation in this growing country.

The flue dust chamber and the smoke stack contain nearly 2,500,000 brick. The main building and flue chamber have been built to take in seven smoke stacks. The boiler house has room for two more boilers. The calcining building is 84x101 feet, and the two furnaces—already erected—are each 17x71 feet. The interior of these furnaces are lined with fire brick that cost 5 cents each.

The flue dust chamber is 10 feet square and 440 feet in length; this is connected with the chimney, which is of the same diameter at the base.

Each of the two furnaces will smelt 80 tons per day, and will require 25 tons of coke.

The smelter will be prepared to handle gold, silver, lead, and copper ores, and will start up with these two completed furnaces and employ 150 men. When the full complement of seven furnaces is finished, 1,000 men will be necessary to do the requisite work of smelting the 560 tons of ore daily required. At present the capacity will be 160 tons of ore daily, with 150 employes, on three eight-hour shifts—day and night. A consignment of 1,000 tons of lead-silver "concentrates" from Dennis Ryan's "Gold Hunter" mine in the Cœur d'Alene, is expected soon to arrive, when work will then commence. The syndicate is now making arrangements to contract to smelt 5,000 tons of Alaska ores per month, and it will also receive silver ore as ballast from South American lumber vessels. Surely, the day of small things in the mining industry of Tacoma has passed, and we are well on our way to become a mining center.

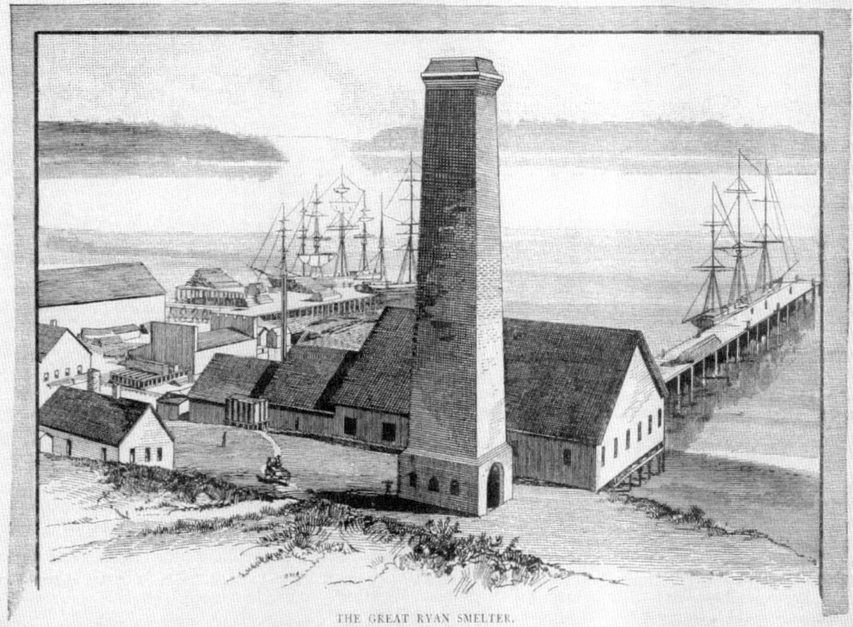

THE GREAT RYAN SMELTER.

There are few persons who can realize what the smelter will do for Tacoma in a financial way. The shipping from this city of quantities of precious ores to our Eastern financial centers, will make Tacoma the principal point for the buying of exchange, and will so help to make her the great financial center of the Pacific coast.

This may seem rather a broad assertion, but why so? The Alaska resources of precious ores are practically boundless, as are also those of the Cœur D'Alene and other districts; precious ores will be sent continually to New York and thus there will at all times be a balance in favor of Tacoma, which naturally will give this city the prestige when exchange on New York is wanted.

No one can compute the extent of the benefit from a smelter the size of the present one at Tacoma, particularly in view of the city's superior location for everything pertaining to transportation, general commerce, manufactures and finances; we wish to bring this as strongly before the reader as possible.

WHEAT.

TACOMA THE GREAT OUTLET—HER IMMENSE EXPORTS OF THIS CEREAL.

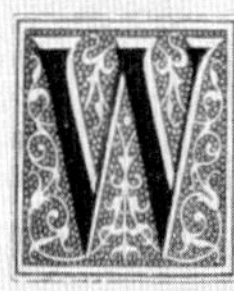

HEAT has made cities. Some of the greatest cities on the American continent owe their growth largely to the wheat trade which has come to them because of their situation at the outlet of some great wheat district, their railroad facilities, or their position on some great river, lake, or better yet, one of the two great oceans. To their location Chicago, New York, St. Louis, San Francisco and Duluth owe their greatness as grain markets or grain exporting cities. Tacoma is thus blessed. Her situation makes her the natural outlet of the great grain producing districts of Washington, Idaho and Oregon. She has the best railroad facilities of any city in the Northwest, and she is situated on Puget Sound, the great inlet of that greatest of oceans—the Pacific.

Tacoma has more than this. She has at her back one of the greatest wheat producing districts of the world. The grain region tributary to Tacoma includes a number of the largest counties of Washington, Idaho and Oregon, making in all a territory considerably larger than many of the Eastern States possess, and certainly much more fertile and productive.

If an Eastern farmer gets twenty or twenty-five bushels of wheat per acre from his farm, he thinks he is doing well. The Washington farmer's acres average fairly well at fifty bushels to the acre, though a higher average is not unusual. The grain district in the southeastern part of Washington is known as the Walla Walla wheat district. This district also includes the northeastern part of Oregon and several counties in the western part of Idaho. The other great grain district of Washington is known as the Inland Empire. It comprises the region lying between the Snake and Columbia Rivers. This grain district is also known as the Big Bend country, from the fact of its being bounded on three of four sides by the great Columbia River. There is no real dividing line between the Walla Walla grain district and the Inland Empire. The two districts together comprise the whole of eastern and southeastern Washington, but the opposite boundaries of the grain producing region are so far apart that it is more convenient to know the grain region as two wheat districts. The Walla Walla wheat district is the older of the two in the matter of cultivation. Wheat has been grown in this region for over twenty years, and the land now produces as much wheat per acre as it ever did. This district is connected with Tacoma by two entirely different lines of railway. To begin with, the Oregon & Washington railroad, better known as the Hunt railway system, taps the leading centers of the wheat district. The Northern Pacific railroad and the Oregon Railway and Navigation company's lines both traverse the grain region also. The wheat is brought by the farmers to stations along one of the three lines of railroad and sold. The grain is bought by one of several elevator companies, or by private wheat buying firms. The Northern Pacific Elevator company, which is the most important one buying wheat in this district, has wheat elevators or warehouses all along the lines of the Northern Pacific and the Oregon and Washington railroads. This company, which is one of the wealthiest in the Northwest, has its great elevator at Tacoma where all of its grain is shipped to be transferred to the vessels that are to carry it to Europe. The wheat buyers and elevator companies buy the wheat and store it in the warehouses or elevators along the railroads until they are ready to ship it to Tacoma. The Oregon and Washington road is a feeder of both the Northern Pacific road and the Oregon Railway & Navigation line, though now, by a close traffic agreement, most of the wheat sold along the line of that road is transferred to the Northern Pacific line for shipment to the tide water.

The wheat picked up on the Northern Pacific and Oregon & Washington roads is shipped over the former line to Pasco Junction and thence over the Cascade division of the same road to Tacoma. The other route by which wheat is shipped to Tacoma is over the Oregon Railway & Navigation company's line to Portland, Oregon, and thence to Tacoma over the Pacific division of the Northern Pacific road, or by water on ocean vessels or steamships. The latter route is the longest, but the charges for the shipment of grain to Tacoma are the same, whichever route it comes by. The cost for the transportation of grain to Tacoma is $4.70 per ton. The wheat from the Inland Empire is shipped over the Northern Pacific road or its branches.

The wheat is gathered up on the main line of the road, the Spokane Falls and Palouse branch and the Washington Central road, which is another branch of the Northern Pacific. The Northern Pacific Elevator company also has wheat warehouses and elevators along the line through the wheat district of the Big Bend country. After the wheat is bought and stored in the warehouses and elevators along the railroad, it is shipped by rail to Tacoma. Arrived in Tacoma, the wheat is stored in the immense elevators and warehouses. Among the principal firms exporting wheat from Tacoma are Balfour, Guthrie & Co., the Portland Shipping company, C. Cæsar & Co., McClaine, Wade & Co., Reese, Redman & Co., the Puget Sound Flouring and Milling Company, the Tacoma Warehouse and Elevator Company, the Northern Pacific Elevator Company, Reed & Co., and Dusenberry & Co.

Tacoma has an aggregate warehouse and elevator capacity of over 4,000,000 bushels of wheat. It is the only seaport in Washington which has elevators or warehouses, and her grain handling and shipping facilities are vastly superior to those of any city on the Pacific coast with the single exception of San Francisco. Among the large elevators and warehouses here are the Northern Pacific Elevator company's new elevator, just completed, the warehouse of the Tacoma Warehouse & Elevator company, the Puget Sound Flouring & Milling company's warehouse, and the new elevator now being built by the latter company. There is a large flouring mill at Tacoma which uses nearly 1,000 bushels of

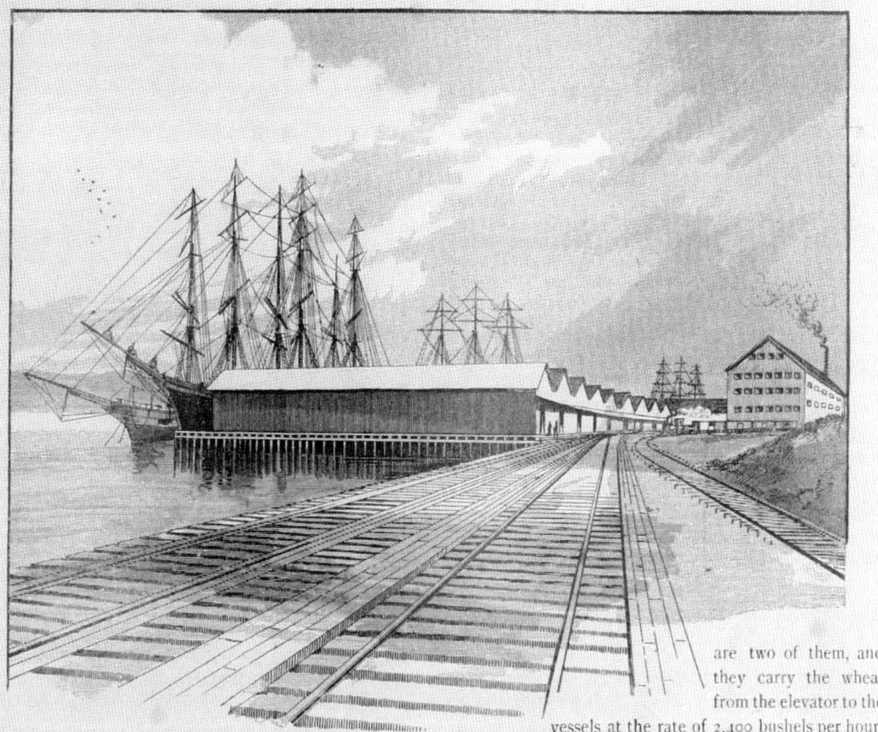

wheat per day, and the Puget Sound Flouring & Milling company is now erecting a large flouring mill, one of the finest in this country, which will, when completed, turn out flour from 1,000 bushels of wheat per day.

Nearly 10,000,000 bushels of wheat can be stored in the elevators and warehouses at Tacoma and along the railway lines through the grain districts. As the wheat comes in, after the wheat harvest begins in the summer, the warehouses and elevators at Tacoma are quickly filled up and then the grain is stored in the grain district to be shipped on to Tacoma after the export shipment to Europe by vessel begins. It will thus be seen that, though Tacoma is a young city and has not shipped any grain until within the last two or three years, she already has one of the best and most fully equipped systems of handling wheat, that there is in existence in the world. The method employed at the Northern Pacific Elevator company's big elevator is a good example of how the wheat is handled after it reaches Tacoma. The cars of wheat are taken right into the elevator and there unloaded by steam power at the rate of a car every ten minutes on each of the two tracks which pass through the elevator. The wheat is carried to the top of the elevator, and emptied into immense bins. As this is written, the British iron bark Dumbartonshire is loading wheat at this elevator. She is the first vessel to load there, as the elevator was completed only a few weeks ago. When the vessel has reached the right position, one of the grain carriers is set in motion. There are two of them, and they carry the wheat from the elevator to the vessels at the rate of 2,400 bushels per hour. With these two carriers, two large vessels can be loaded at the same time and at this rate a large vessel can be readily loaded in the extremely short space of three days.

In 1887, the ship Persian sailed for Europe from Tacoma with 45,000 centals of wheat valued at $50,000. This was the first cargo of wheat shipped from Tacoma, and the only cargo for that year. During the year 1888 there were shipped from Tacoma twenty-nine cargoes of a total weight of 1,517,040 centals, or nearly 3,000,000 bushels of wheat. The value of these twenty-nine cargoes aggregated $2,127,974. This jump at a single bound from shipping one cargo of wheat in 1887, to twenty-nine cargoes in 1889, demonstrated that Tacoma was to be a great grain shipping port. The export of wheat from Tacoma for the year 1889 will at least double that of last year. A vessel's expenses in coming in from, and going out to the sea from Tacoma, are several thousand dollars less than a vessel's expenses in going up to Portland from the sea and back again. The grain buyers now have representatives in the grain districts, and the farmers are selling their wheat at from 62 to 66 cents per bushel. At $4.70 per ton for transportation, the rate per bushel is about 14 cents, so that the wheat is worth from 76 to 80 cents per bushel at the very lowest price when it reaches Tacoma. The Tacoma Produce Exchange was incorporated several months ago. The exchange has an office in the Chamber of Commerce building, and daily market reports are received from the principal grain markets of the world.

BANKS AND BANKING.

FACTS AND FIGURES SHOW TACOMA WILL BE THE GREAT FINANCIAL CENTER OF THE NORTH PACIFIC COAST.

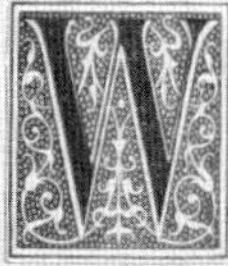ERE it not for the fact of its universally conceded advantageous location it would be a difficult task, even for men eminent in finances, to account for the almost universal desire of new-comers to engage in the banking business. Her rapid growth since the completion of the Northern Pacific R. R., three years since, is evidenced forcibly by the increase of the banks.

Ten years ago when Tacoma was merely a hamlet, containing not to exceed seven hundred souls, she had no bank; now, with a conservative estimate in population of at least 30,000, there are nine commercial and two savings banks; of the commercial banks six are National, and three private.

The first bank established in Tacoma was organized about eight years ago by the late A. J. Baker, with a capital of $35,000, and was known as the Bank of New Tacoma; it was successfully conducted for a period of three years, when it was purchased by the Hon. Walter J. Thompson and his associates, who, in May, 1884, merged it into the Merchant's National Bank with a paid up capital of $50,000; the very rapid and successful growth of this bank is a fair index of the standing and rank of the "City of Destiny" in financial and commercial circles, and we shall later refer to its management, first in the order of banks in order that existing conditions may be properly understood, and we shall now proceed to the completion of our theme based upon the record before us. We premised by stating that, while ten years ago Tacoma had no banking institutions within her limits, she now has eleven, including two savings banks. We shall enumerate them in the order of their organization, viz., Merchants' National, capital $250,000; Tacoma National, capital $100,000; Pacific National, capital $100,000; National Bank of Commerce, capital $200,000; Traders' Bank of Tacoma, capital $100,000; Citizens' National, capital $100,000; Washington National, capital $100,000; West Coast Fire and Marine Insurance Co. Bank, capital $180,000, and the Security Bank, capital $60,000.

This makes an aggregate capital in the commercial banks of $1,190,000, which with their surplus fund, which aggregates $210,000, gives us fourteen hundred thousand dollars of banking capital for commercial purposes in a city of thirty thousand people, in addition to the deposits which reach about four million of dollars.

The Savings Banks, known as the Tacoma Trust and Savings Bank, and Tacoma Building and Savings Association, having an aggregate capital of $130,000, are safe, conservative institutions, located finely, and doing a good business.

It is stated, as an everlasting truism, that bankers are the most conservative of all professional men; if this be true, then must Tacoma, the "City of Destiny," become what her many friends have been predicting for years, viz., "The financial center of the North Pacific Coast." Furthermore, as an evidence of the fact that the banking business is not overdone, it has been stated to us that the managers of the Bank of Montreal and of the Bank of British Columbia, have signified their intention of opening branches at Tacoma, and it is everywhere regarded as good evidence of the advantages of location when these foreign institutions seek them out.

MERCHANTS' NATIONAL BANK BUILDING.

In the preparation of this article we have endeavored to place only well-known facts before the reader rather than mere metaphor or brilliant description, but if it shall aid any one to determine in his own mind the important future which lies before this proud city on Commencement Bay, in Puget Sound, at the foot of the grandest mountain peak on earth, Mount Tacoma, raising its snow-crested head, 14,444 feet above the sea, we shall be content.

THE MERCHANTS' NATIONAL BANK.

This bank, which ranks first in amount of paid up capital in the State, was, as we have before stated, organized in May, 1884, with a capital of $50,000; in May, 1888, its directors finding that the large line of deposits necessitated more capital, the capital stock of the bank was doubled, and again last August their deposits having reached nearly a *million* of dollars, the amount of paid in capital was increased to $250,000. In the five years of its existence it has acquired a standing in financial circles which in the older cities of the Eastern States would have taken years, yes twenty years, to accomplish. Its leading position gives it facilities for collection and correspondence which are excelled by no other banking institution in the State. The total resources of the bank according to its last statement, are $1,285,972.72.

At this date the Merchants National Bank has the largest capital, more country correspondents, and transacts more business than any other bank in the State of Washington.

The phenomenal prosperity of this institution can be accounted for by the way it is officered. Walter J. Thompson, the President, is a man who is universally admired and respected by the entire community in which he lives, and it is safe to say that there is not a man in Tacoma to-day who so justly deserves respect. Although but thirty-seven years old, Mr. Thompson is to-day a self-made man and a millionaire at that. While living in Hebron, Neb., Mr. Thompson forsook law, a profession he had originally intended following, and entering the principal bank of that city, he remained there until his removal to Tacoma in 1883. Mr. Thompson is also a prominent candidate for United States Senator on the Republican ticket, and as the new State Senate is composed of a majority of Republicans, there is a very good prospect of his attaining his ambition.

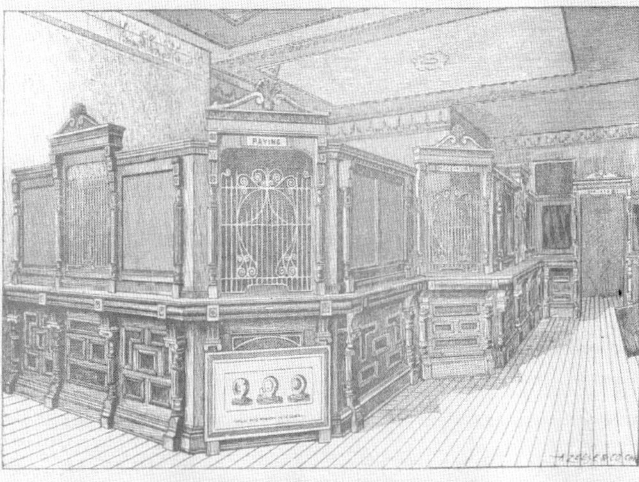

INTERIOR OF THE WASHINGTON NATIONAL BANK.

The Vice-President, Mr. Henry Drum, is also a young man. He is a brother-in-law of President Thompson, and comes from the same town. Mr. Drum, when Mayor of Tacoma from 1888–9, proved himself an able and clear headed business man. He has recently been elected to the State Senate. Mr. Drum is a Democrat in politics, and the very fact that the constituency which he represents is strongly Republican, proves beyond doubt his popularity. The cashier of the bank, Mr. Samuel Collyer, although only a resident in Tacoma since June, 1888, is now looked upon as a most successful business man. To him credit is chiefly due for the prosperity of the bank. His sound judgment has gained for him the respect of every one in Tacoma. He is a member of the executive committee of the Chamber of Commerce, and has more than once been called upon to represent the City of Destiny in commercial conferences in distant cities. To Mr. Collyer we are indebted for the history of Tacoma's banking interests, as also for many courtesies extended us, and it is hardly necessary to say that Mr. Collyer's position in financial circles is established when it is understood that he is president of the Tacoma Clearing House, secretary of the Washington Bankers' Association, First Vice-President of the Pacific Coast Chamber of Commerce, and Vice-President of the American Bankers' Association. He is for Tacoma first, last, and all the time, and is ever ready to give his time and money to maintain the prestige of the city. Mr. Collyer comes originally from Chicago, and he is a son of the Rev. Robert Collyer, the eminent divine of New York City. Mr. R. J. Davis, the assistant cashier, started in the bank as office boy. His business ability and general integrity are unquestioned, and he has no superiors in the knowledge of banking.

The present offices of the bank have recently been renovated, but the new Safe Deposit Block, a magnificent edifice built by the Merchants' National Bank and the Tacoma Trust and Savings Bank, will be occupied by this bank. A cut of their new building will be seen on the opposite page, and as will be seen, it will indeed be an ornament and pride to the city.

THE WASHINGTON NATIONAL BANK.

This bank has not been in operation one year, and yet in proportion to the other banking houses in Tacoma its business is larger. The bank was organized last spring by Messrs. E. L. Scarritt and C. S. Bridges, two energetic and thoroughly capable banking men from Watertown, Dak., and Greencastle, Ind. They were readily welcomed with open arms by the citizens of Tacoma, and but a few days passed before the Washington National Bank was incorporated with a capital stock of $250,000. The following directorship shows the names of some of Tacoma's best known citizens: L. F. Thompson, A. A. Honey, A. A. Knight, A. J. Littlejohn, E. N. Ouimette, Chas. Reichenbach, C. S. Bridges and E. L. Scarritt. The officers are: E. L. Scarritt, president; E. N. Ouimette, vice-president, and C. S. Bridges, cashier. Of President Scarritt it can be truthfully said that the Washington National Bank is fortunate in having such a clear and level-headed business man at the head of it. He comes from a fine New England stock. He has practiced as a lawyer with great success, and his knowledge of legal matters is of great value to him now in his everyday business. Since his residence in Tacoma he has become identified with some of the leading industries of the city. He is a man of quick and unerring judgment in business. Mr. C. S. Bridges was born at Morton, Indiana, in 1862, but until coming to Tacoma spent most of his life in the city of Greencastle in the same State. For many years he acted as assistant cashier in the Central National Bank.

Of Mr. Ouimette but little can be said that is not already detailed in a special detail on his large interests in Tacoma, which will be found in this book.

This bank transacts a general banking business, loans on collateral and personal security; discounts liberally for its customers, and accords to each and all as favorable terms as is consistant with judicious and conservative banking. The funds and securities of this bank are protected by the Corliss safe, the only one in Tacoma.

The offices of the bank are at 1314 Pacific avenue, a cut of which will be found on this page.

The following is a statement of the bank's resources and liabilities Sept. 30, 1889:

RESOURCES.

Loans	$172,774 23
Overdrafts	2,403 00
U. S Bonds to Secure Circulation	22,500 00
Real Es ate Furniture Fixtures	4,718 01
Expenses	3 091 94
Premiums	6,518 75
Redemption Fund	1,012 50
Cash	44,115 55
Total	$257,133 98

LIABILITIES.

Capital Stock Paid in	$100 000 00
Undivided Profits	4,448 05
National Bank Notes Outstanding	20,250 00
Deposits	132,435 93
Total	$257,133 98

PACIFIC NATIONAL BANK.

This institution has been established nearly four years in Tacoma, and is at present located in the Chamber of Commerce Block, but the rapid growth of Tacoma, and consequently the increase of business with this bank, demand more commodious quarters, and it is the intention of the directors to build a large and handsome block on the southwest corner of Pacific avenue and Thirteenth street. Work will be commenced on this structure in the near future, and when once started, will be pushed rapidly. The officers of the bank are as follows: President, C. P. Masterson; Vice-President, T. B. Wallace; Cashier, L. R. Manning; Assistant Cashier, S. B. Dusenberry, while the directors are C. P. Masterson, W. D. Tyler, J. P. Stewart, L. R. Manning and T. B. Wallace.

The bank is not only known as one of the largest and strongest of Tacoma, but for the liberality extended to its customers. The officers are men of high social standing and strict integrity.

The paid up capital of this bank is $100,000 with a surplus of $35,000. A general banking business is transacted.

The following is a late statement of its financial condition:

RESOURCES.

Loans and Discounts	$493,567 87
Overdrafts	4,007 78
U. S. Bonds	25,000 00
Other Stocks and Bonds	26,476 34
Cash on Hand	104,859 22
Due from Banks	192,621 15
Real Estate and Fixtures	19,370 17
Current Expenses and Taxes	4,554 38
Premiums	1,875 00
Due from U. S. Treasurer	1,125 00
	$873 456 91

LIABILITIES.

Capital Paid in	$100,000 00
Surplus	35,000 00
Undivided Profits	13,844 26
Circulation	22,500 00
Deposits	702,112 65
	$873,456 91

THE TACOMA TRUST AND SAVINGS BANK.

This institution may be termed one of the most profitable businesses in the State of Washington.

In 1887, when about a dozen of the most influential business men of Tacoma decided to incorporate a savings bank for the handling of trust funds, even the most sanguine scarcely thought that it would be such a successful business venture, or such a great boon to the public, especially that class who desire to place their hard earnings in safe keeping and receive a liberal interest on their deposits, but such it has turned out to be.

This bank is authorized to receive, hold, and disburse money securities in trust, and act as financial agents for individuals, corporations, or estates, besides negotiating the sale of mortgages.

Under the able management of Mr. W. B. Allen, the secretary and cashier, who was also one of the incorporators, all communications of a business nature will at once receive prompt care and attention.

The following gentlemen are the incorporators of the bank: W. J. Thompson, president; Nelson Bennett, vice-president; W. B. Allen, secretary and treasurer; Jesse M. Allen, Rev. W. H. Sampson, M. J. Cogswell, M. F. Hatch, A. C. Smith, Geo. F. Orchard and C. S. Barlow.

The offices of the bank are on the corner of Pacific avenue and Eleventh street, but the present quarters are to be torn down, and the Safe Deposit block, a structure 100x120 feet, and six stories high, will be erected on the site. The trust and savings bank will have handsome offices in this building when it is completed.

This is the block which we have displayed in our pages, and which is being built in connection with the Merchants' National Bank.

THE CITIZENS NATIONAL BANK,

on Pacific avenue, near Fifteenth street, is doing business under the National Banking Law, and although the enterprise is of comparatively recent establishment, it is already upon a substantial basis, and doing a large and flourishing business. Among its officers are Mr. O. B. Hayden, well known in real estate circles, who is president. He has his pleasant real estate offices on the floor above the bank, and is well known as a man whose conservative judgment and sterling business integrity make a very safe guide to intending investors in property in the vicinity of the City of Destiny. The other officers of the bank are H. S. Huson, vice-president, who was for several years Assistant Engineer of the Northern Pacific Railroad. Mr. L. J. Pentecost, the cashier, was formerly the cashier of the Guthrie County National Bank of Panora, Iowa, for fifteen years. Mr. Hayden is also from Panora, and it was there that the friendship was formed which led to their present partnership. The statement published below represents the business done up to the close of Sept. 30, 1889.

RESOURCES.

Loans and Discounts		$85,871.37
Overdrafts		73.10
U. S. Bonds		25,000.00
Other Stocks and Bonds		6,068.45
Banking House		35,000.00
Furniture and Fixtures		3,719.63
Current Expenses and Taxes		1,625.85
Premium on Bonds		7,156.25
Eastern Exchange	$57,127.67	
Cash	41,312.30	
Redemption Fund	1,125.00	
		100,004.97
Total		$264,579.62

LIABILITIES.

Capital Paid in	$80,000.00
Undivided Profits	2,349.45
Circulation	22,500.00
Deposits	159,730.17
Total	$264,579.62

Attest:
O. B. Hayden, H. S. Huson, Thos. Carroll, } Directors.

L. J. PENTECOST, Cashier.

Sworn to before me this 3d day of October, 1889.

FRED F. LACEY, Notary Public.

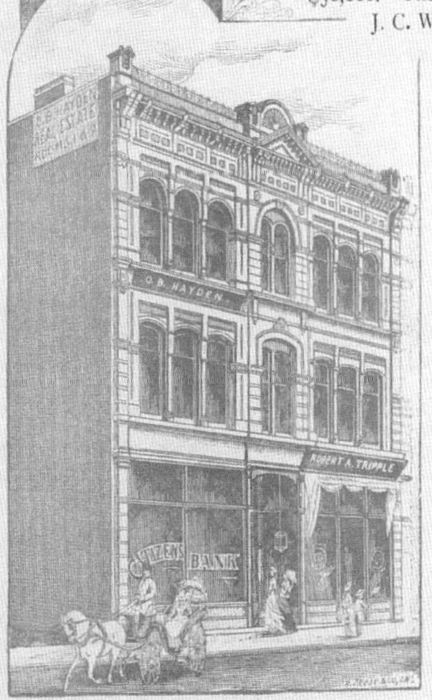

CITIZENS BANK BUILDING

OTHER BANKING HOUSES.

The Tacoma National Bank, located on Pacific avenue and Tenth street, has a capital stock of $100,000 and a surplus of $100,000. The officers are: W. B. Blackwell, president; Edmund Rice, vice-president: W. Fraser, cashier, and H. O. Fishback, assistant cashier. The directors are Robert Wingate, Edmund Rice, Jr., I. W. Anderson, W. B. Blackwell, and Geo. E. Atkinson. A general banking business is transacted.

The Oakland Land, Loan and Trust Company is situated at 111 South Tenth street. Their capital stock is $300,000, paid in capital $256,400, and surplus $11,197. Mr. Harry M. Ball is the president; S. M. Clark, vice-president and treasurer, and Merton H. Corey is assistant treasurer. The bank does a large general trust and investment business.

The Tacoma Building and Savings Association Savings Bank. This concern has its present office on the corner of Eleventh and C streets, and is transacting a general banking business. Its paid up capital is $100,000, and E. H. Hatfield is the president. The other trustees are W. H. Woodruff, vice-president; Linus E. Post, secretary and cashier; Thos. L. Nixon, treasurer, and Theo. L. Stiles, Geo. P. Eaton, and C. P. Ferry.

The National Bank of Commerce has a paid up capital of $200,000, with a surplus and undivided profits of $50,000. The officers are F. M. Wade, president; J. C. Weatherred, vice-president, and A. F. McLane, cashier. The offices are at 930 Pacific avenue, where a general banking business is transacted.

The Security Bank is a private corporation, and only just started. Its business is rapidly growing, and under the able direction of A. J. Hayward, president, its success is assured. The other officers are: W. H. Bradley, vice-president; R. H. Passmore, cashier, and A. F. Eastman, assistant cashier. The capital stock of the bank is $100,000.

The Traders' Bank, with a capital of $100,000, is located in the Fife Block, cor. Pacific avenue and Ninth street.

The West Coast Bank, located temporarily in the new Bostwick Block, is newly organized. Its capital stock is $100,000, and the bank is doing a good business.

Much more could be written of the banking institutions and general banking of Tacoma, but our limited space will not permit of it; in different parts of our work we have referred to the existing conditions which influence banking here and have shown how these favorable conditions, with proper energy on the part of the citizens and bankers of Tacoma, may make the city the great financial and exchange center on the Pacific coast.

By a proper husbanding of these great resources it is firmly believed our predictions will be fulfilled. If in the short space of five years from this time the "City of Destiny" has not fulfilled these expectations, it will certainly be because the city has been engulfed by some of nature's freaks, or that the citizens have not shown the proper energy to improve her chances.

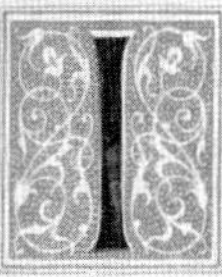

IT is now nearly a century since Washington, in his farewell address to the people of the United States, said: "Promote, then, as an object of primary importance, institutions for the general diffusion of knowledge. In proportion as the structure of a government gives force to public opinion, it is essential that public opinion should be enlightened."

The commonwealth now assuming statehood and destined forever to bear the proud name of Washington, has, with great cordiality and promptness, adopted this lofty sentiment, embodying the same in a well-sustained public school system.

Tacoma in its wonderful development materially has not forgotten the wise counsel of the father of his country.

The public school system is firmly established in the affections of the people, the work and discipline of the schools are well supported, while a liberal policy marks the treatment the schools receive from those who pay the taxes. The system is thoroughly established and wisely administered by an active Board of Education, and a carefully selected corps of teachers. During the school year of 1887-88 there were enrolled in the city schools 1,401 different pupils. The entire enrollment for the school year of 1888-89 was 2,294, an increase of over 63 per cent.

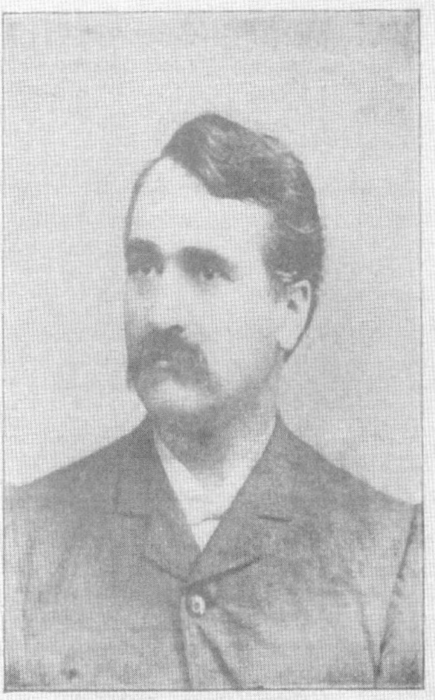

PROFESSOR F. B. GAULT,
Superintendent of Public Schools.

The school census taken June, 1888, showed 2,139 school youth (five to twenty-one years of age) in the district. It will be seen that the school enrollment exceeded the census enumeration, an evidence of remarkable growth, corroborated by the census of June, 1889, which gives the city a school population of 3,281, or a gain in one year of 1,142 school youth. At this writing there are now enrolled in the schools 2,000 pupils who are carefully instructed by forty-five teachers.

The board of directors consists of three members, each elected by the people for a term of three years, one new member coming upon the board annually. The present board is composed of S. T. Armstrong, president, Henry Drum and J. A. Wintermute. The system comprises five school wards or districts, known as the Central, the Lincoln, the Hawthorne, the Longfellow and the Emerson Schools. These buildings are attractive in external appearance, the rooms, without exception, being commodious, pleasant and well furnished.

The Emerson, when occupied in January, will afford suitable accommodations for the High School and highest grammar schools; it will also contain the offices of the board and superintendent, and several rooms for the primary grades of the immediate locality.

The corps is made up of teachers who have been connected with the best systems throughout the country, and is essentially cosmopolitan. The management aims to encourage the individuality of teachers, holding each responsible for results without limiting or thwarting the activities by narrow rules and details of supervision. In the course of instruction the aim everywhere is thoroughness. There is to be no hurry, cramming or confusion; there is to be time enough to do everything well. Hence it has been necessary to lighten the grade work and reduce the number of subjects allotted to the various years of school life. But the grade of the school is to be just as high as in those schools where the work is done with more pressure and worry. Non-essentials are to be excluded, and essentials magnified. It is believed that pupils who are well grounded in the early part of the course will make more rapid and more certain progress in the upper grades.

In harmony with this plan of work, reading, which is a fundamental branch, receives marked and enthusiastic attention. Pupils read often, and a great deal each day. To this end carefully selected sets of supplementary readers are provided for the different grades. These extra reading books are historical, biographical, narrative, or scientific, being well calculated to draw out the tastes of children toward those useful lines of reading. This is an excellent foundation for subsequent school work and for after life. "While pupils learn to read they should also read to learn," is the motto in this school.

Recently the Hon. Walter J. Thompson, of Tacoma, offered the board the munificent sum of $10,000 for the founding of a manual training department in connection with the city schools, the money to be devoted to equipment, the board to furnish the room and instruction.

An additional $10,000 was also placed in trust by Mr. Thompson to aid in the further extension of the enterprise, which sum is conditioned upon the faithful application of the first ten thousand dollars and the success attained by the manual training school. This makes available twenty thousand dollars, an amount sufficient to guarantee the complete success of the department. The department will be opened as soon as the Emerson building is finished. Half of this sum is to be applied to a boys' school, and the other half to a girls' school for domestic economy. Doubtless the same motive of generosity and public spirit that prompted Mr. Thompson to make this gift will actuate others to assist in this beneficent enterprise, and in time the Tacoma Manual Training School will develop into a broad course of study and wide range of technical instruction, with laboratories, workshops, draughting rooms, etc.

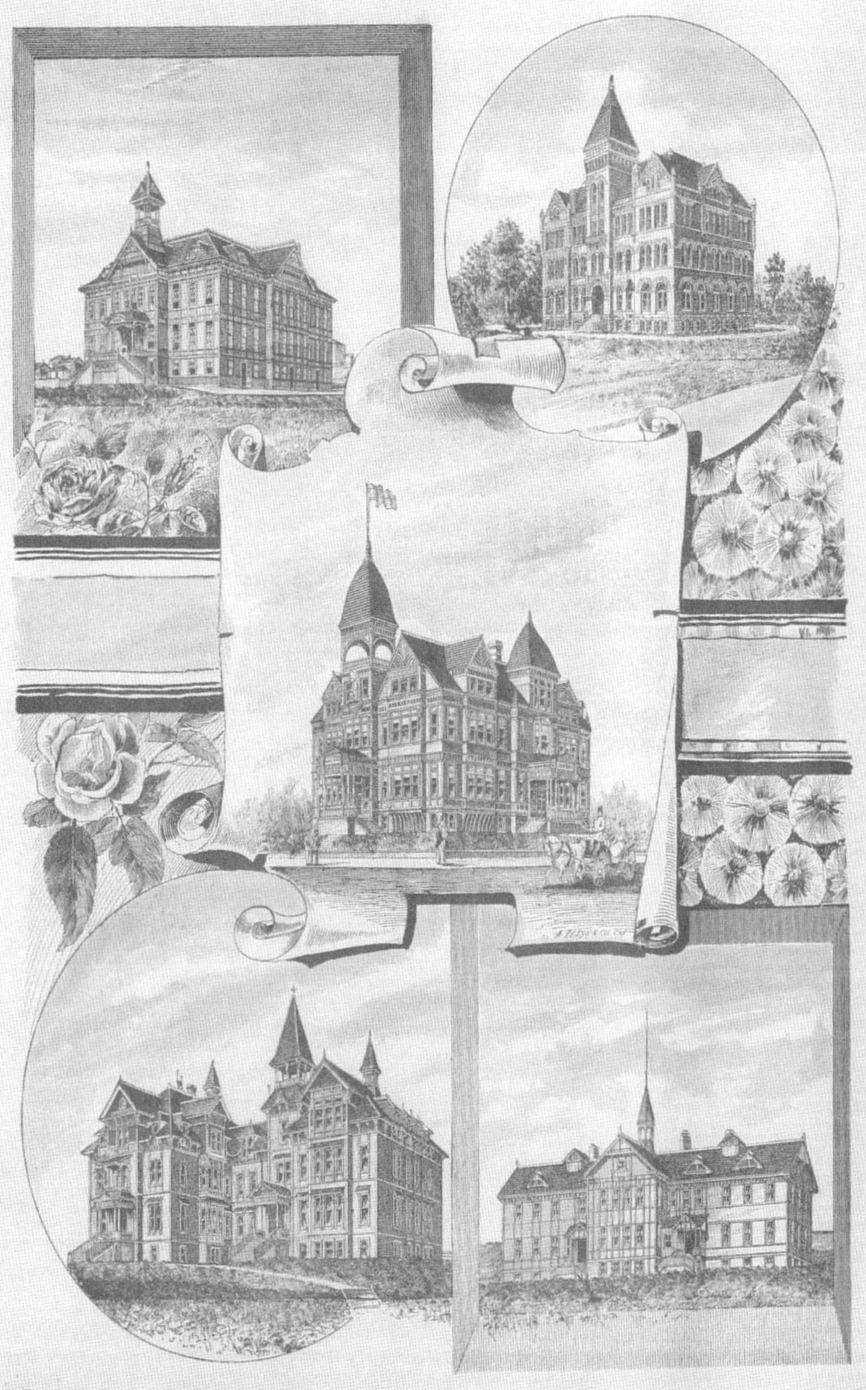

CENTRAL SCHOOL. ANNIE WRIGHT SEMINARY. EMERSON SCHOOL. PUGET SOUND UNIVERSITY. HAWTHORNE SCHOOL.

THE CHURCHES.

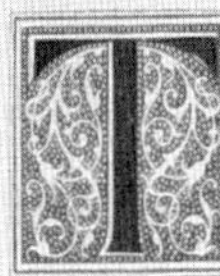

THE class of people that settled Tacoma, and has continued to pour in during these years of great growth, has made churches and Sunday schools strong and prosperous.

The first church to enter the field and make good her pioneer record was the Methodist Episcopal. The First Church was organized December 11, 1875. The first sermon preached by a Methodist preacher on this town site was delivered in a tent where the first Congregational Church now stands. The church on the corner of C and Seventh was built in 1878 under the leadership of Rev. Martin Judy. The old parsonage was built by Rev. J. F. DeVore in 1882. The church was greatly enlarged in June, 1889, during the pastorate of Rev. Geo. C. Wilding. In the spring of this same year, the new parsonage, corner of G and Eighth streets, was built and furnished at a cost of about $4,500; and the Epworth Church in Coulter's Addition was erected by the Young People's Methodist Alliance of the First Church at a cost of $3,000. The following pastors have served this church, viz: Rev. C. H. Hoxie, two years; Rev. Martin Judy, two years; Rev. John Parsons, one year; Rev. E. Dudley and Rev. Spaulding together, one year; Rev. J. Miller, one year; Rev. J. F. De Vore, three years; Rev. J. A. Ward, one year; Rev. T. J. Massey, two years; Rev. D. G. Le Lourd, one year, and Rev. Geo. C. Wilding, the present pastor, took charge of the church in September, 1888. Present membership, about 450.

THE OLD TACOMA CHURCH

Was organized by Rev. J. F. DeVore, October 30, 1884. The present church was built in 1885. The following pastors have served this church: Rev. J. F. DeVore, two years; Rev. G. A. Landen, two years. Rev. R. H. Massey, the present pastor, took charge of the church September, 1888.

A mission Sunday school was started in 1882, which grew into the present Central M. E. Church. The church was built by Rev. J. F. DeVore in 1884, and greatly enlarged by Rev. W. B. McMillin in 1889. The society was organized in 1887, and the first pastor was Rev. G. A. Landen, who was followed in 1888 by Rev. W. B. McMillin, the present pastor. The present membership is about 150.

A small society has been formed at Fern Hill, and in June, 1889, Rev. Geo. C. Wilding dedicated a handsome little church that cost about $3,000.

Lots have been secured in East Tacoma, and a church will be commenced in a few weeks. Rev. B. F. Brooks is the pastor.

THE GERMAN M. E. CHURCH

Was organized in April, 1883. A church and parsonage was built on D and Thirteenth streets and the property was sold and buildings erected on I and Twenty-eighth streets. The present membership is about 50. The following pastors have served the church: Rev. Fr. Bonn; Rev. Mr. Sinclair; Rev. J. Braner; Rev. Mr. Hansen, the present pastor, was appointed in the autumn of 1887.

Rev. C. J. Larsen was appointed to work among the Scandinavian people of Tacoma in 1884, and he organized a Methodist church soon after his arrival. In 1885 they built the church on Tacoma avenue near Sixteenth street. They have a membership of about 80. Rev. C. N. Hauge, the present pastor, took charge in September, 1887.

THE METHODIST UNIVERSITY,

On Twenty-first and I streets, to cost $65,000, is completed to the top of the first story, and will be completed in six months.

THE FIRST CONGREGATIONAL CHURCH

Has been organized quite a number of years, and is become quite strong and prosperous. They are now enlarging their house of worship on St. Helen's avenue, and when completed it will be one of the best church buildings in the city. They also have a church in East Tacoma, and will soon have one in North Tacoma. Rev. M. S. Hartwell has been pastor of the church for about one year. Rev. Thomas Sims is pastor of the churches in East Tacoma and North Tacoma.

THE FIRST BAPTIST CHURCH

Was organized, corner of Ninth and D streets, March 28, 1883. Its first pastor was Rev. J. Beaven, who served the church one year; his successor was Rev. B. S. MacLafferty, who remained nearly four years. He was followed by Rev. A. B. Banks, the present pastor, on May 1, 1888. The church edifice was built in 1884, and dedicated on March 16. This church has been very prosperous, and has now a membership of 225. A mission church has been started in the East Addition and lots secured for future churches at Fern Hill and Junett's Addition. The church has been recently enlarged, and is now quite an attractive room. Rev. G. B. Douglass is in charge of a Second Baptist Church, which has purchased the old Presbyterian church building and located at the corner of Tenth and K streets.

THE CHRISTIAN CHURCH

Was instituted the first Sabbath in February, 1884. The church building is located on the corner of E and Thirteenth streets. It has had a season of prosperity, and now has an enrolled membership of 200. A peculiar feature of this society is that it is now entirely out of debt. The pastors have been Revs. Bruce Wolverton, Andrew Sweeney, H. K. Sicafoose and the present pastor, Rev. M. F. Redlien.

On August 30, 1885, the First Unitarian Church was organized, with Rev. Geo. H. Greer, pastor. In January, 1888, the church edifice on Tacoma avenue and Third street was dedicated. In December, 1888, Rev. W. E Copeland took the pastorate. There are now about 100 names on the church roll, and the Sunday school numbers about 75. A fine new parsonage has recently been built.

ST. LEO'S CATHOLIC CHURCH,

Corner of D and Eleventh streets, was erected in 1883. Rev. P. F. Hylebos is rector. The congregation is large, and there is every indication of thrift and growth.

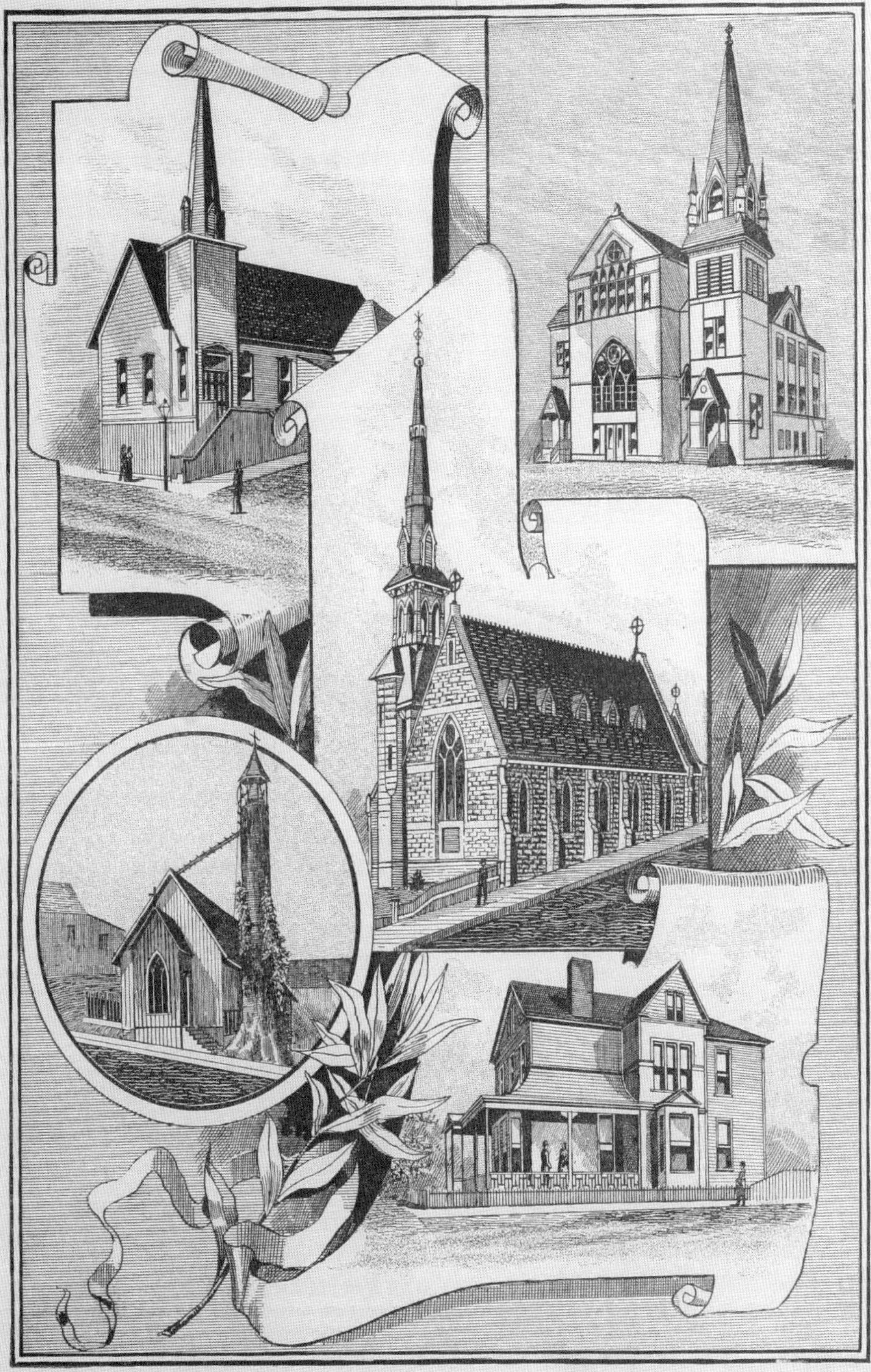

FIRST M. E. CHURCH.
THE OLD TOWN CHURCH.

ST. LUKE'S EPISCOPAL

LUTHERAN CHURCH.
PARSONAGE OF THE FIRST M. E.

THE LUTHERAN CHURCH

Is making great progress in this city, and has quite a number of societies.

The First Norwegian Evangelical Lutheran Church, of which the Rev. Ingebrigt Tollefsen is pastor, though recently established, is moving forward encouragingly and is doing a good work. This church is located on I street, between Twelfth and Thirteenth streets.

THE GERMAN LUTHERAN CHURCH,

Located at 1307 I street, is one of the old and strong ecclesiastical organizations in the city. Rev. F. N. Wolf is the untiring pastor of this church. Not content with the large field he cultivates in the body of the city, he has recently built a mission church in East Tacoma.

Rev. G. A. Anderson is the pastor of the Swedish Evangelical Lutheran Church. The congregation was organized in July, 1882, by Rev. Carlson. In the summer of 1883 the first church was built on Tacoma Avenue. In the spring of 1884 the present and first pastor took charge of the church. The old church was sold, and their present commodious edifice erected in the spring of 1889, at a cost of $15,000. The membership is 150.

THE FIRST PRESBYTERIAN CHURCH

Is one of the strong and influential churches of the city. Several years ago the society was organized, and a neat church building erected on the corner of C and Eleventh streets. In the spring of 1889 the old church and site were sold for $50,000; lots were purchased on the corner of G and Tenth, and immediately was begun the erection of a handsome church to cost some $40,000. In the meantime the congregation worshiped in a tabernacle on the corner of G and Eleventh. The membership of the church is almost 300. Rev. W. A. Mackey is and has been the pastor for a number of years.

THE SECOND PRESBYTERIAN CHURCH

Was organized in January, 1888. Rev. Thomas MacGuire took charge of the congregation in December, 1888. A corner has been secured at North J and Ninth, and a church will soon be built.

THE THIRD PRESBYTERIAN CHURCH

Was instituted Jan. 28, 1889. A neat church was soon built on the corner of A and Thirtieth streets. The pastor is Rev. J. Osmond.

THE PROTESTANT EPISCOPAL.

Among the churches that very early began their work in this city, is to be placed the Protestant Episcopal. It has become a strong, influential, and wealthy organization. Through the generous beneficence of Mr. C. B. Wright of Philadelphia, the St. Luke's Memorial Church, corner of Sixth and C streets, was built at a cost of some $30,000. Rev. Lemuel H. Wells is the rector. In Old Tacoma is St. Peter's Church, with the "oldest church tower in the United States," being simply a great cedar tree beheaded. The Church of the Holy Communion is on E street near Seventeenth, Rev. R. S. Carlin, Rector. Right Rev. John A. Paddock, D. D., Bishop of the Diocese of Washington, resides in Tacoma. Under the direction of this branch of the church is the Annie Wright Seminary for girls, and the Washington College for boys. They are doing a good work in the Fannie Paddock Hospital, the fine new building being almost ready for occupancy. We learn that a handsome church is to be erected near the hospital.

THE SCANDINAVIAN FREE EVANGELICAL CHURCH

Is located at the corner of G and Thirteenth streets, and Rev. C. O. Torgerson is the pastor.

THE SEVENTH DAY ADVENTISTS

Have a church at the corner of K and Sixteenth streets, with a small organization.

THE NEW JERUSALEM CHURCH

Holds occasional services, but has not as yet effected an organization.

GEO. C. WILDING.

TACOMA SOCIALLY.

No Eastern city of Tacoma's size can boast a better class of citizens than those who form the body of this community. Indeed, it is almost wholly made up of young men and women who left the East to link their fortunes with this city, knowing its destiny; many of them with large means, and all of them with strong and well-defined purposes in life, and ambition to rise and prosper. It is the class of men with their wives, mothers, daughters and sisters, who, accustomed to the refinements, pleasures and luxuries of the East, with broad ideas ánd busy hands and brains have undertaken to build a city on Commencement Bay that shall copy only the best features of the cities they have left behind, and avoid a repetition of their mistakes. Benevolent, beneficial, church, Masonic, fraternal, literary, amateur theatrical, musical, bicycle, riding, and other social clubs are numerous. Perhaps the most notable of these is the Union Club, an organization formed of a number of the foremost young men in the city. The club is now building a handsome clubhouse to cost $15,000. The members are young men of means, and propose to perfect an organization and equip their resort in a fitting manner.

THEATERS OF TACOMA.

A beautiful structure, the New Tacoma Theater, which will be found in our pages, has just been completed, and will furnish the finest attractions. Mr. John W. Hanna, a gentleman of large experience is manager, and Mr. Thomas G. Moses scenic artist.

Germania Hall is a handsome building and fine playhouse under the management of Mr. J. Howe, and presents fine attractions.

Mr. J. M. Junnett, who has managed the Alpha Opera House and given pleasure to thousands, intends building a fine new theater in the near future, and intends to make it one which will rival in point of beauty and magnificence the new Tacoma theater

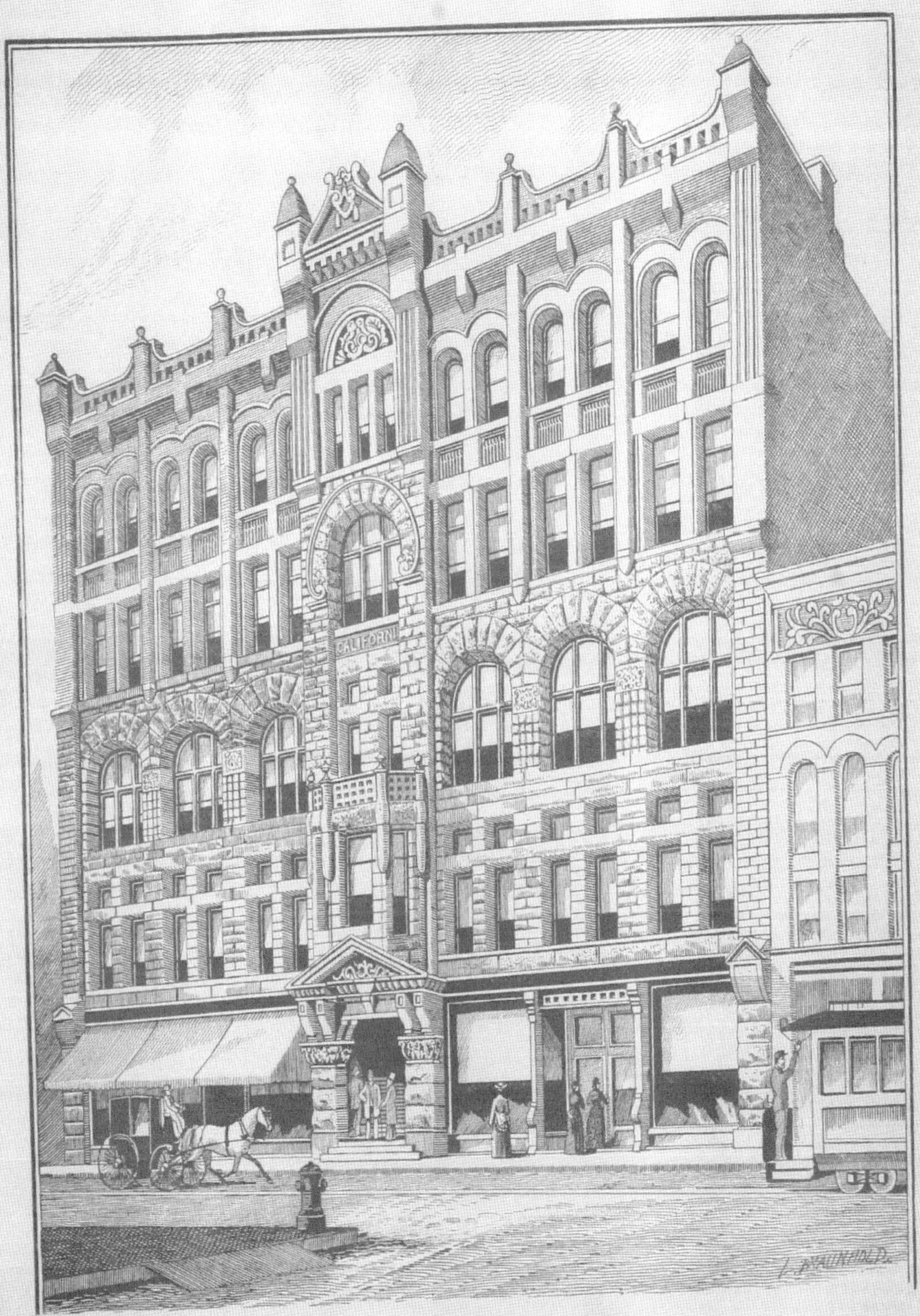

THE WILSON BLOCK.

MINERAL WEALTH.

How it is Tributary to Tacoma—Iron, Coal, Clay, Gold, Silver, Lead, Copper, Rocks and other Minerals.

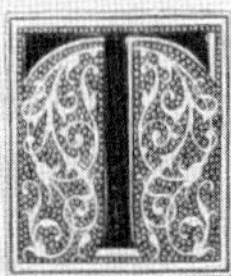

THE facts regarding these enormous and valuable interests have been furnished us by Dr. Willis E. Everette, an eminent mining expert and geologist of Tacoma, who has made the mineral deposits of Washington, Idaho, British Columbia and Alaska a study for many years past. He gives true and unvarnished facts, and comprehensively shows the almost unlimited wealth that this new State possesses. A sketch of Dr. Everette's business will be found in our columns.

"IRON."

Near the eastern border of King county are two immense veins of iron ore, locally known as the Guy mines, and which are composed of varieties of "hematite"—both of the *specular* and Bog Ore varieties—and a high grade of "magnetite" ore. This iron ore has given, upon personal analysis, over 69 per cent. of metallic iron. The veins are very long and will average over 500 feet in thickness, and in one place over 1,800 feet thick. Nearly two miles northwest from these Guy veins are the Denny iron properties which contain the same class of ore. They are practically inexhaustible, and are of great value by reason of the large quantities of marble in variegated colors which have been found near by these Denny iron veins. This marble will furnish all the lime that is necessary to flux these iron ores for reduction into pig iron, and being found directly on the ground, or almost so, increases the value of these iron ore veins very much.

The Skagit River country, and in fact, the entire Puget Sound basin, contain iron ores, and their corresponding fluxes, of such value and of such great magnitude, and so easily accessible, that there should be no hesitancy in saying the *cities of Puget Sound can be built up by their iron industries alone* (as was the case with Birmingham, Alabama, and other towns), by reason of the enormous extent of our Puget Sound iron ores and their great suitability for the making of Bessemer steel rails. Furthermore, it is an acknowledged fact among Eastern iron men that the iron ores of the Puget Sound basin produce the best iron found in America, and, in order to show the appreciation of this fact, a two million dollar *steel plant* is about to be erected on Puget Sound to reduce these ores and prepare them for the market in the shape of Bessemer steel rails and other manufactures of steel. The value of the proximity and easy transportation of iron to Tacoma in building up her manufacturing industries, can hardly be realized.

"CLAY."

Within seven hours' ride from Tacoma there are immense beds of clay of every description, *i. e.*, kaolin or porcelain clay, pipe clay, yellow brick clay, fire clay, fat clay, sand clay, slip glaze clay, red and brown brick and tile clay, and finally beds of infusorial silica and sharp sands in inexhaustible quantities, easily accessible, and of very high grade.

The importance of these "clays" lies in the fact that they are close to the waters of Puget Sound and near both rail and inland river transportation, are in large quantities, and of sufficient variety to warrant the erection of pottery works which could produce porcelain and chinaware, fire brick, pressed brick, drain pipe, common brick and tiles, etc., in quantity sufficient to supply the entire home market, and also considerable outside demand.

The writer recently returned from a personal examination of these clay stratums and has brought back with him 102 varieties of clay of every technical kind, description and color; these different varieties give very interesting information relative to the "Keramic" industries and possibilities of our Puget Sound basin. These clays are now being subjected to a thorough practical test, and it may already be said that some kaolin clays have been secured which will make beautiful porcelain ware, fire clays which have stood over 3,300 degrees Fahrenheit, and tile and brick clay which will make a beautiful yellow red tile or a bright red pressed brick.

These heats can be relied upon, as only the best imported "Pyrometers" were used, and which came from the Prussian Government Factory of the Royal Berlin Porcelain Works at Charlottenburg, near Berlin, Prussia.

"COAL."

Although the coal measures of the Puget Sound basin are principally of the tertiary formation, still, occasionally, we find that the metamorphose of a lignite vein into a bituminous vein has been almost complete enough to change the lignite into a high grade bituminous, and also with evidences of semi-anthracite. This metamorphism has evidently been caused by recent (geologically speaking) local changes, which have been produced by the enormous pressure and the resulting heat of that pressure from the eruptive strata which were thrown out of the earth by volcanic and seismic energy, possibly not later than the upper Post-Pliocene period. But whatever period our coals belong to, we have unmistakably immense and inexhaustible quantities of the very best grades of "lignite," both of the dull brown, and the glossy black, crystallized or *anthracitized* varieties, furnishing a superior household fuel. Of the "bituminous coals" we have many large and important veins that are at present being worked to supply the local demand for steam power, and also export purposes. Of "coke" we produce a local variety, equal to the very best of Connellsville, Pa., and only second in its heating qualities to that of Cardiff, Wales.

The analysis says:

Pierce County Coke, fixed carbon......60.67
Connellsville Coke, fixed carbon.......60.02

This fact is of immense importance to the owners of the large smelter being built here, as it gives them a cheap and high grade fuel always at their very doors.

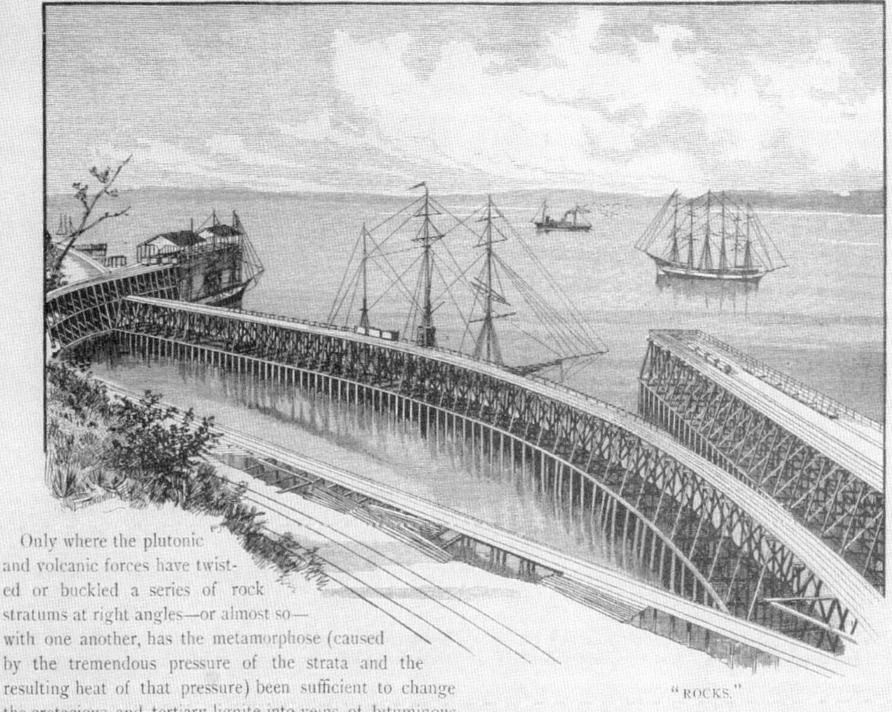

Only where the plutonic and volcanic forces have twisted or buckled a series of rock stratums at right angles—or almost so—with one another, has the metamorphose (caused by the tremendous pressure of the strata and the resulting heat of that pressure) been sufficient to change the cretacious and tertiary lignite into veins of bituminous coals, and thence into a true "anthracite." Therefore, as yet, we have not been able to find any appreciable quantity of anthracite coal, although semi-anthracite, with impure cannel coals, and a glossy black—anthracitized—hard crystallized lignite with a conchoidal fracture, is found in this Puget Sound basin in large quantities. Recently, however, reports have come in relative to the finding of large beds of true anthracite coal on the head waters of one of the rivers in the Cascade range.

To show our steadily increasing coal mining industry, enough to say that the Puget Sound basin in the year of 1888, besides supplying the greatly increased home demand for coke and coal, actually shipped to San Francisco and other places, over 557,000 tons of coal; being an increase of over 37,000 tons from the preceding year of 1887. In fact, the total official yield of our coal mines for 1888 was 1,046,243 tons, of which a little over 557,000 tons were exported to other cities; and, finally, as there are several new mines being opened, and many of the old mines themselves being supplied with new and improved mining machinery, it is safe to presume that the output of coal for the fiscal year ending June 30, 1890, will double the above named amounts.

The most improved coal bunkers have been built in Tacoma receiving their supplies direct from the railroad and discharging by the most labor-saving methods into the vessels constantly awaiting cargoes. The facilities used can be seen by the accompanying view of the bunkers.

"ROCKS."

Of rocks we have large deposits of granites, sandstones, syenites, porphyrys, and many varieties of the trap rocks, with immense cliffs and mountain sides of variegated limestone and marble of all colors, and nearly all close to water or rail transportation.

The sandstones of Bellingham Bay, the limestones and marbles of the Cascade Mountains and the Columbia River, and the granites of Snake River and elsewhere, are too well known to need any description. Suffice it to say, that we have building material of the very best description almost at our very doors, and sufficient to supply all possible demand.

"GOLD."

Our best ores of gold are found in the Cœur d'Alene and Okanogan districts, the first in North Idado and the latter in North Central Washington. The north fork of the Cœur d'Alene River has given thousands of dollars in rich quartz and placer gold, and the gold ores of Wanicutt Lake, Palmer Mountain, and Similikameen and Sinilikaheekan Rivers of the Okanogan district, are very promising, and by deeper development and economical, scientific working, will prove to be very rich. The Peshastin district is also again attracting attention.

"SILVER."

The silver ores that will come to the smelter at Tacoma, will come from the ores of the south fork of the Cœur d'Alene River from the mining camps of Mullan, Burke, Wallace and Wardner. The enormous extent of these veins being so well known, it is not necessary to go into detail with regard to the actual amount of ore turned out from them, as space forbids a proper enumeration of it.

In the Okanogan district of North Central Washington the several mining districts of the "Lime Belt," South Fork, Ruby, Conconully, Mineral Hill and Arlington or Loop Loop, will be able to furnish many tons of average, fair, good, and high grade silver ores to the great Ryan smelter which fires up next month here in our city.

Already a very large "Russell Leaching Process" mining plant is being erected on the Arlington mine in the Okanogan country, and this plant will also demonstrate the value of the Okanogan district as a mining country and a mineral producer.

The west side of the Cascade Mountains is now attracting the attention of miners, as lately very rich silver ore has been found in the foothills of the western slope between here and the "divide."

"LEAD."

The Cœur d'Alene mining districts, especially the camps and concentrators of the south fork of the Cœur d'Alene River, will furnish the principal supply of lead ores to our smelter. The writer has personally assayed ores from this section that have given him over 70 per cent. lead and over 100 ounces of silver per ton. The supply is simply enormous, and too well known to go into detail. The camps of the Okanogan district will also furnish lead ore and it is fair to presume that the discoveries in the western slopes of the Cascade Mountains will also prove valuable, and send their quota of ore to our smelter for reduction.

"COPPER."

An antimonial galena—erroneously called a gray copper ore by the miners—containing some lead, antimony, zinc, silver, and copper, with silica, sulphur and iron, is found in large paying quantities in many of the mining districts of the Cœur d'Alene and Kootsnai, Okanogan and Cascade mining camps. Also a good quality of copper oxide and sulphide is found on the eastern slopes of the Cascade range, and also on the headwaters of the Yakima River. The writer recently received a consignment of copper ore—found on the western slope of our noble mountain peak—that was a combination of copper carbonate, bi-carbonate, oxide and sulphide, with iron pyrites carrying gold—a most beautiful ore. Personal analysis gave over 33 per cent. of metallic copper. This, for surface croppings, is very rich. Some ores will run over 65 per cent. of copper, and it is fair to presume that we can supply our smelter with all the copper ore it desires.

"OTHER MINERALS."

Our various mining camps in Oregon, Washington, Idaho, and British Columbia, that are tributary to Tacoma, or can be made such, have abundance of zinc antimony, arsenical pyrites, mercury, asbestos, and chromic iron ores, with a recently discovered vein of tin. There is also a large deposit of manganese in the shape of a ferro-mangan ore near the Puget Sound basin, which can be worked profitably.

"ANTHRACITE."

Judge E. F. Russell of Tacoma, has furnished us with further facts on the anthracite discoveries; he states that recent developments and investigations show that at a greater elevation on the western slope of the Cascade Range, and farther east than the present discoveries of the bituminous coals in a southeasterly direction from Tacoma, a number of veins of semi tolerable pure anthracite coal—containing a large percentage of fixed carbon, have been discovered. These veins are of good size. Some of these are now being opened, and others prospected, while the railroad is being extended from South Prairie to the anthracite fields, for shipping this coal to the Tacoma market.

The want of roads through the heavy growth of timber upon the mountain sides has retarded exploration in that direction, and yet an occasional prospector through these great forests has often found the croppings of coal, cleaned away sufficient surface debris to satisfy himself of its existence, carefully taken his bearings, that he may be able to find the same spot again when he wishes to return, snugly covered up his "find" and wended his way out through the tangled undergrowth, toward civilization in the valleys below.

The following is an official statement of the output of coal for the past fiscal year ending Oct. 18, 1889:

DISTRICT NO. 1.

Report of Coal Mine Inspector H. C. Paige, District No. 1:

Northwest Coal Company of Bucoda—Output, 26,600 tons; men employed, 35.

Carbon Hill Coal Company of Carbonado—Output, 195,387 tons; number of men employed, 350.

South Prairie Coal Company of Burnett—Output, 45,107 tons; men employed, 40.

Wilkeson Coal and Coke Company of Wilkeson—Output, 6,738 tons; men employed, 13.

Tacoma Coal and Coke Company of Wilkeson—Output, 8,081 tons; men employed, 40.

Total output for the year, 281,913 tons.

One fatal accident. Mines in good repair.

DISTRICT NO. 2.

Report of John Sullivan, Coal Mine Inspector for District No. 2:

Newcastle Mine—Total output for year, 76,102 tons. Mine in poor condition. One accident during the year; not fatal. Number of men employed, 226.

Franklin Mine—Good condition. Total output for the year, 136,044 tons. The monthly pay roll for this mine averages $17,000. Number of men employed, 381. No accident during the year.

Black Diamond Mines—These mines are superior to any other mines in the district. Total output for the year, 105,255 tons. Number of men employed, 285. One fatal accident during the year.

Cedar Mountain Mine—Partly abandoned. Total output for the year, 23,120 tons. Number of men employed, 10. One fatal accident.

Gilman Mines—Condition good. Total output for the year, 41,482 tons. Number of men employed, 225. One accident during the year.

Roslyn Mines—These are the only mines in operation east of the Cascades. Condition good; ventilation fair. Total output for the year, 230,548 tons. Number of men employed, 850. Two fatal accidents during the year, and five accidents serious, but not fatal.

Durham Mine—The mine is now abandoned. Total output for the year 636,430 tons. Number of men employed, 68. No accidents during the year.

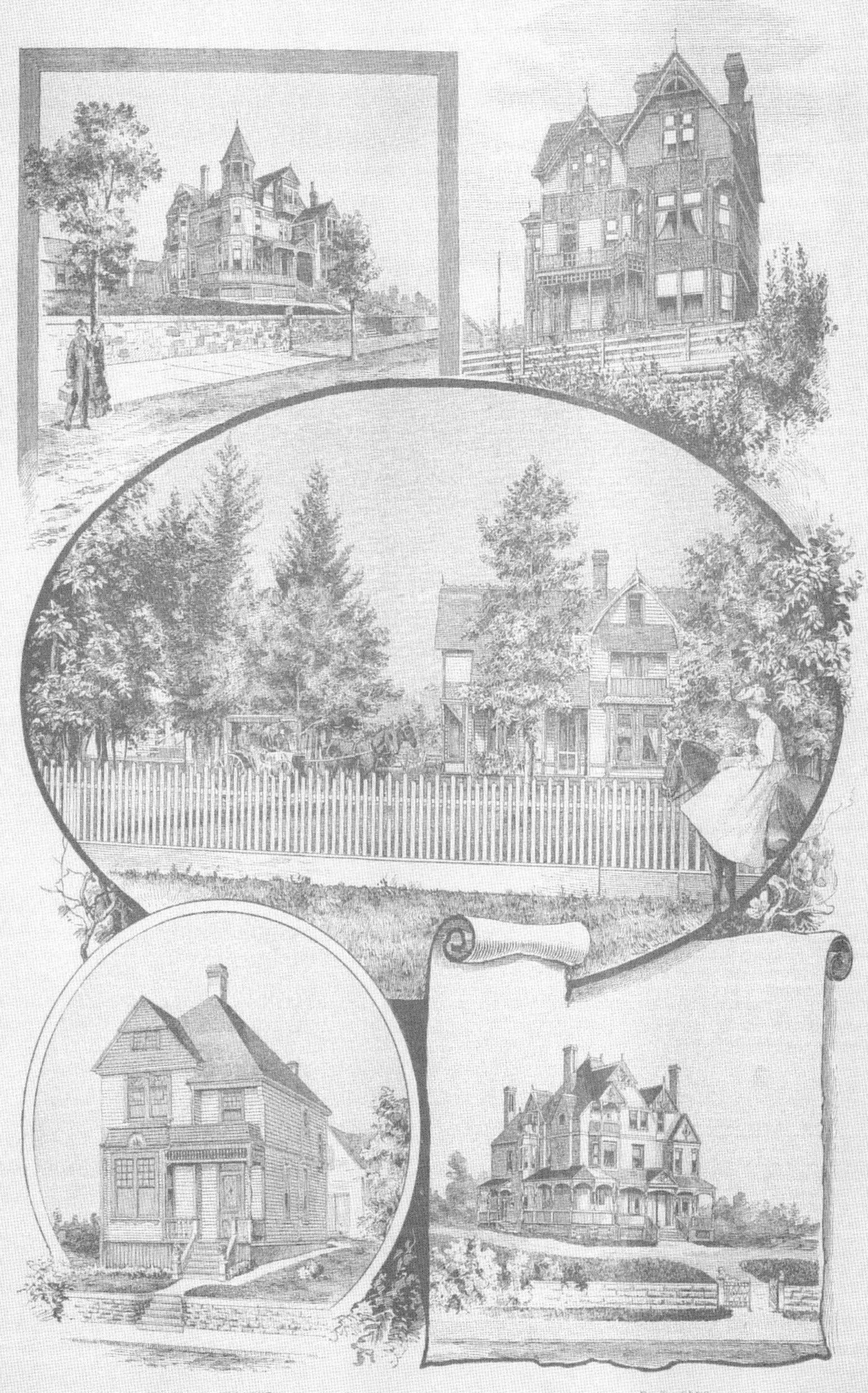

GEN. J. W. SPRAGUE.
COL. J. D. SMITH.

GEO. W. TRAVER.

F. T. OLDS.
THEO. HOSMER.

RESIDENCES OF TACOMA.

TACOMA AS A LUMBER CENTER.

NOWHERE in the world are there such magnificent forests as in Western Washington, forests of such vast extent and covered with such enormous trees, that the eastern lumberman can scarcely credit the truth concerning them. The value of this timber is just making itself known in the East. It has been shipped to California points and to foreign countries for years, and Douglass fir is as well known and more eagerly sought for in some parts of the world than the white pine of the East, on account of its greater strength and tenacity.

Vessels have been loaded at the mills on the Sound with this lumber for twenty years and more, but it was not until 1873 that any lumber was sawed in Tacoma. Then the mill of Hanson & Co. was built in the first ward of the present city. The second mill was not built until more than ten years later, when Mr. M. F. Hatch erected one on the railway wharf, and afterward another in the woods back of the little village.

Now there are nearly a score of sawmills proper, beside planing mills, sash and door factories and other wood working establishments, and several of them are of large capacity, especially the Pacific, St. Paul & Tacoma, the Gig Harbor, Tacoma Lumber & Manufacturing Co., and Mt. Tacoma Manufacturing Co.'s mills. The total cut of the Tacoma mills every day is 1,100,000 to 1,500,000 feet in ten hours. During the year ending June 30, 1889, the output of the mills in the city was about 210,000,000 feet, and the estimated cut for the year ending Dec. 31, 1889, is about 260,000,000 feet. Most of this is Douglass fir, with some cedar and a little spruce. More than one-half of this enormous product was consumed in the city itself, and the remainder was shipped to various parts of the world, including Great Britain, Australia, China, Japan, Peru, Chili, the Argentine Republic and Southern California, by water, and there have been an average of over a dozen large ocean vessels loading lumber at Tacoma every working day of last year. Some of these vessels have for a long time been engaged regularly in the business, and one of them, the Dashing Wave, owned by the Tacoma Mill Co., has made as many as ten round trips between Tacoma and San Francisco in a single year.

Beside the shipments by water, there was also a considerable quantity of lumber sent by rail to points along the line of the Northern Pacific Railway as far east as St. Paul, and even to Chicago, while considerable quantities have been sent to St. Louis. Much of the lumber sent by rail was either bridge timber or car and tank material. The Douglass fir is without a rival for these purposes. Its great strength and enormous size make it the very best timber in the world for Howe truss bridges, and the fact that such extraordinary length of absolutely clear lumber can be cut here, makes it the finest and best material for railway cars and tanks.

The value of the sawmills to Tacoma can hardly be overestimated. These mills employ over a thousand men every day, at an average of $2.50 each, which makes the total amount paid out in wages during the year over $750,000 by the sawmills alone. But beside the sawmills there are many other wood-working establishments, such as planing mills, sash and door factories, furniture factories, and a new building has been erected to manufacture balusters and other turned materials under the patents of the National Lathe and Torc company, which will revolutionize the wood turning on the Pacific coast, and also will employ a small army of men in Tacoma. The wood working establishments of Tacoma, outside of the sawmills, employ just about as many men as the sawmills themselves, and at a similar rate of wages, so that the lumber industry of Tacoma may be said to be worth in wages to the city about a million and a half of dollars, and to employ about two thousand men, who reside there with their families. There is every probability that in a year from now Tacoma will cut more lumber and have more wood working establishments of various kinds than any other city in America. She now has more than any other city on the Pacific coast, and they are unrivaled in the general excellence of their design and fitting up, and in the quality of the material produced.

THE GREAT TIMBER BELTS OF WASHINGTON.

The heaviest growth of timber in the United States is in the western part of Washington, and between the Cascade Mountains on the east, and the Pacific Ocean on the west. While the heaviest in growth, this forest is far from the most varied in character. The causes which have led to its greatest density are to be found in the large amount of annual rainfall and the mildness of the climate. There are no heavy frosts or extremely cold weather to interfere with the growth of the trees, nor is the summer heat sufficient to deprive the ground of the necessary moisture. This growth varies from two cords to 200 cords to the acre, with an average of over 100 cords. Following the foothills of the Cascade Mountains from the British Columbia line to the Columbia River, with a line drawn south from Semiahmoo Bay through Puget Sound to the Columbia River as a western boundary, the reports show that the western part of Whatcom County, the most northerly in the State, has a forest growth computed at 200 cords of wood to the acre. Two hundred cords of wood would represent over 300,000 feet, board measure, but this would include the limbs that cannot be utilized in making lumber, and large quantities of standing timber of various kinds that cannot be called "merchantable timber" as the term would be used on the Pacific coast. Merchantable timber here means timber that is not more than sixty inches in diameter at the top of the butt log, nor less than sixteen inches at the top of the smallest log. Nothing outside of these diameters is ever scaled. It is therefore a reasonable estimate to call a cord of wood 500 feet of lumber, board measure, or about one-third of what it will actually show.

This growth of over 200 cords to the acre, or say 100,000 feet, extends from the shores of the Gulf of Georgia eastward to the foothills of Mount Baker. At the foothills the growth is less dense, and at the foot of the mountain is only from 50 to 100 cords to the acre, and this decreases again on the other side till the Cascade Range is met, and between Mount Baker and the Cascade Mountains there will be only from twenty-five to thirty cords to the acre, or following the estimate given above, only from 12,000 to 15,000 feet.

Skagit County has the same general growth, with the exception that the density decreases more slowly as the Skagit River is ascended. In the next county to the southward—Snohomish—the growth of timber on the immediate shore line is only from five to ten cords, or say 3,000 to 5,000 feet, but at from one to five miles back the forest becomes as dense as in the more northerly counties, but the very heavy growth extends only for about an average of ten miles back, when it again decreases to between 100 and 200 cords to the acre, and thirty miles back from the shore only shows from twenty to fifty cords to the acre. West of these counties are the counties of Island and San Juan, composed of groups of small islands in Puget Sound, none of which, with the exception of the southern parts of Whidby and Camas, have more than five or ten cords to the acre. The Southern parts of these counties had at the time this report was made over 200 cords to the acre, but much of this has been cut down.

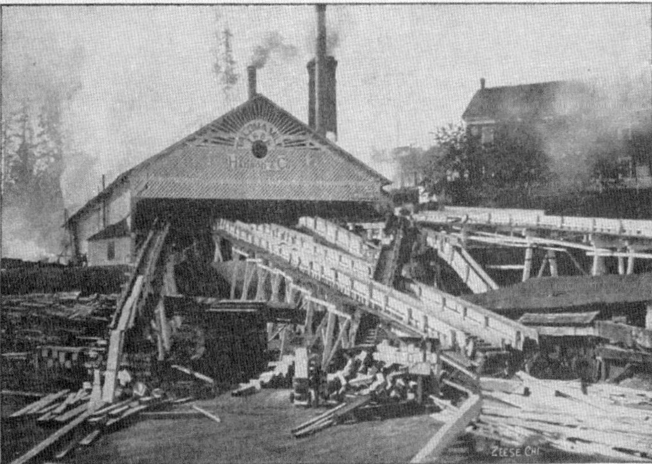

HANSON & CO.'S MILL.

King County, lying immediately south of Snohomish, and containing 2,000 square miles, has the same dense growth of over 200 cords to the acre for about fifteen to twenty-five miles from the shore line, thence rather suddenly decreasing to the foothills, where it has but from twenty to fifty cords to the acre.

Pierce, the next county south, has the same general conditions, except through a portion of its area and that of the adjoining county of Thurston. With the exception of this small treeless waste, Pierce is remarkably well timbered, the high average of more than 200 cords to the acre extending over a greater area than in any of the other counties named above, while the area containing between 100 and 200 cords to the acre extends to within a short distance of the foot of Mount Tacoma. But little timber in Pierce county has been cut, except close to Puget Sound. Thurston is the southern county of Puget Sound, and has the same heavy growth for five or ten miles from the upper shores, but this soon falls to between 100 and 200 cords.

Following the line down the western boundary of Thurston, between that and the Cascade Range, the next county south of Pierce and Thurston is Lewis, which, except in the fertile but narrow valleys of the Cowlitz and Chehalis Rivers, has a density of growth varying from 100 to 200 cords to the acre, and the timber of this section is of fine quality and very easily marketed, as all the streams have good logging waters in ordinary seasons, while the timber being sheltered from wind storms, has no shakes, and grows to large proportions, with long, straight trunks, clear of limbs to a height of 100 to 150 feet or more. Cowlitz and Clarke Counties have the same general characteristics as Lewis, being lightly timbered in the valleys of the Cowlitz and Columbia Rivers, and heavily timbered a mile or two back. Skamania County has some fine timber south of Mount St. Helens, but the growth is not as heavy as in the other counties, and will nowhere exceed 100 cords to the acre, the average of the better land being but a little more than fifty.

Turning west to the coast counties, the small county of Wahkiakum has a considerable amount of Columbia valley land, which, while very fertile, has but little timber, not cutting more than five or ten cords to the acre. This belt extends back nowhere more than six miles, when the heavy timber lands, containing 100 to 200 cords to the acre, are again met with. Pacific County is, with the exception of the sand spits along the immediate ocean, heavily timbered, and will average throughout its extent nearly 200 cords to the acre. The same dense growth prevails through the counties of Jefferson and Clallam, to the straits of San Juan de Fuca. The land in the Jefferson and Kitsap counties bordering on Hood's Canal and Puget Sound, with the exception of from one to five miles of shore line, was similarly well wooded, and the whole, or almost the whole of Mason County, which occupies the land in the southwestern part of the Puget Sound region, and the southern part of Hood's Canal region, has a forest of about equal density.

THE TACOMA MILL COMPANY.

Their mill as pictured in our cut, was established in 1868, and was one of the first started on Puget Sound. It is a general saw milling business, both wholesale and retail. They do a very large foreign business, shipping quantities of lumber to China, Australia, South America, East and West coast of England and even Spain, as well as the Atlantic seaboard. The Spanish business is a new departure, this being the first cargo of lumber ever shipped to Spain from the shores of Puget Sound. It is probable that this first order will open up a new field, and lead to a large trade in this direction.

The Northern Pacific R. R. runs through the premises of the company, which gives them unusual facilities for shipping lumber, as they possess a switch track of their own, thus expediting transportation.

The mill is the most completely fitted up imaginable, and contains the latest improved machinery. The average daily output of sawn lumber is 250,000 feet, although on one occasion 465,928 feet were turned out in ten hours. The mill is a gang mill and can cut timber 140 feet long and 30x30 inches; 1200 horse power is employed, necessitating 18 boilers. This power is used in running two double circular saws, two gang saws, two gang edges, one pony saw, two lath mills, four planers. Drying kilns are connected with the mill, which employ 250 men on the premises, and the company has over 500 more constantly engaged in logging for them.

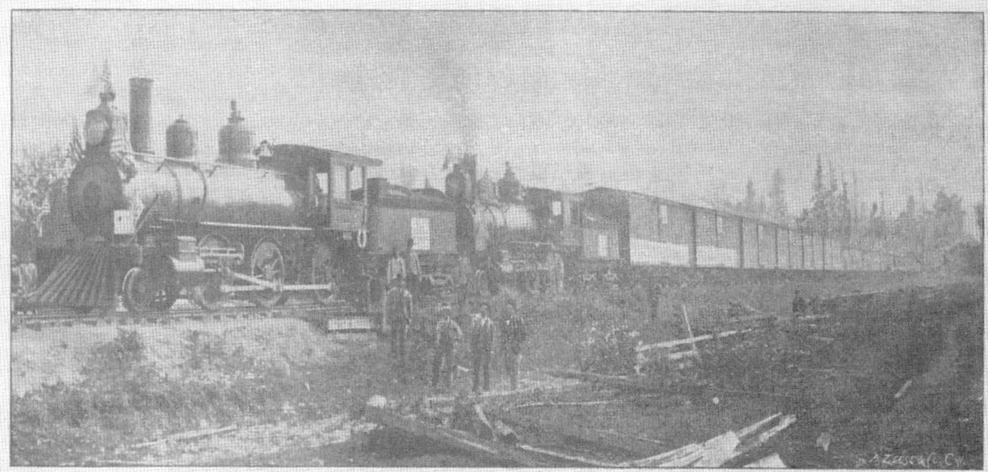

THE FIRST TRAIN LOAD OF RED CEDAR SHINGLES SHIPPED EAST OVER THE NORTHERN PACIFIC.

Hanson & Co., 48 Market street, San Francisco, are the agents. Mr. Charles Hanson may be called the Tacoma Mill Co., as he and his son, William H. Hanson, are the sole proprietors. Mr. Hanson is a native of Denmark, and came to San Francisco in 1853.

He was a "rustler," and embarked in the lumber business, handling redwood chiefly. Later he came to Puget Sound and noting with keen business sagacity the advantages of the location, he built the mill on the present site. Tacoma did not have enough population to unload the vessel that brought down the mill plant. When one looks at it to-day and sees ten or twelve vessels loading at the company's wharves, it seems hardly credible that a great city has grown here in so short a time.

Young Mr. Hanson is the practical manager of this great concern, and makes his home in the city of Tacoma.

J. T. L. HARRIS.

J. T. L. Harris, whose photograph is given in "TACOMA ILLUSTRATED," among the representative citizens, as will be seen, is a man with the best part of his life before him. He came to Tacoma a short time ago from Sioux City, Iowa, and is now permanently established here with his family. When Mr. Harris came to the Pacific coast it was with the intention of engaging either in banking or the lumber business. After looking the field over and seeing what a magnificent field for the latter business Washington is, he decided to erect a sawmill for the production of cedar shingles which are becoming so popular with builders throughout the United States.

The Tacoma Cedar Lumber Company was thereupon organized by Mr. Harris, with a capital stock of $25,000, he holding a controlling interest. The mill is situated on the shore line of Commencement Bay, between Old Town and the Pacific Mill, and has a capacity of 100,000 shingles per day. The mill is operated night and day by two shifts of men, and has jumped right into a profitable business. Carload shipments have already been made to Cortland, N. Y., cities in Missouri and Illinois, and Sioux City, Des Moines, and other Iowa points. All kinds of fancy shingles are manufactured by this company, and they are the sole makers of the Star Brand of cedar shingles.

The Tacoma Cedar Lumber Company is one of the very few firms on Puget Sound that does not belong to the shingle trust. The company's office is at 928 Pacific Ave.

ST. PAUL & TACOMA LUMBER COMPANY.

It requires courage of no mean order to fight the long established prejudices of a trade or occupation, and no people are more tenacious of their prejudices than lumbermen. When the St. Paul and Tacoma Lumber Company began to build their mill on the flats in Tacoma, and announced that they had ordered a band mill and would use it without a circular saw, the old-time lumbermen scoffed at these "new fangled notions," and could by no argument or persuasion be induced to consider the possibility of success.

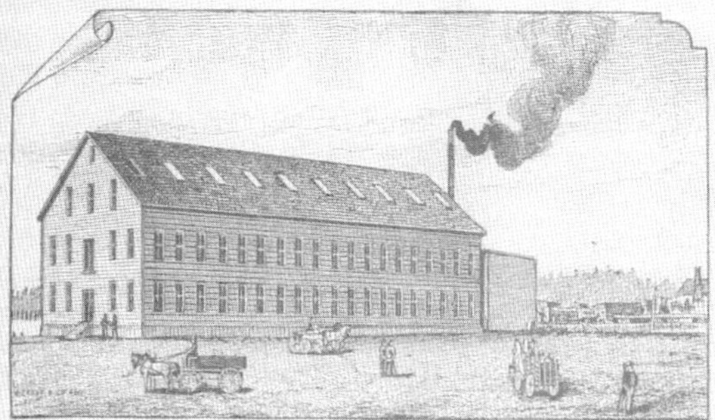

WHEELER, OSGOOD & CO.'S SASH, DOOR AND BLIND FACTORY.

Time has shown that the new company was wise in its determination to introduce an improvement, and that the band saw makes as good, if not better, lumber than the circular saw, and is far more economical.

The result is a triumph for the company, and will make a revolution in the whole system of lumber sawing on the Pacific coast. The St. Paul and Tacoma Lumber Company, which made this successful experiment, is composed almost entirely of St. Paul and Minneapolis capitalists, some of whom have been engaged in the lumber business in Minnesota and Wisconsin. The officers are Col. Chauncey W. Griggs, president; A. G. Foster, vice-president; George Browne, secretary; Henry Hewitt, Jr., treasurer, and P. D. Norton, assistant treasurer. The mill has been running about six months, and was designed to cut lumber for the Eastern markets. The local demand in Tacoma has, however, been so great that the whole product has remained in this city, and has been used to build houses for the enormous population that has come to make the city of Tacoma their home.

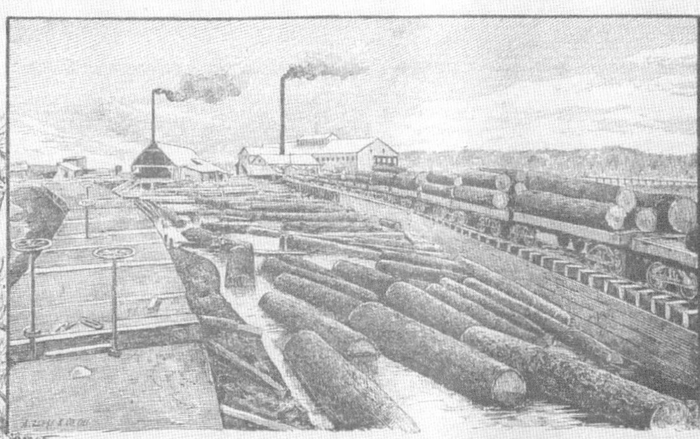

THE ST. PAUL AND TACOMA LUMBER COMPANY.

Situated directly opposite the Tacoma Hotel, the mill is a prominent feature of the landscape, and is a handsome structure. The proprietors have made many innovations in the established practice of sawing on this coast, besides the adoption of the bandsaw. Among these are the endless chain with fixed dogs to haul the logs from the pond on to the mill floors, and the steam nigger for turning logs on the carriage. These were improvements that they were told would prove useless, but they have more than justified the expectations formed of them. The mill now cuts 175,000 feet of lumber every ten hours, and works six days every week, and every week in the year except when temporarily closed for repairs. Over two hundred men are employed in the mill or in the yard, and a large force in their logging camps. At the corner of Twenty-third and Adams streets the store and general offices are established in a very handsome building erected by themselves. The store has one of the largest and most complete stocks of general merchandise to be found in the Pacific Northwest, and does a large business with the general public as well as with the employes of the company. In the rear is the city yard, which occupies two blocks of land, and whence any kind of lumber can be furnished to all parts of the city.

WHEELER, OSGOOD & CO.

In the month of July last a pile driver at work on the tide flats at the head of Commencement Bay, could be plainly seen from the business portion of the city, and gradually there towered up to a great height above the piles, story by story, a large structure which, it was then said, would be a sash and door factory. Of its magnitude and the influence it would have upon the future growth and prosperity of the city of Tacoma, little was then thought. To-day it stands there complete, a monument to the manufacturing interests of this city, unequaled anywhere in the Pacific Northwest in capacity or excellence of construction.

The relation that the establishment, covering a floor space of 29,484 square feet and employing 150 skilled workmen, bears to the industrial growth of Tacoma, is evidenced by the fact that already more than twenty-five skilled workmen, with their families, have come from the East to make this city their home, and secure employment in this factory. This concern is rated at 300 doors per day, which means that it will turn out in one day not alone 300 doors, but from 400 to 500 sashes, and a proportionate amount of finishing moldings, casings, etc., in one day for fifteen houses, such as would cost to build $2,500 each.

The machinery is all of the latest and most improved pattern. Of the many new machines in the building there is one deserving of especial mention, there probably being nothing like it on the coast. It is called a "sander." By the old method the smooth finish was given to doors, sashes and the like, by hand labor. With this machine a door is made as smooth as glass in about one minute. The work is much more perfect than if done by hand.

Everything about the building, in fact, is on the latest and most improved plan. The exhaust fan is, perhaps, a feature new to many. It is used for carrying away from the different machines the shavings and other debris that would otherwise endanger the premises by their likelihood to catch fire. A large fan is so constructed that the shavings and other debris are drawn up from the machines and forced through the flume to the shaving room. From there it finds its way into the furnace, and in the shape of smoke, out through the smoke stack.

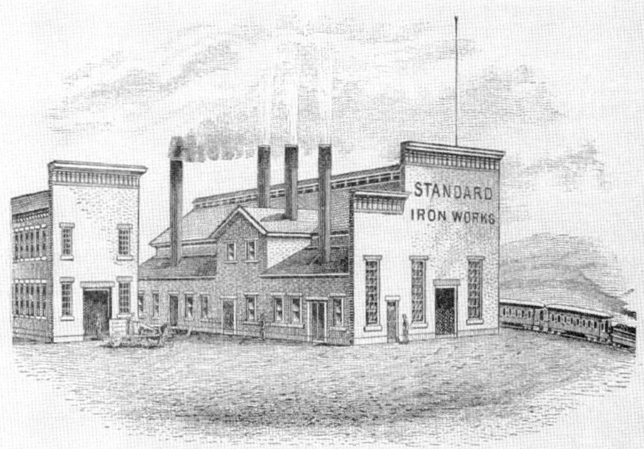

A steam elevator, 6x9 feet in size, will be used to facilitate the handling of materials between the different floors.

There will be in use, when the machinery is all set in motion, over 3,000 feet of belting. The shafting runs the entire length of the building on the first floor, and instead of the usual cast iron pulleys wooden split pulleys are used, so that should a mishap occur it would not be necessary to stop the machinery for repairs but a few minutes.

The members of this firm are W. C. Wheeler, G. H. Osgood, and D. D. Clark, all of whom are thorough business men.

THE GIG HARBOR LUMBER COMPANY

has its retail yards and main office on Dock street below Fifteenth. It has only been in existence a year, but during that time the amount of business done by it is phenomenal. The mill is situated on Gig Harbor opposite Point Defiance, and is fitted with the latest improved machinery, and capable of an output of one hundred thousand feet per diem.

The export trade is by far the most important feature of this company's business, and they ship large quantities of lumber to China, Australia, South America, and to the Eastern seaboard. The following from a trade paper is interesting, as illustrating the facts above noted :

"On Tuesday, Sept. 17, the Gig Harbor Mill cut six sticks of timber 24x24 inches, 110 feet long, which were loaded on the ship Earl Granville for China."

The officers of the company are Francis Hall, President; Geo. S. Atkinson, Superintendent; J. H. Parker, Secretary, and E. S. Prentice, Treasurer.

LINK'S PLANING MILLS.

The factory and office of this flourishing concern are on Adams St., south of Twenty-fifth. The business has been established a little over a year, but is already on a substantial basis and turning out a large quantity of good work. Mr. Link manufactures windows, doors, mouldings and brackets, and does stair-building, band-sawing, turning, etc., to order. The machinery plant is very complete, and of the latest and most scientific designs.

The ownership of the mills is invested entirely in Mr. A. R. Link. He was born in Floyd Co., Indiana, but lived afterward near Terre Haute, where he was in business for eighteen years. He was a carpenter in early ife, and being one of that class of men that is hard to hold down, he soon began contracting on his own account, and accumulated capital. Later he moved to Wichita, Kan., and after a residence there of two years, came here, and established himself at once in the business as has been stated.

THE STANDARD IRON WORKS.

J. H. Lister & Sons are the proprietors of these works, the oldest of this description in the city, as they were established in 1886. The principal feature is the manufacture of architectural iron work and machinery castings. Their works are situated in the southeast portion of the city, on the line of the Northern Pacific Railroad Company, and near to the new freight warehouses, at the corner of East E and Twenty-third streets. Teir switch runs into the yard of the works. Since their establishment they can point to many ornaments of their handiwork, having furnished all the iron and steel used in the erection of many of the most prominent buildings in Tacoma, among which may be mentioned the Fife, C. B. Wright's, Bostwick's, Wilson's, Campbell & Powell's, Mason's, the Sprague Block, Catlin & Barlow's, and the Gross buildings. It is evident that these are among the best buildings in the city. Outside they have done good work in the cities of Olympia, Port Townsend, Ellensburgh, Yakima, and Spokane Falls. Every year has shown for them an increase of at least 200 per cent.

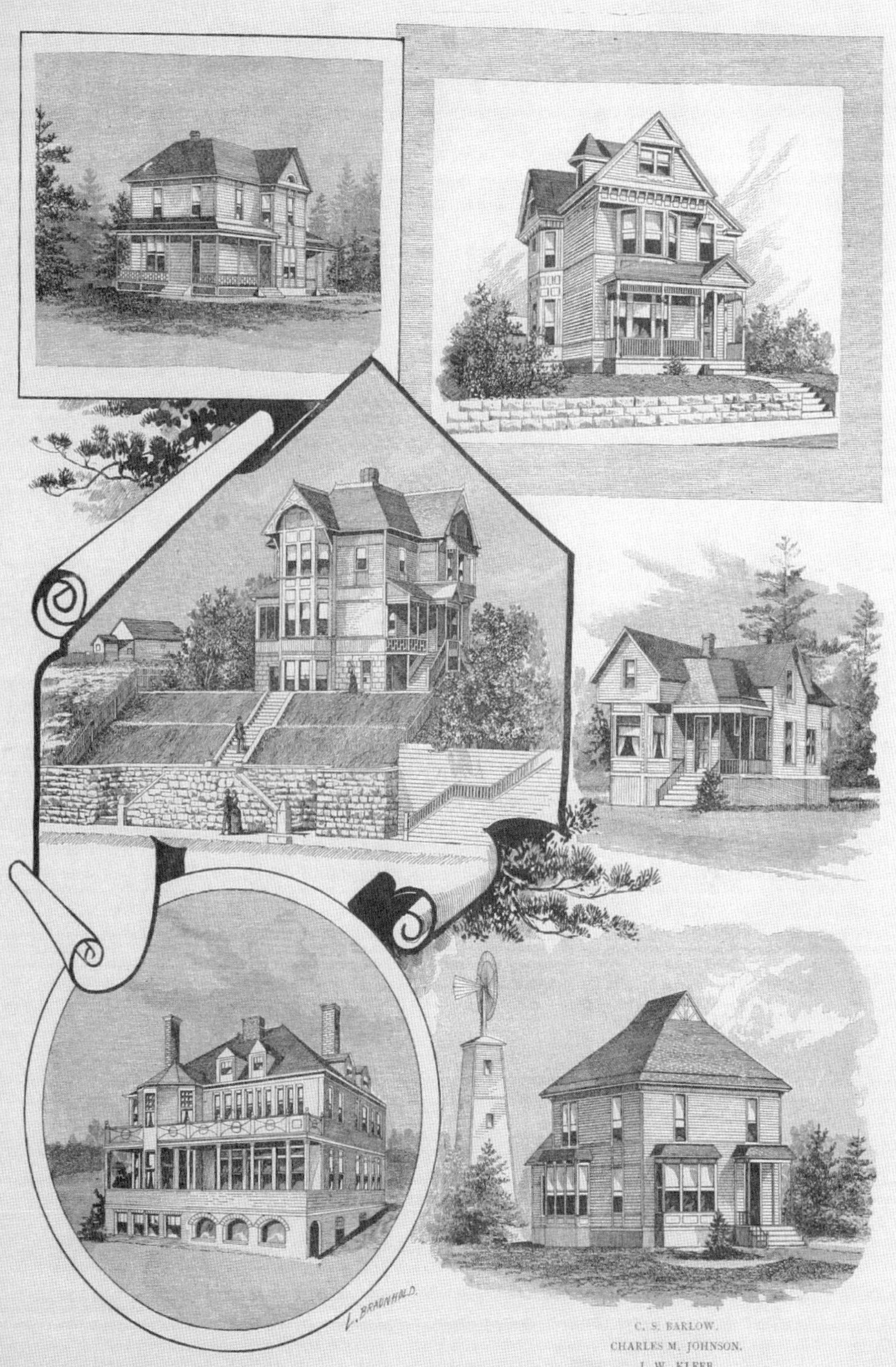

C. S. BARLOW,
CHARLES M. JOHNSON,
J. W. KLEEB.

O. W. BARLOW,
F. M. WADE,
NEW CLUB HOUSE.

RESIDENCES OF TACOMA.

REALTY AND BUILDING.

GENERAL REVIEW OF ITS HISTORY TO PRESENT DATE.

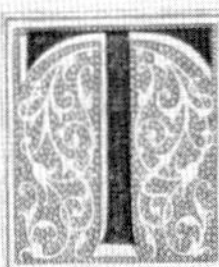

THE following able article on Tacoma and its rapid growth and advancement is contributed to TACOMA ILLUSTRATED by Col. C. W. Hobart, the editor of the Tacoma Real Estate *Journal:*

Real estate has been a leading factor in the phenomenal growth and wealth of Tacoma. Prior to the time, June, 1873, that it was determined by the Northern Pacific Railroad management that its Western terminus was to be at this point, the land within and around the limits of the proposed new town could command but little more, if any, than the government rates per acre. But this event stimulated values thereof at once, and speculation therein began its career to a moderate extent. Then the town site was laid out and the purchase of lots began, with the more far-seeing and venturesome people. Not only in lots within the limits of the new terminal town did real estate deals extend; but by some who were inspired with greater confidence in the future of the location and had faith in the ability of the Northern Pacific R. R. to carry out its design, they extended to purchases of acre propery outside.

Matters thus went forward until the cessation of work on the Northern Pacific, through the failure of Jay Cooke, when all transactions ceased. Those who still had faith in the revival of the enterprise held on to their property, while others who were discouraged, disposed of their holdings with but slight advance. Thus every one who had pinned their faith upon Tacoma were suspended upon the ragged edge from 1873, until C. B. Wright came to the front and organized a syndicate, and thus secured the capital to push the railroad project forward. Later, Henry Villard came into the management as President, and under his administration the road was completed to the Columbia River, there connecting at Wallula with Portland by river and rail. Here the Northern Pacific had another set-back by the failure of Mr. Villard in 1883. During the period of Villard's administration the anxious investors of Tacoma were in a condition of suspense through the supposed intention of Mr. Villard to not extend the road across the Cascade Range, or if he did to make Seattle the terminus instead of Tacoma, but rather make Portland its terminal point. But after Mr. Villard retired, other gentlemen connected with the company, faithful to the original purpose to make Tacoma the western terminus, inaugurated plans to build the line from the Columbia River near the junction of the Snake, across the Cascade Range to Tacoma, which was accomplished July 4, 1887.

From this time the building of the Northern Pacific to Tacoma was definitely assured, real estate began to advance from primitive values, and from the consummation of the enterprise in 1887, its advance was marked.

Not until just before or at the beginning of 1880, was anything accomplished toward clearing the forest and laying out the first streets of the new town. Settlers then began to appear, and arrangements were begun for building, and wharves constructed for the landing of steamers. Within four years from the time the first forest trees were felled, a $200,000 hotel was commenced in June, 1883; a female seminary, a public school edifice, and gas and water works were erected by the railroad company, mainly through the efforts of Mr. Wright.

The establishment of these enterprises began to stimulate the value of real estate. After the completion of "The Tacoma" hotel in 1884, lots in the center of business would bring from $1,000 to $1,500 per lot of 25x 120 feet, and fine residence lots in the most desirable localities, would bring from $100 to $1,500, according to eligibility of location. The Northern Pacific Railroad located the original town site, and purchased other lands about it from the government,and afterward sold them to the Tacoma Land Company, an auxiliary of the former company. During the last months of 1884, the Land Company sold to private individuals for residence purpose, several hundred lots, the sales amounting to about $25,000 per month. The entire real estate sales in Pierce County, in 1882, which included but few outside of Tacoma, were $573,466. The next year, 1883, the first improvements began. The sales were $1,392,296, double those of the prior year. For the year 1884, the sales were $1,027,911. For 1885, the sales were only $667,356, and for 1886, they were $747,371. It will be observed that there is a sudden falling off in sales during the two years last named about one-half over the two years of 1883-4. This was during the construction of the Cascade division from Pasco to Tacoma; the result of a change in the policy of the road after the retirement of Henry Villard from the presidency thereof. It was opened to Tacoma July 1, 1887, and it will be observed that the real estate sales for that year, which were $2,078,531, were a large advance over all former years, largely due to this event. From this year, 1887, began the growth of Tacoma, and transactions in real estate began in earnest, and have continued thus to the present time with no reaction in values, as is shown by subsequent sales and prices. The sales for the year 1888 were $8,853,598, an increase of sales over those of the previous year of over 400 per cent. The rapid additions to population, and the steady and firm growth of building and business enterprises caused an increase in the demand for real estate, and a consequent increase of values. For the first ten months of the present year, 1889, the sales reached $11,313,245. Estimating the sales for the two last months of 1889, as equal to those of the two months prior, they will reach for the year $13,500,000 in round numbers, which is an increase of nearly five million dollars over the year 1888.

Tacoma has never had any "boom" in real estate or business. The rapid increase in population since 1887, from about 9,000 to about 30,000 in October, 1889, as indicated by the vote at the general election on the first of that month—an increase of over 300 per cent., has produced the demand for real estate, and the consequent increase of values therein. Values in real property have never de-

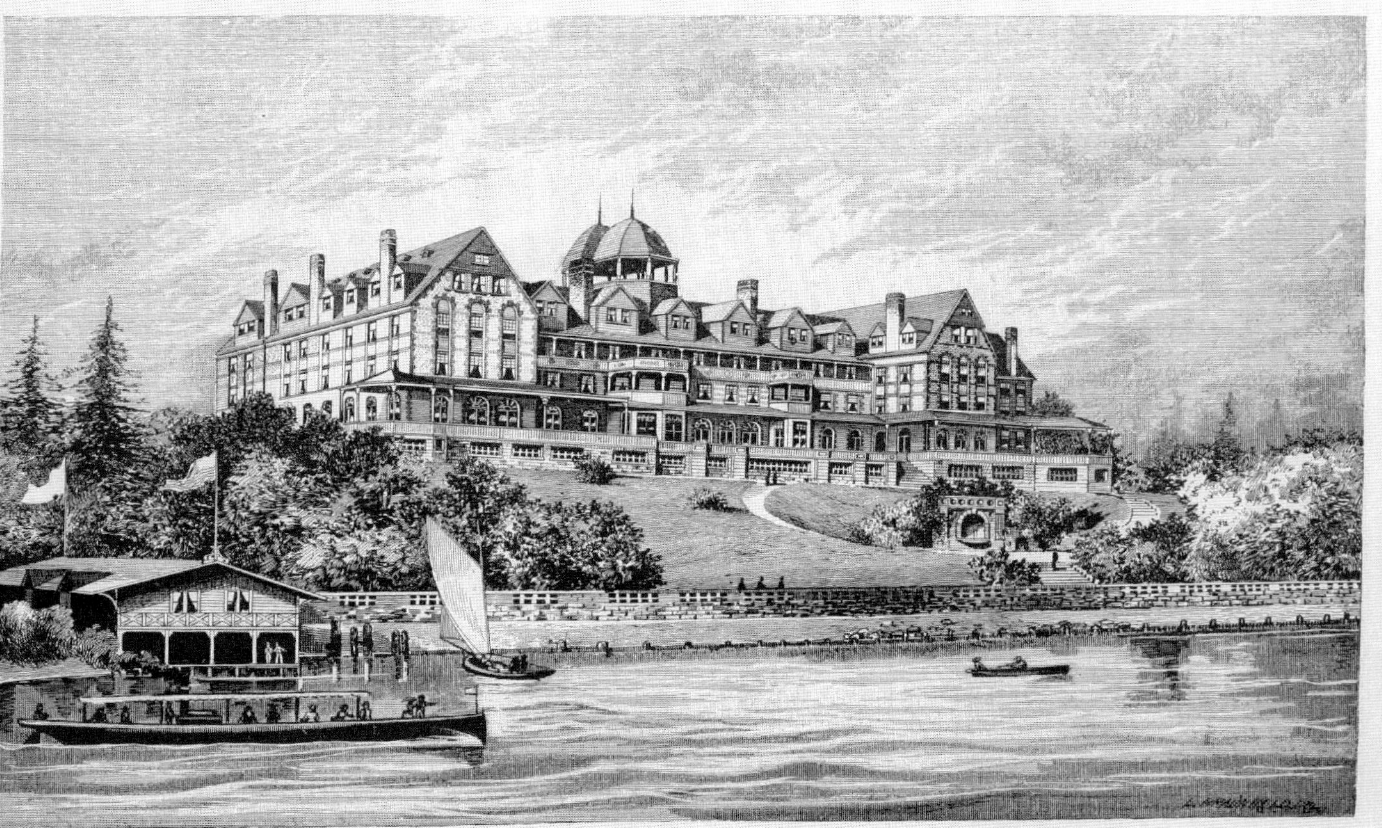

HOTEL TACOMA. (A View from the Sound.)

creased a day since the founding of the town, and since the completion of the Cascade Division of the Northern Pacific Railroad to Tacoma the increase has been steady, firm and upward, and thus they continue to-day.

During the year 1887, the price of real property on Pacific avenue—the leading business street of the city, was from $200 to $400 per front foot, while the ranging price of property on other business streets was $50 to $150 per front foot. Fine residence property in the most desirable location ranged from $25 to $40 per front foot, while residence lots in other localities within a mile of the business center ranged from $5 to $15 per front foot. During the same period acre property within a mile and a half of the business center sold from $400 to $500 per acre, while within two and a half miles of the same point, similar property brought from $150 to $200 per acre, all according to locality and improvements.

During the year 1888, the population continued to increase to a rapid extent, thus enlarging the demand for real estate in the interest of the growing trade, commerce and manufacturing. Business property during this year brought from $500 to $1,000 per front foot, on Pacific avenue, and similar property is largely in advance of these prices to-day, because of the steady increased demand. This demand for business extends to more than six streets, which are parallel with Pacific avenue, besides occupying various cross streets, In fact, business has extended to J street, eight blocks west of Pacific avenue, which has a tendency to increase values in both residence and business property.

While inside business property has thus advanced in value from government price in 1873, to $1,000 per front foot in 1888, outside timber and farming lands have also increased in value, more than quadrupled since 1887. This is largely due to the extension of additions to the city in almost all directions for three and four miles out and the existence of motor railroad lines through them. So widely is the pulse of Tacoma's growth in population and permanent business felt that it affects real estate prices for ten miles around—in fact, throughout Pierce County. To-day $200 to $500 per acre for outlying acre property is moderate.

The building enterprises of Tacoma have been enormous during the past three years, as a result of the steady and large advance in real estate. It has been utterly impossible to supply lumber and other material fast enough for the demand in building. During the year 1888, over 1,000 houses were put up, yet the demand was not supplied. This with a population of about 20,000 at the end of the year. At this rate with a population of over 30,000 at the end of 1889, there will have then been erected over 2,000 buildings, because the supply of material has increased with new lumber mills, and yet the demand for more houses is as extensive at the end of ten months of 1889 as it was at the end of 1888.

Real estate being the basis of all material and industrial interests, they all keep pace one with the other, hence the phenomenal growth and prosperity of Tacoma, the coming metropolis of the Pacific Coast.

SLAUGHTER & CO.

This firm has its offices at 112 Tenth Street. As good wine needs no bush, so the old and well known firm of Slaughter & Co. needs no introduction to the people of Tacoma and those dwelling on the shores of Puget Sound. They have made some of the largest sales of real estate that have ever been made in this vicinity, and in no single instance have they failed to make money for their patrons. They have been in business ever since 1882.

Messrs. Slaughter & Co. will shortly place upon the market one of the most beautiful pieces of property near Tacoma to-day. It is known as Lake Steilacoom Park, and lies in a southwesterly direction, just seven miles distant from this city. It is readily accessible however, and reached by the Lake City Railroad which runs through the tract. The scenery of Lake Steilacoom is unsurpassed for beauty, variety and grandeur; Mount Tacoma looms majestic in the distance. The Park itself is a lovely stretch of prairie land dotted with groves of trees. Springs of living water abound and the lake itself lying there like a jewel adorning the face of the landscape, is a constant dream of delight to the lover of nature. It is also a paradise for any one who properly appreciates pure air, fine scenery, a genial climate, and outdoor life. In the above described vicinity Slaughter & Co. offer to the people of Tacoma an opportunity of purchasing the most charming residence sites near town. Illustrations, plats, maps, etc., will be cheerfully given on application. They are also selling acre-lots at American Lake at a very low figure. This is another lovely location developed through the energy and far-sightedness of Messrs. Slaughter & Co. Considerable property has already been sold at American Lake Park, and some elegant residences are now being projected there.

Although Messrs. Slaughter & Co. offer for sale sites for beautiful suburban homes in the above mentioned localities, it must not be forgotten that they are agents for some of the choicest and most desirable property in the business and inside residence portion of the city. Any applicant to this firm for information concerning these properties will at once receive full particulars.

W. B. SOMERS,

of 920 A street, is one of the prominent real estate men of the City of Destiny. He only located here in the month of January, 1888, but even in that short period has succeeded in making himself an enviable position among the better class of the business community. Despite his comparative youth Mr. Somers has had extensive experience in the real estate business, having formerly been successfully engaged in it in Council Bluffs, Iowa. He is a man of the rarest business integrity, and the accuracy of his judgment is unquestioned by all who have had dealings with him.

Mr. Somers has lately moved into his new, commodious and elegantly furnished offices, where he will attend to the wants of investors in a thoroughly satisfactory manner. Also all correspondence will receive his prompt and personal attention.

THEO. HOSMER.

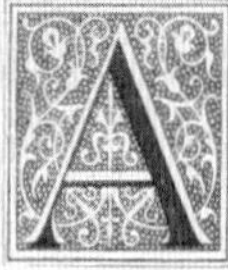

A GREAT deal of Tacoma's magic development is attributable to Mr. Theo. Hosmer, and it is with pleasure we introduce in the pages of "TACOMA ILLUSTRATED" his familiar features. Mr. Hosmer was born in Sandusky, Ohio, and when quite young left his native city for Philadelphia. In the year 1873 his health having been somewhat impaired through constant application to business, and deeming a change of air and scene would be beneficial, he accepted the Northern Pacific Railroad's proposition and became secretary of the commission which afterward located that company's Western terminus here.

His original intention when leaving Philadelphia, was to remain here just three months; the climate agreeing with him so well, however, he was induced to remain and take charge of the immense work laid out by the officers of the Commission prior to their departure for the East.

The dense timber of a thousand acres had to be cut down and cleared away; roads laid out and graded, and the perspective of a future great city clearly defined. Mr. Hosmer, with the exception of three years spent in the East on account of sickness in his family, has lived in Tacoma ever since, watching with pride the development of the many enterprises with which he is connected, and the growth to a metropolitan city of the little hamlet which he saw when he first arrived. He has been constantly identified with the Tacoma Land Company, and is at the present time Comptroller of that Company. He is also president of the Light and Water Company, having been its general manager since its beginning up to 1882, president of the Tacoma Opera House Company, president of the Wilkeson Coal and Coke Company, vice-president of the Union Club, trustee of Annie Wright Seminary, and director in several other leading institutions of the city, many of which owe a large measure of success to his untiring and aggressive energy and enterprise, always mindful of the public welfare.

WILLIAM H. FIFE.

Some men are born great, some have greatness thrust upon them, while others achieve it. To the latter class belongs William H. Fife, one of Tacoma's best and truest pioneers. The subject of this sketch was born in Peterborough County, Ontario, in the year 1833. His early boyhood was spent upon a farm, and it was not until he had reached the age of seventeen that he left the parental roof and started out to seek his fortune. In the town of Kent he obtained employment in a general merchandise store, receiving five dollars per month the first year, and seven dollars per month the second year, for wages. At the age of twenty-one he engaged in a similar occupation in the neighboring town of Norwood and married Miss Harriet A. Johnson, to whom he attributes to a great extent the wonderful prosperity he has experienced. When the Caribou gold excitement was at its height, Mr. Fife moved to British Columbia, remaining there three years. On his return to Canada, he moved with his family to Vassar, Michigan, where he engaged in the merchandise and sawmill business. In 1870 he again moved to Cherokee, Iowa, where he built the first store and laid the foundation of a prosperous and growing city.

When Mr. Fife left Canada he had his eye on the Pacific Coast, and in 1873 started for the Puget Sound terminus of the Northern Pacific Railroad, and located among the stumps that then covered the town site of Tacoma. He established the first general merchandise store, laid the first water main in the streets of Tacoma, and was the first postmaster, acting in that capacity for eight years. Since his arrival in the City of Destiny his financial success has been phenomenal. To-day he pays as much taxes, if not more, than any other man in the new State of Washington. The Hotel Fife, one of the handsomest and costliest buildings in Tacoma, was erected in 1888, by Mr. Fife, at a cost of $125,000. The structure is of brick, five stories high, and has a frontage of 330 feet. He owns a great many other buildings besides this, as well as some valuable property in the very best portions of the city. His fortune is variously estimated at between one and two millions.

CAPTAIN W. J. FIFE.

Capt. Fife, whose picture is given in this work among the representative citizens of Tacoma, may well be termed a man of energy and zeal. His residence in Tacoma dates back to the time, when, a mere lad, he accompanied his father, W. H. Fife, from Iowa to take up his permanent residence in the City of Destiny. At that time he had received little or no scholastic training, and Tacoma, unlike what it is to-day, possessed extremely limited facilities in this respect. Young Fife managed, however, to devote all his leisure hours to his studies, at the same time acting as assistant postmaster.

In 1876 he entered the California Military Academy at Oakland, Cal., and only left it when he had attained the highest possible honors in a competitive drill between three companies of the academy. The institution presented him with a massive gold medal, and promoted him from a cadet to the captaincy of Company A. He is also a graduate of the Columbia Law University of Washington, D. C., taking the junior and senior courses. In 1883 he was admitted to the Pierce County bar, but on account of the large interests of his father and his own private affairs, he does not follow his profession, although before a jury, or on the rostrum, he has proved himself an eloquent pleader, and a logical and clever speaker. As commander of the Tacoma Guards, Company C, First Infantry Regiment of the National Guard of Washington, Capt. Fife is looked upon by the entire company with the highest esteem, and their trust in him has been fully demonstrated on more than one occasion. In May, 1882, Capt. Fife married Miss Flora J. Thompson, the eldest daughter of Senator L. F. Thompson, of Sumner.

Mr. Fife is deeply absorbed in the public interests of Tacoma, and the zeal displayed by him in these interests has made him a very popular citizen.

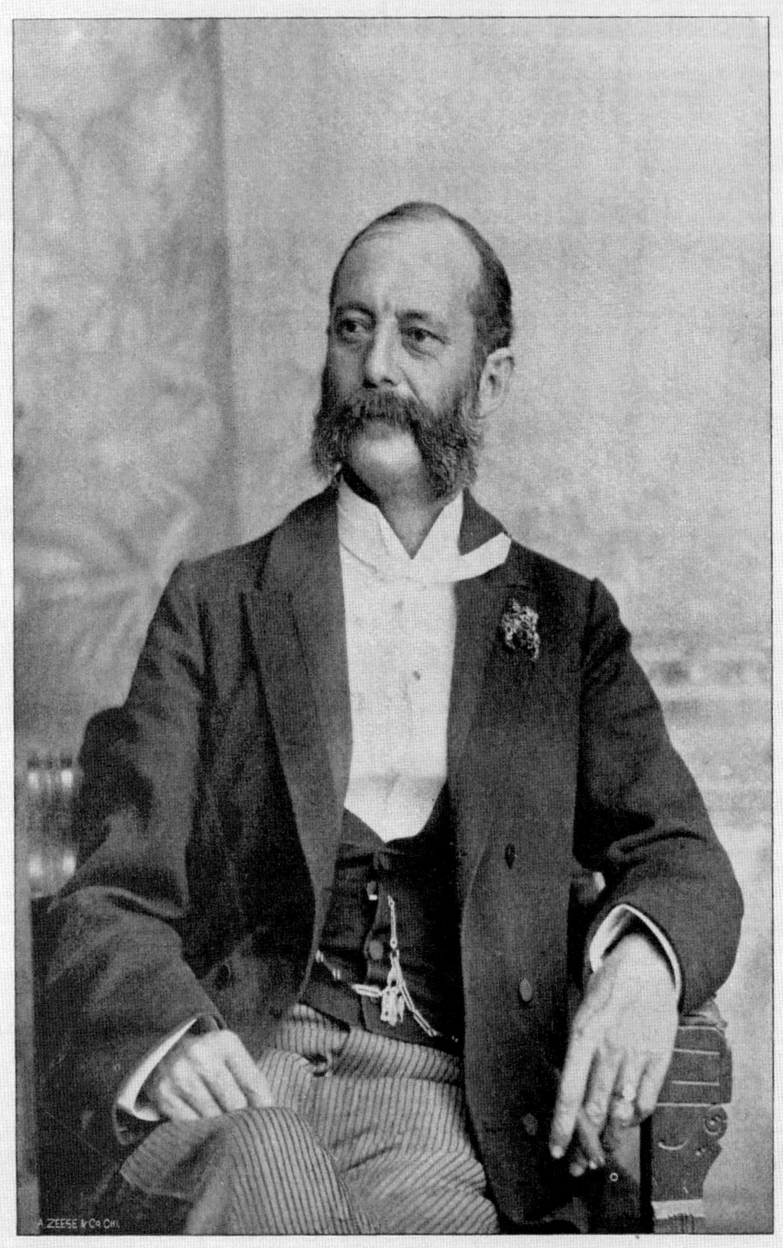

CLINTON P. FERRY.

CLINTON P. FERRY.

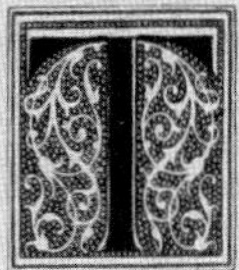

HE subject of this brief sketch, Mr. Clinton P. Ferry, to whom the writer, as well as many other visitors to Tacoma, is indebted for many acts of kindness and courtesy, is a character within himself. Mr. Ferry is a self-made man; born at Fort Wayne in 1836, after the age of 12 years he took upon himself his own education, meanwhile being his own support. He left school when 19 years old, having passed through a commercial college, and become cashier for the Toledo, Wabash & Western Railroad, leaving his position two years later to go to the Pacific Coast, where he spent about twenty years between Portland and San Francisco. In 1868 Mr. Ferry came to Tacoma, then nothing but a forest, and invested in real estate. Many persons looked upon his investments then as a pure act of folly, and thus it was that they dubbed him the "Duke of Tacoma," a sobriquet which has followed him to the present day, and is so identified with Mr. Ferry that he is known everywhere as "the Duke." Mr. Ferry is of French descent, his grandfather having been chef de battalion under Napoleon the First. The present Governor of Washington is his uncle. Much of Mr. Ferry's tenacity, one of his greatest characteristics, can be judged of by his strength of conviction in the natural resources and location of Tacoma. Much of the real estate bought by him twenty-one years ago is to-day the finest property in Tacoma, and still held by him. He has in fact for that period of time subordinated everything to the maintenance of his interests in Tacoma, and has naturally reaped a handsome reward.

Mr. Ferry, however, has been always active in the public interests of Tacoma, and although not a politician uses his money and influence in all good acts of charity and public good. His zeal, vitality, perseverance, honor, polished manners and good fellowship have secured for him the best legacy any man can wish—firm and devoted friends.

GEO. P. BALDWIN.

W. J. D. FRASER.

The above named gentleman has a commodious office in Exchange Block, corner of Tenth and A streets, and is well known in Tacoma as a pushing, energetic, active business man. He does a general real estate, loan brokerage and commission business, and is one of the firmest believers in the future of this city that can be found. His interest in the city is absorbing, and he has identified himself with it so closely that he is sure to prosper as the city itself does.

Mr. Fraser represents, and is in fact the principal owner of the Ravenswood Addition which is one of the choicest bits of property lying adjacent to Tacoma. It is all on high ground, and faces Commencement Bay, commanding one of the most beautiful views in the vicinity.

Mr. Fraser has a large business connection in Great Britain, and has already been commissioned to act as agent for several influential capitalists.

BUCEY & WILLIAMS,

REAL ESTATE INVESTORS AND BROKERS.

This firm, composed of Henry Bucey and Herbert J. Williams, is located in the Wright Block in Rooms 10 and 11 corner Pacific avenue and Ninth street, and is doing a very large general Real Estate and Brokerage business; the greater portion of their real estate transactions are investments for non-residents, and their success in the business is due to their careful and judicial investments made for strangers. Their reputation for honesty and reliability is well known and established. They have handled some of the finest and most valuable property in the city, and their judgment is greatly relied upon in all matters pertaining to investments.

Mr. Henry Bucey, who is the head member of the firm, is an attorney at law of acknowledged ability. He is from Ohio, but has been on the Northwest coast since 1876. His judgment led him after careful study of the country to the conclusion that Tacoma was destined to be the great metropolis of the Northwest, and in the fall of 1884 he left a very lucrative practice at Pendleton, Oregon, and moved with his family to Tacoma. His early life having been spent in horticultural work which he had great love for, and discerning that this Territory was destined to be a great fruit producing country, he originated and effectually organized the Washington Horticultural Society in 1885 and has been its president ever since, which society has accomplished a vast amount of good for the whole Territory; and to aid the society he originated and published the *Northwest Horticulturist*, a monthly journal, which immediately became under his able editing, the leading and most popular paper of the kind in the Northwest. His legal practice and real estate business having become so great, he disposed of the paper to its present managers and editors. His last and greatest undertaking of a public nature is the establishing of a large Exposition building in this city; he has succeeded in forming a corporation with a capital stock of $125,000 and has secured two blocks of land in the city. The building will be completed by September 1st, 1890, when the exposition will take place. The building is near the Sound, and he proposes to make one of the leading features of the Exposition the establishing and maintaining of large aquariums, a venture which will net him a handsome return.

Herbert J. Williams is from Michigan, and has resided in this city about two years, in which time he has by his honesty and ability to transact business earned an enviable reputation, and he is universally respected.

He is a graduate of the Medical Department of the University of Michigan, class of 1881, but after practicing for five years in Eastern Oregon devoted his attention entirely to the drug business. Upon coming to Tacoma two years since, seeking some business in which to engage, he became associated with Mr. Bucey in the business which they have made such a success. He still takes an active interest in matters pertaining to the advancement of the medical profession, being a charter member of both the County and State Medical Societies.

LOMBARD INVESTMENT COMPANY.

CORNER OF C AND ELEVENTH STREETS, TACOMA.

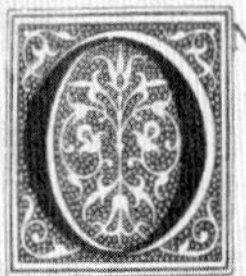

ONE of the oldest established, best known and strongest of loaning companies in the United States, having a capital fully paid up of $1,250,000, with a surplus of $750,000. The Eastern office of the company for making loans is located at Kansas City, Mo., which is under the direct charge of Mr. James L. Lombard, Vice-President of the company, and the Eastern office for disposing of loans is at No. 13 Sears Building, Boston, Mass., under the direct charge of Mr. B. Lombard, Jr., President of the company, who has been identified with the business for over thirty years, having commenced the loaning of money for Eastern capitalists in the State of Illinois when a mere boy, and having devoted his entire time to it to the present date. The company is represented by branch offices in the States of Minnesota, Iowa, Nebraska, Colorado, Kansas, Oregon, Utah, Tennessee, Texas and Washington (all of these branches being directly under the management and control of the Kansas City office), in which are competent employes who have been with the company for greater or less periods of time. The company averages from $10,000,000 to $12,000,000 per year of loans, and in all the business they have ever transacted no investor has ever been known to lose a cent. The office at Tacoma is under the charge of Mr. S. S. King, who has been in the employ of the company for the last eight or ten years, and who was sent to this coast in the summer of 1886 for the purpose of looking it over and seeing whether it would be a good field for investment. Upon his report to the company they decided to open an office, which they did at Portland, Oregon, in the summer of 1887, placing him in charge. The business of the office having increased so rapidly that it was deemed advisable to divide the work and make two offices, in April of 1889 Mr. King moved the headquarters of the company to Tacoma, Washington, placing Mr. J. A. Arment, who had been with him since commencing business here, in charge of the Portland office. Since opening the office here the company have placed over 2,000 loans, amounting in the aggregate to $2,500,000. In all of this business they have never had a foreclosure, and have not up to the present date ever been obliged to take a single tract of land, and have never carried delinquent interests any month to exceed $300, making a splendid showing for the conservative manner in which loans have been placed and demonstrating that they are worthy of the confidence in which they are held by Eastern investors. The office in this city employs fifteen people, and judging from appearances when it was visited by our reporter, we are satisfied that they have sufficient work to keep them all busy, and could probably employ a larger force to good advantage.

With the growing field and a thrifty population before them, it is hardly necessary to bespeak for the Lombard Investment Company, a further brilliant success in their undertaking in the City of Destiny.

SNELL & BEDFORD.

The pleasant offices of this firm are at 1405 Pacific avenue. These gentlemen are both well known in Tacoma, and possess a large and flourishing business. Mr. W. H. Snell is city attorney of Tacoma. He fairly represents the best type of Western men. He is rather small in physique, but evidently possesses one of those alert, vigorous organizations that is capable of any amount of exertion. His brain is apparently of the same sinewy quality as his body, and equally fitted to sustain hard work. Mr. Snell was born in Mechanicsburg, in July, 1852, but while he was still a boy his parents moved to Nebraska, and settled in Lincoln, the capital city. Here Mr. Snell entered the Nebraska University, and graduated therefrom in 1873. He then went into the office of Philpot & Curran, and studied law. He was admitted to the bar in 1874, and went to Georgetown, Col., where he was assistant prosecuting attorney. While here he made the acquaintance of Miss Mary Alice Bates, and to her was united in the bonds of matrimony in 1876. Shortly after this event Mr. Snell found his health breaking down, and moved back to Nebraska, where he located in Fairbury, and began to practice. In 1885 he was elected as representative from the 22d Senatorial district. He was re-elected to the Senate in 1887, and served his term. Then he came to Tacoma, and his interests have ever since been identified with the City of Destiny.

Charles Bedford, the other member of the firm, is of English birth, but he came with his parents to this country before he was six years of age. His father settled at first in Illinois, but afterward removed to Nebraska. Mr. Bedford, who is of a scholarly turn of mind, was during his younger days a teacher in some of the best schools in Jefferson County, Neb. Then he took up the study of law, and shortly after he was admitted to the bar, met Mr. Snell, and they formed a partnership which bids fair to last for a lifetime.

STEPHEN O'BRIEN,

of 1342 Pacific Avenue, has a large general practice, and is regarded as one of the rising legal luminaries of Washington.

He was born in Belleville, Ontario, in 1863. He was university bred, and one of the most promising graduates of the class of 1880. He left Belleville when still a lad in years, and commenced the study of law at Osgoode Hall, the famous Toronto law school. He obtained his degree and was admitted to the bar in June, 1885. He then took up the practice of his profession in his native town. As his powers developed themselves he found the field too contracted for his growing energies, and migrated to the Pacific Coast. He settled in Tacoma in the summer of 1888, and has since become identified with some of the largest business enterprises in this city. He is attorney of the Tacoma Electric Soap Company, and Milwaukee Furniture Company, and in fact is already in possession of a lucrative general practice.

PINKHAM & WALKER.

REAL ESTATE AGENTS, CORNER PACIFIC AVENUE AND S. TENTH STREET.

THIS firm has from the very first day that their sign appeared, a year ago, enjoyed an enviable position among the prominent and substantial real estate agents in Tacoma. Previous to deciding that the City of Destiny should be his future home, Mr. L. Hampden Pinkham held positions with high-class financial firms in the East. At a comparatively early age he filled the responsible position of general representative for several noted paint houses throughout New England, but subsequently drifting West, became secretary and treasurer of the Kansas City Investment Company of Kansas, and afterward cashier for the Minnesota Loan and Trust Company of Minneapolis, Minn. For the past nine years Mr. Pinkham has been so closely identified with the real estate and loan business that he may now be considered an important authority on all matters appertaining thereto.

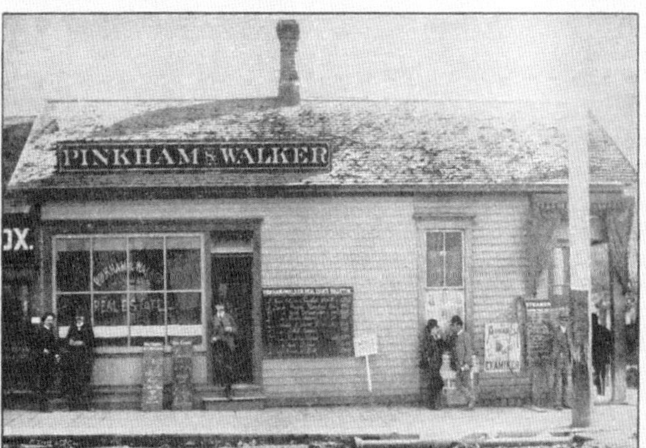

OFFICES OF PINKHAM & WALKER.

Mr. Richard E. Walker has been a resident of the Pacific coast for a number of years. About two years ago he decided that Tacoma was the metropolis of the entire Pacific northwest, and since that time he has made himself extremely popular by his sound business qualifications and general geniality, qualifications without which no business man can hope to be successful, so quickly is human nature attracted toward the man who is always pleasant and good humored.

Both these gentlemen have become heavy property holders. The past summer with them has been exceptionally good, and their prospects for a brisk business during the coming winter and spring, are most promising. At present they are handling inside and acreage property, and are making a specialty of investing money in Tacoma realty for Eastern capitalists. Mr. Pinkham, through his numerous Eastern acquaintances, commands an almost unlimited amount of capital from savings banks, trustee and guardian funds, and the firm will in the near future organize a real estate mortgage and loan company in Tacoma, on a large scale, and commensurate with the deserts of both the gentlemen composing it. Thus our city draws to itself clear-sighted men, who work for its future greatness with a right good will.

E. N. OUIMETTE.

Among the representative citizens of Tacoma few are more widely known or generally respected than E. N. Ouimette. Although at present an enthusiastic American citizen, Mr. Ouimette first saw the light of day in St. Eustache, Canada, where he passed his earlier years. He was a graduate of the well-known university of his native town, and on finishing his collegiate course betook himself to commercial pursuits at the early age of eighteen years. As time passed on, and the ambitious youth developed into a man of alert and vigorous intellect, he found the field about him all too restricted to afford exercise to his growing energies, and in the year 1865, he emigrated to Portland, where he engaged in the drygoods business. He remained there about four years, gaining business experience, and acquainting himself with the possibilities of the Pacific coast, and the new people among whom his lot was cast. At the end of that time the star of Olympia rose above the horizon, and among other wise men Mr. Ouimette "went for it there and then." He engaged in the same business, and remained in the new town ten years, making himself a reputation for business integrity and enterprise, that rendered him a marked man in commercial circles in the rapidly growing Territory of Washington.

At the end of the decade Mr. Ouimette, with his usual vigor and determination, made another migration, and finally arrived on the scene of his present successes, Tacoma. In 1884 he forecasted with unerring sagacity the future importance of the City of Destiny, and divesting himself of all other interests, threw himself heart and soul into the real estate and insurance business in Tacoma. Since then his shrewdness, his knowledge of, and judgment in real estate, and his public spirit, have placed him in the foremost rank of our citizens. His handsome offices are daily thronged by the best class of investors; he is a director of one of the most important banks in Tacoma, has plotted several of the most important additions to the city; in short, he is among the first to push any undertaking that promises to advance the interests of his adopted city, and add to its stability. He has proved the wisdom of his choice, as also his excellent foresight and judgment, and though still a comparatively young man, he has already carved out a career such as his fellow citizens may well point to with pride and envy, and endeavor to emulate.

E. F. RUSSELL & CO.

REAL ESTATE AND MINING BROKERS.

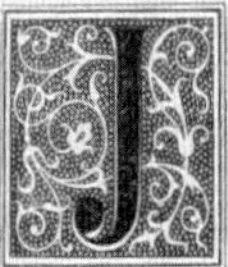

JUDGE E. F. RUSSELL and his son Everett F. Russell compose this firm. Both gentlemen are well known in Tacoma, and along the Pacific coast. There is not a man upon the western slope of the dividing mountains who is better known as a mining man, and whose opinion on all appertaining thereto is more trusted, than that of Judge Russell. He has, during his thirty years' residence on the coast, devoted most of his time to mines and mining, and the working and reduction of all classes of ores. In this last respect he has gained considerable fame as the inventor of the Russell Roasting Furnace for the reduction of rebellious ores. This class of furnace is now very generally used in all sections where ores of difficult reduction are found.

Judge Russell has lived a greater portion of the thirty years of his residence on the Pacific coast at San Francisco, but he may also be termed an old-timer in Tacoma, for in the early days, long before the advent of the Northern Pacific Railroad into Washington, he invested largely in Tacoma realty, and also in other lands in this State; and he still retains possession of many of them. His faith in Tacoma is unbounded. For this reason, as well as because the mining outlook is much brighter in Washington than in any other State in the West, he came to the City of Destiny, and since his arrival here has carried on a very extensive business in the buying and selling of real estate, mines, coal, and timber lands for numerous customers. Without counting mines and coal lands, the firm of Russell & Co. have to-day for sale over $1,000,000 worth of property. Some of the heaviest realty transactions in Tacoma have been made through them, and all their transactions have had one termination, viz.: An advantageous transaction for the buyer and seller. This firm offers only first-class property for sale, and by this have made a success in business.

Soon after his arrival on the coast, Judge Russell engaged extensively in the practice of law in the courts of Oregon and Washington Territory, living at the time in Oregon; but since 1870 he has devoted his whole attention to mining and real estate.

THE ALKI REAL ESTATE CO.

This corporation has its offices in rooms 4 and 5, Union Block. The company consists of H. F. Garrettson, president; Emmet N. Parker, secretary, and W. J. Werner, manager. Its chief business is the buying and selling of real estate for itself and on commission, and negotiating mortgages, loans and other securities. One of the choicest tracts of suburban property ever placed upon the market, is the Alki addition to Tacoma, located in the southern portion of the city. When the company placed this addition upon the market it was with the idea of offering a delightful location for suburban residents, and they have carried out their idea in a most thorough manner. The tract is situated in the vicinity of the Tacoma and Fern Hill Street Railway, and the motor line is now being constructed through the center. Residents in the Alki addition, who purchased their lots when first offered, have secured cheap homes within a few minutes' ride of the business portion of the city, that are now worth double what they paid for them. The company has only been established since the beginning of last March, but the reputation of the organizers was amply sufficient to assure the public of its reliability. The president and secretary, Col. H. F. Garrettson and Emmet N. Parker, are partners in law, and as counsellors in all legal matters, rank among the first of their profession in the city. Mr. Werner is comparatively a newcomer to Tacoma, but he is now well known as a thorough and reliable business man. His former home was in Wichita, Kan., in which place, as well as elsewhere, he has been engaged extensively in the real estate business.

GLOYD & SPINNING.

These well known gentlemen, whose offices are in the Merchants National Bank Building, constitute the oldest firm in Pierce County engaged in business as abstracters of land titles. Their books were opened by E. C. Pentland of the firm of Hall & Pentland in 1883. The celebrated Thora Numerical Tract Index is the system on which they are conducted. Mr. Frank H. Gloyd bought the books from Hall & Pentland in the month of February, 1884, and in March of the same year he formed a copartnership with Wm. N. Spinning.

Messrs. Gloyd & Spinning at first did a general real estate business as well as abstracting of titles, but since 1887 have dropped that, and now handle only their own property. This includes a building now in process of construction on the corner of Fifteenth and C streets, which will be four stories in height, with a frontage of sixty-five feet. This will be devoted to business purposes and contain three stores and thirty-nine offices. They also possess very considerable water-front property, and a large hop farm. Their main business, however, is as abstracters, and in this they do far more than any other firm in town.

Mr. Gloyd was born in Shelby County, Kentucky, spent his boyhood in Illinois, and as a young man studied law in the office of a brother of Chief-Justice Waite in Ohio. Then he went to Kansas and remained a year, came across the plain in a prairie schooner and landed in Oregon, where he rested another year, and then came here, where he made the success of his life, and settled down.

William N. Spinning has the right to be called a true Washingtonian, as he was born in Chehalis. His father was a well known physician, and was several times appointed as Reservation Doctor by the Government. As a young man he studied law, but later on, desiring a more robust life, he became a farmer. Then he took a turn at school teaching. After this last experience he and his father went into the real estate business together. Four years later he and Mr. Gloyd became partners, although he continued to retain his interest with his father until 1887.

ROSS & NAUBERT.

REAL ESTATE BROKERS, MASON BLOCK.

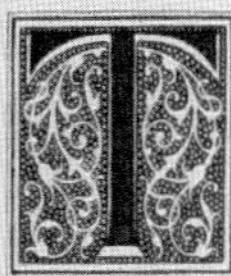HERE is no better evidence of the faith men have in the community in which they do business than is to be found in the liberality they display in making their places of business inviting to their clientage. It is not always, however, that a lavish expenditure of money succeeds in attaining the object desired, namely attractiveness. In addition to luxurious appointments, there must be confidence on the part of the public in the sincerity of the welcome of those who extend the invitation. When the combination of luxurious surroundings and good fellowship is happily insured, the object is attained.

Messrs. Ross & Naubert, each the prince of good fellows, have the keynote in the decoration of their splendid offices in the Mason Block, and situated as they are on the corner of A and South Tenth streets, they hold the combination referred to. Both gentlemen are thoroughly well known in Tacoma. Mr. Frank C. Ross landed in the City of Destiny from Pittsfield, Ill., on Christmas day, 1879, and has been engaged in the real estate business since 1882, handling only his own property until the present copartnership was formed, about eighteen months since. Mr. C. A. E. Naubert, a native of Montreal, Canada, on first coming to the Pacific coast located in Portland, Oregon, but saw the opportunities that Tacoma offered, and straightway came here. This was in 1881. For five years after his arrival, Mr. Naubert was cashier of the Northern Pacific Railroad Company, and only left that important position to engage in his present business.

OFFICES OF ROSS & NAUBERT.

Besides being owners and dealers in property located in the very best parts of the city, Messrs. Ross & Naubert, together with other prominent business men, have platted and are handling in one of the most picturesque suburban districts of Tacoma, Lake City, a location with enchanting surroundings and bordering on American Lake, the finest sheet of fresh water in Western Washington. This town site will be connected with Tacoma by a railroad that is now nearly completed. More particulars of this beautiful place will be found upon another page.

Another very important enterprise in which these gentlemen are interested, especially Mr. Ross, is the construction of a wharf and warehouse on the tide flats at the head of Commencement Bay, that portion of the city where several important industries enumerated in the article on the city at the beginning of this work, have been, and are being constructed. Some months ago Mr. Ross and his associates purchased forty-eight acres of this valuable land. They have now conceived the idea of building a wharf a mile and a quarter long for the accommodation of ocean going vessels. The necessary piling is now being driven. At the end of the wharf a warehouse 300 feet in length, and proportionally wide is being constructed. These improvements will be approachable from several points. The Northern Pacific Railroad will build a branch line across the flats to the warehouse, and an immense bridge will open the wide arm of the Puyallup River from either Ninth or Tenth streets to the flats. The Northern Pacific is continually extending its docks for the accommodation of the ever-increasing trade that Tacoma is building up with all parts of the world.

Outside of Tacoma Messrs. Ross & Naubert also have large interests. Mr. Ross' gold, silver, copper and iron mines in the Cle Elum mining districts have already proved rich, and when the more extensive improvements that are soon to be made are completed, there is no reason to doubt that they will be the richest mines in the district.

It is such men as Messrs. Ross & Naubert who have labored so earnestly to bring Tacoma to that destiny that she has attained, namely the metropolis of the Pacific Northwest, and who will be pointed to by future generations as pioneers.

GEO. W. TRAVER.

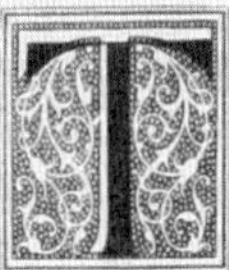

HE REPUTATION OF THE GENTLEMAN whose name forms the caption of this article is as familiar as a household word to residents of Tacoma, and, in fact, to most of the inhabitants of Washington Territory. He is engaged in business as a real estate and investment agent in the Fife Block, and it is a safe statement to venture that few, if any, offices in this city conclude so many important transactions in a given period of time, and of so varied a character.

Mr. Traver, who settled in the City of Destiny, in the year 1882, is one of the citizens that Tacoma may well be proud to boast of possessing, for since identifying his interests with those of this city, he has done perhaps as much to forward its fortunes, blazon its advantages to the world, and develop and foster its financial affairs, as any other one man who ever cast his lot among us.

Mr. Traver is a typical Western American, and could his life and career be written, it would be found to abound in exciting incidents and thrilling adventures, sufficient to set up a romance writer in material from which to grind out novels for a lifetime. He is one of the "old timers" in Oregon, and all the earlier residents of that State know him like a book, and would follow his lead like a flock of sheep after the bell-wether. He was a resident of California in its palmy days of prosperity, having been engaged in business in Alameda on a large scale and with the most successful results. It may be mentioned in this connection that Mr. Traver is Commissioner of Deeds for Oregon, and that during the past year he has been Commissioner and taken most of the depositions in regard to the Indian complications at the Puyallup Reservation. It was, in fact, he who was mainly instrumental in bringing about the favorable consideration of their claims which was given to them by the United States Government through the Indian Department at Washington, D. C.

On becoming a resident of Tacoma in 1882 Mr. Traver at once took rank, by virtue of his reputation and character, as one of the leading citizens of the then rapidly growing little town. His keen judgment and business acumen at once discerned the vast future possibilities of the City of Destiny, and his hand was forthwith put upon the throttle, and he has held the valves open ever since, keeping steam up in the engine and speeding the city of his adoption upon its course at a pace that few other engineers could have equaled. He has spent thousands and thousands of dollars in showing up the advantages of Tacoma to outside capital, and has sounded the fame of the city as far abroad as the Atlantic coast.

The well known Traver's Addition was projected by Mr. Traver's fertile brain, and has proved in every way one of the most successful and desirable locations ever added to the city. The property consists of about 40 acres of most admirably situated land, and the lots, when put upon the market, sold like hot cakes to the most desirable class of purchasers.

Mr. Traver has also been installed by E. Bennett, of Topeka, Kansas, as his agent and attorney in placing Hunt's Prairie upon the market. This is a beautiful tract of land in the southwestern suburbs of the City of Destiny. It has only been placed upon the market a comparatively short time, but has already attracted a vast deal of attention among speculators as well as that class of investors who play principally for "keeps." In fact, this property may be confidently recommended as containing some of the choicest lots now remaining open for purchase in the neighborhood of the fair city of Tacoma. In addition to these, however, Mr. Traver is interested in many other properties in the southern and western portions of the city, and, in fact, his keen eye and alert judgment are constantly on the lookout for the choicest bits, and those in the market for a real fancy, gilt-edged article cannot do better than allow themselves to be guided by his judgment and experience.

The elegant residence of Mr. Traver is one of the show sights of Tacoma, and among the earliest drives that a newcomer or visitor to the city is shown is that leading to "Oak Grove," as the happy possessor, with peculiar aptness, has christened it. It is indeed led up to by one of the loveliest drives of four miles that imagination ever pictured, or eye gazed upon. The broad panorama embracing every scenic effect—rugged mountain, broad, smiling savannah, forests, rearing their lofty heads to the skies, clothed in living green, make the landscape one that Whittier would yearn to depict. At the end of the lovely drive Oak Grove forms the fitting climax to the picture the feeble pen has vainly endeavored to put before the reader. The house is situated upon a gentle eminence embowered and enshrined in a grove of oak trees whose umbrageous propinquity suggested the name to the fortunate owner of this little paradise. The scene involuntarily suggests to the spectator the words of the grand old hymn:

"Where everything is lovely,"

and in this case not even "man is vile."

The house is unobtrusive in its order of architecture, but so constructed that while the building completely and beautifully harmonizes with every feature of the surrounding landscape, each convenience also with which modern science has equipped household affairs, is obtained in the complete menage. The picture that will be found of Oak Grove among the residences of Tacoma, will give the reader a more complete idea of the entourage, and convince him that the homes being constructed are of a character which will lend permanence to the outlook.

The commodious offices of Mr. Traver are in the well known Fife Block, as advantageous a situation as is probably to be found in the city. Any caller there will always find the courteous proprietor invariably ready to welcome him and give him the benefit of his ripe judgment and years of experience in real estate business, an experience which has taught him how to distinguish at a glance between the "paper" and "sand lots" of the town which is merely boomed as a money-making speculation, and the town which has come to stay, to be as it were a lasting monument to energy.

JOHN C. BROCKENBROUGH, JR.

Real Estate, Insurance and Loans—in Rear of Traders' Bank.

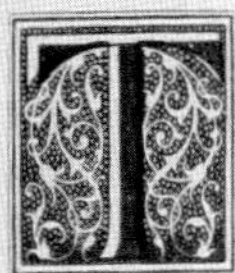

THE steady advance in Tacoma realty during the past few years has brought within her gates a number of enterprising, bright business men. Prominent among them is Mr. John C. Brockenbrough, Jr., who came from Lafayette, Indiana, last year, and he then decided on the City of Destiny as his future home.

After carefully reviewing the ground he made some investments and embarked in the real estate, loan and insurance business, opening up the handsome offices where he is at present located, and on acount of his ability and integrity his business soon assumed large proportions. In fire insurance he probably is doing the largest business in the city to-day, as he represents the most prominent insurance companies in the Union. The sums of real estate transfers which have been transacted through his office, aggregate hundreds of thousands of dollars, while through his loan department he has invested over a quarter million of dollars of Eastern capital. His knowledge, both of the value of real estate and of the credit and solvency of borrowers, has given him a leading position in the city as a lender of money on real estate security. Through this department of his business many large and important trusts are confided to him, and it is a fact, perhaps without precedent in such a business, that of the many thousands of dollars loaned on mortgages by him, every one has proved profitable to the investor, thus adding to his reputation for judgment and foresight.

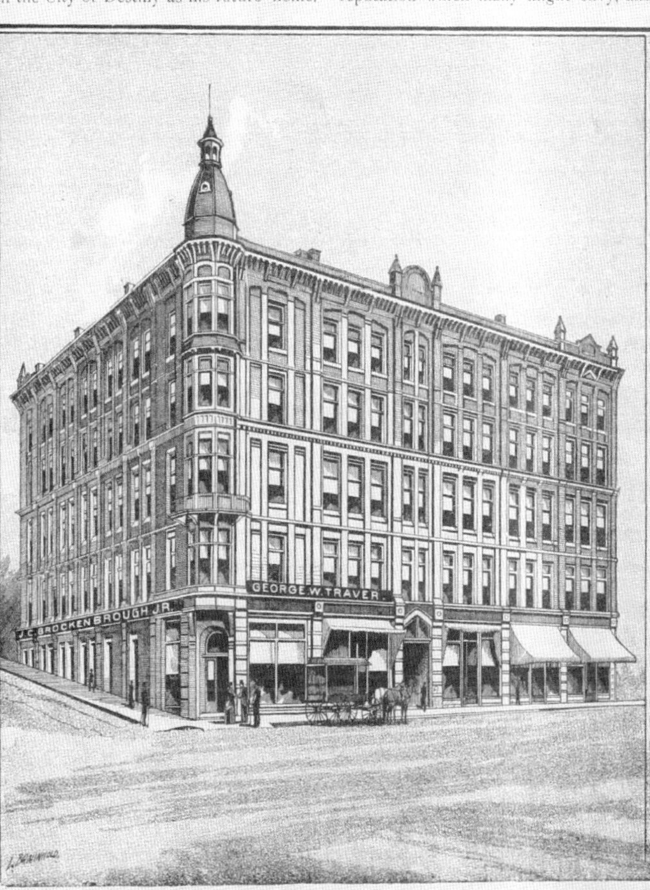

FIFE HOTEL AND BLOCK.

Experience shows that in addition to their thoroughly tested security, wisely chosen real estate mortgages yield a larger income than any other safe form of investment accessible to the people. The remarkably cool judgment displayed by Mr. Brockenbrough, in his selection of only the best loans, both in respect to the character and standing of the borrower, and the value of the property sought to be mortgaged as security, has procured for him a reputation which many might envy, and will undoubtedly very much increase his business in this department.

Mr. Brockenbrough, although careful, has proven himself both far-sighted and energetic, and when he first settled here, he saw the chance to make some money on a tract of land on the south side of Tacoma and which up to that time had not attracted much attention and he bought it. Portions of this tract were eligible for residence sites, and others admirably adapted for business blocks and for warehouses, by reason of their being adjacent to the tracks of the Northern Pacific Railroad. Mr. Brockenbrough's likeness will be found in our columns and he is, as will be seen, a young man; he however is (to use a rather coarse though expressive term), a hustler, and, although but a very short period in Tacoma, is well known to almost every man in the city; he is fineiy educated, a refined, gentlemanly, courteous and polished man and withal modest: in combining these qualifications with strict business integrity it is hardly to be wondered at that he has been so successful. It will be seen by the cut that he and Mr. Traver are in the same block.

DES MOINES.

TWELVE MILES FROM TACOMA.

A GROWING YOUNG CITY.

The sun looks forth in glad surprise!
What miracle this that greets her eyes—
Where yesterday Nature reigned supreme,
A new-born city lies!

—*Le Duc.*

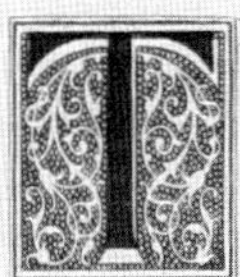

HE thought expressed in Jack Spratt and wife (the fable which is so well known to all children) conveys, like La Fontaine's fable poetry, a metaphor which to older persons appeals in more ways than one.

It is a Godsend to humanity that the human thought is not always in the same channel, that our tastes differ, so like the "girouette" on the housetop; many persons are so wedded to the rush, dash, and excitement of our large cities, and are so accustomed to them, that they would feel like strangers were they to commence a new life in a small and growing hamlet, even though at the end of the year the fruits of their exertions should be tenfold the amount of their accumulations in the city; there are others who for many reasons (of less means perhaps, or for the love of quietude, or the knowledge of their ability to economize more and accumulate faster in a pioneer town) prefer to place their fortunes in a young city like Des Moines.

Leaving Tacoma and steaming up the beautiful shores of Puget Sound, passing Point Brown, Ash Point and the little village of Adelaide, noting on every hand small clearings made in the timber, and fruit farms dotted here and there, we arrive after a charming sail of an hour at the young city of Des Moines, where a few months ago not even a building marked its present site.

What a change the enterprise and energy of man can make in such a short space of time! As short a time ago as last July the town was located and platted by several gentlemen of Tacoma, who, recognizing the natural advantages of the location for a harbor and town site, organized a company known as the "Des Moines City Improvement Co.," with a capital of $100,000; no time was lost in erecting a saw mill, and thus furnishing the building material for the requirements of new comers; so rapid, in fact, has been the growth that Des Moines to-day has in addition to the saw-mill (which employs some twenty-five men, and has a capacity of 20,000 feet per day) ten substantial residences, a well-appointed general merchandise store, a schoolhouse, and about 880 feet of wharfage, the surface of which has required 200,000 feet of lumber. In addition to the improvements already made twenty more houses are in course of construction. The firm of Young Bros. is about to open another store for general merchandise, a church is being built at a cost of $2,500; a brick yard employing forty men, and pottery works employing a like number, a shingle-mill employing twenty hands, and with a capacity of 100,000

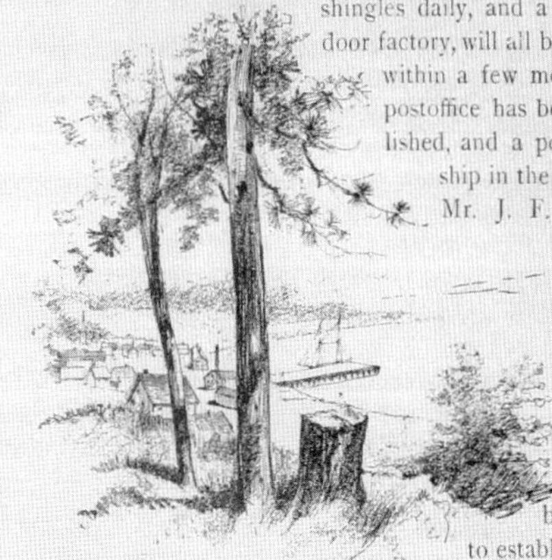

shingles daily, and a sash and door factory, will all be running within a few months. A postoffice has been established, and a postmastership in the person of Mr. J. F. Hiatt, a native of Indiana, who has for the past five years resided at Tacoma, but left it to establish a general merchandise business at Des Moines. Besides doing an extensive business Mr. Hiatt finds time to extend the courtesies of the town to all new-comers, and being a notary public, attends to what legal matters are required. The Des Moines City Improvement Co. is building at a cost of about $5,000 a steamer which will make the trip to Tacoma (about twelve miles) twice a day in the space of one hour, including stops.

Thus it is that Des Moines has become a city almost in a night, and her location is such that she can hardly help becoming a large place. Situated as she is in a quiet harbor midway between the two cities of Tacoma and Seattle, all vessels plying between these two cities pass Des Moines; in the immediate vicinity of it are islands where extensive potteries and brick yards are located; these islands, as also Chatauqua Beach, obtain their supplies from Des Moines, while back in the clearings are some of the finest fruit-orchards, richest bottom lands covered with farms, where hops and all kinds of vegetables are raised; all this produce is marketed through, and supplies obtained from, Des Moines; the timber lands are of immense value, and are almost inexhaustible.

As fast as this magnificent timber is cut, so fast appear beautiful fruit and other farms in its stead, and so the steady march of civilization wends its way through these giants of the forest, as the tilling of a naturally rich soil must of necessity build up immense cities, whose prestige shall be known from the East to the West.

For a beautiful resort none could be found superior to Des Moines, lying as she does on a gentle rise from the most beautiful sheet of water in the world, and with a fine view of the snow peaks of grand old Mount Tacoma and the Olympia Range.

And above all, the climate, where the summers are never too warm, and the winters never too cold; where the flowers bloom, and the grass remains green in the winter, and where nature thrives the year round; where the finest fishing in the world can be had by a few strokes of the oar; where game of all descriptions is plentiful, and where man's hand and brain are building up a beautiful young city in the midst of nature's sublimity.

REALTY LOAN AND INVESTMENT CO.

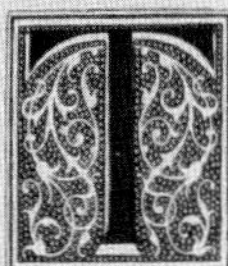

THIS company is situated in the Tacoma National Bank Building, Tacoma, and is organized with a capital of one hundred thousand dollars. The officers are as follows: Charles M. Johnson, President; J. W. Kleeb, Vice-President, and O. W. Barlow, Secretary and Treasurer.

The company does a general real estate and mortgage loan business, invests money for non-residents, and looks closely after the interests of its customers after the investments have been made by them.

Mr. Johnson, the president, came from Aberdeen, Dakota, in November, 1887; Mr. Kleeb, the vice-president, from Council Bluffs, Iowa, in February, 1888, and Mr. Barlow, the secretary and treasurer, from Doland, Dakota, in December, 1888. In December, 1888, the company was organized, and considering the short time which has elapsed since then, the growth of the business shows a remarkable display of energy on the part of the incorporators.

This business, which is of immense magnitude, may be said to have been confined principally to two places, Tacoma and Des Moines, and as we have devoted some space to the latter investment made by them, we will here finish up this subject in as short a space as possible.

The gentlemen forming the Realty Loan and Investment Company came into communication with Mr. F. A. Blasher, a resident of that now thriving young place; recognizing the great importance of the location of Des Moines for not only a supplying station for the surrounding country, but a manufacturing and commercial town as well, they organized the Des Moines City Improvement Company with a capital of one hundred thousand dollars, and elected the following officers: J. W. Kleeb, President; F. A. Blasher, Vice-President, and O. W. Barlow, Secretary. A history of their movements from that time forth, and the unprecedented way in which the town is growing are given in our short review of the fair city of Des Moines, but it must be acknowledged that the gentlemen interested in this object certainly showed more than the average amount of foresightedness and pluck to assume such an undertaking. That they have been eminently successful is evinced by the growth and prosperity of this pioneer city, built up as it is by hewing the timbers which were its only adornment; this, however, was necessary in the case of Tacoma. But to their business investments in this city. The Realty Loan and Investment Co. celebrated its advent in Tacoma by a purchase of two of the best known subdivisions adjoining the city limits of Tacoma; these two additions are the Woodlawn, which lies due west on Eleventh street, and the Elmwood addition, which lies due southwest. The purchases were singularly successful ones, and this fact has been proved by the demand for lots in both subdivisions. They are of nearly the same size, and the Woodlawn contains six hundred and seventy-two, while the Elmwood contains six hundred and thirty-four lots; both additions have been divided off with streets eighty, and alleys forty feet in width; the fact that they nearly adjoin one another, and that they are similarly situated, will suffice us to describe their location as one. In the first place it may be said that there are only two or three such peculiar locations adjoining Tacoma; the drive to them is by way of the road to that Divine gift of nature, "American Lake," and it may be said that there is no more artistic and beautiful a drive in the country; it is the favorite one of the residents of Tacoma and where it passes through these additions presents a most picturesque vista on each side; the eye notes that the land is singularly level, and that the hills and dales of many of Tacoma's subdivisions are not here; and over the tree tops in the distance it lights upon the majestic, snow-capped peak of Mount Tacoma.

Turning a little to the right one views the grade of the Lake City Railway and Navigation Company, where the tracks are now being laid, and where by February 1st trains will be running to and from the lake, stopping each time at the Elmwood station, and thus making the trip to the business part of Tacoma in less than ten minutes, and to American Lake about the same time. Here, in this lovely as well as convenient spot, are situated the three residences of Messrs. Johnson, Barlow and Kleeb; the very fact that these gentlemen have located their homes and families here ought to be a sufficient guarantee to anybody that they have confidence in the sites which they possess; all three residences will be viewed in our pages of the fine residences of Tacoma, and it will readily be seen that in point of beauty they would adorn any Eastern city.

Their position is nearer the business portion of Tacoma than American Lake, to which latter it is, however, only a short drive; this convenience of location must be seen to realize what a haven it is, and there are probably no visitors to Tacoma who have not in their drives to American Lake looked with lingering eyes on these charming residences and that of Mr. George W. Traver, which is only a few rods from them, comparing them with some fine Eastern homes and wondering who the happy possessors were.

In addition to these investments, the company own a very considerable amount of inside property, and have shown a conservative spirit in their investments.

The headquarters of the Des Moines City Improvement Company are naturally in the offices of the Realty Loan & Investment Co., and all matters relating either to Des Moines or to the Tacoma properties of the company will be attended to at the offices as above; those residing in the far East can rely implicitly on the integrity of these gentlemen and the truth of their statements relating to the properties in question, as also all information which they furnish regarding realty.

Personally one could not ask to meet with more courteous treatment than is received at the hands of the gentlemen composing the company; all three are men of energy, discretion, and withal imbued with true Western hospitality; they are men who, while realizing that wealth brings might, are not willing to make themselves slaves to the mighty dollar, and so in retaining their own respect they are able to gain that of others with whom they come in contact.

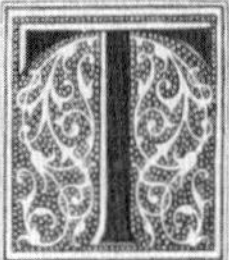

THE new State of Washington comprises an area as large as the combined area of Maine, New Hampshire, Vermont, Massachusetts, and Rhode Island. It is an empire within itself with its immense wealth of coal, iron, lime and gold, its immense timber lands, beautiful and fertile valleys, grand mountain ranges, ever flowing rivers, splendid fisheries, and above and beyond all, its great inland sea, known as Puget Sound, rippling on nearly two thousand miles of shore, where all the ships of the world could find free sailing and good anchorage three hundred and sixty-five days of the year.

All of these resources are tributary to the giant young city of Tacoma, known as the "City of Destiny." Tacoma was, in 1880, the smallest city in the Puget Sound country. Her population at that time was seven hundred and twenty inhabitants. She has grown up step by step, passed in point of population all the other cities in the State, and is now fairly entitled to the sobriquet, "Queen City of Washington," in view of the fact that her population is variously estimated at from 30,000 to 35,000.

The completion of the tunnel through the Cascade Mountains, in 1887, made Tacoma the terminus of the Northern Pacific Railroad, and placed her in direct communication with St. Paul and the East The value of this was at once felt, and the growth of the city became very rapid, not only in population and wealth, but in all lines of import, export, mercantile business and manufacturing. So great has been the advance of all lines of business, and so rapidly has the city been built up, that the facts must be seen to be believed. Tacoma shipped during the year 1888 twenty-nine cargoes of wheat, and eighty-three million feet of lumber. During the past year it can be roughly estimated that three times that amount of both commodities have been shipped from Tacoma. The great tracts of iron in the immediate vicinity, as well as coal, both hard and soft, has given a great impetus to the establishment of large iron works, while the best coke in the world is made in the city. The largest smelter for the reduction of ores on the Pacific coast has just been erected.

The Northern Pacific Railroad Company is spending six million dollars in Tacoma in terminal facilities, depots and new shops; one and one-half million will be spent this year.

The Tacoma Light and Water Company is enlarging its water and electric plants at an expenditure of three hundred thousand dollars, and the Tacoma Street Railway Company, of which Henry Villard is a prominent figure, is spending five hundred thousand dollars in cable and electric lines, and the construction of the finest motor house west of St. Paul.

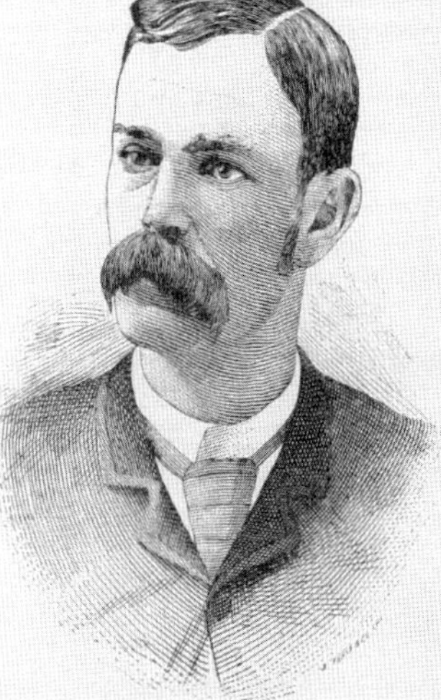

DANIEL McGREGOR.

There are to-day eleven banks in Tacoma, six of them national. There are in addition six building and loan associations. The schools and churches of Tacoma have a special interest. There are to-day eleven hundred buildings in course of construction, at an estimated cost of two million dollars, and the building record for the year reaches about seven million dollars. The transfers for 1888 were nine million, and for the past year about sixteen million dollars.

Meanwhile, the values of real estate have necessarily advanced with the growth and prosperity of the city. Lots on Pacific Avenue, which could be bought in 1882 for one thousand dollars (and were by many considered extremely high) would to-day bring twenty-five thousand dollars. Thus it is no exaggeration to say that there have been fortunes made in buying realty in Tacoma for those who had the foresight and courage to buy and afterward the strength of conviction to retain their holdings. Natural resources, labor and capital are developing the city, and room has to be made for the increasing population and industries. Every residence and place of business has a tenant before it is ready for occupancy.

With the foregoing facts before you, do you think that you can find a better field for investment than in the State of Washington and in Tacoma, its chief city?

The undersigned has resided in Washington since 1881, has spent the last seven years in Tacoma, has seen Tacoma grow from a hamlet of less than one thousand inhabitants to its present population, is thoroughly conversant with the growth and advantages of the city and State, and is familiar with the values of realty in Tacoma and Pierce county. His business is real estate, loans and investments, and he pays particular attention to investments for non-residents; keeps constantly on hand a large list of business, residence and farm property; also acreage suitable for platting and several additions close to the city, on the installment plan. It is therefore safe to say that all investors, for both large and small amounts, can find what they wish, and be sure of good returns for what they place here, in this magnificent region. Those who haven't large amounts to invest can invest what they have, if only one or two hundred dollars; while they are saving more, the amount invested will in all probability grow faster than they can save up more to invest.

The motto of my business is, "A square deal to all, and first come, first served."

DANIEL McGREGOR,
Real Estate and Investments,
1346 *Pacific Ave.* Tacoma, Washington.

R. E. ANDERSON & CO.

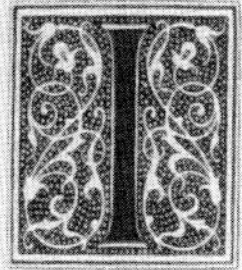T is probable that there are other firms in the city of Tacoma that do more business, but it is certain that none have a better reputation for strict attention to matters confided to their care than the pushing young firm of R. E. Anderson & Co., Investment and Loan Brokers, located at 920 A Street, just opposite the Tacoma Hotel. Trained in the conservative business centers of the East, both Mr. Anderson and Mr. Carman, the other member of the firm, are fully qualified to act intelligently for the best interests of those who seek their advice and counsel; and from the unvarying courtesy and business tact invariably shown by this firm to its callers, it is a matter of very little surprise that it is securing so large a share of the patronage of investors and dealers in Tacoma securities and real estate.

It goes without saying that no better paying investments can be had than those offered who intend locating in this city of progress and enterprise, and a cursory glance at the many great bargains on the list of improved as well as unimproved properties for sale by R. E. Anderson & Co., demonstrate the fact that they should be consulted by the close and careful buyer desirous of getting all that there is in a sale or purchase. As loan brokers they offer for sale first mortgage real estate loans drawing eight per cent. interest payable semi-annually, and running from one to five years. There is nothing better or safer, for the loans are made upon improved inside property in the city of Tacoma, and in no case is more than forty per cent. of the cash value of the security loaned.

A scarcely less desirable investment furnished by them is a first mortgage loan on inside unimproved property drawing nine per cent. interest payable semi-annually, and running from one to three years. Mr. Anderson's experience in the making of loans in the East has been such as to guarantee to the investor that his business will be carefully looked after from a safe and conservative basis. The best of reference is furnished from Philadelphia, New York, Des Moines and Tacoma.

Strangers are always cordially received at their office, conveniently located directly opposite the Tacoma Hotel, and whether they wish to invest or not, they will be shown about the city, and objects of interest they have never dreamed of as existing in this city, and which they themselves might neglect, will be shown to them with pleasure. No mistake can ever be made in looking up this firm by visitors to the "City of Destiny."

ORCHARD & OPIE.

Real Estate Bought and Sold, Investments made for Non-Residents. Office in Rear of Merchants' National Bank.

The rapid growth of Tacoma has been followed by a great advance in the prices of residence property, and so great has been this advance that it is practically impossible for men of moderate means to purchase homes near the business center. Such persons must secure a building site in some of the many eligibly located additions, among which are found the Hosmer's addition, only fifteen minutes' ride over the Fern Hill Motor line, trains running through this addition every hour to the grand Wapeto Lake Park, following Orchard's first, second and third addition, Ferry's addition, and Opie's Tacoma avenue addition.

These gentlemen are doing a very extensive real estate business, and also invest or make loans for non-residents. Mr. Orchard has been a resident of Tacoma about fifteen years, and is an authority on, as well as dealing largely in real estate; he is interested in a large number of enterprises in this city, and has also been identified with the Merchants' National Bank ever since its organization.

Mr. W. H. Opie, of the firm, has resided six years in Tacoma, having been teller of the Merchants' National Bank during that period until January 1, 1889, when he resigned his position there to engage in the present business. We bespeak for these gentlemen a successful business as they are reliable men, and have the confidence and best wishes for success of the entire community. They refer by permission to any bank in the city.

Tacoma, Washington.

Dear Sir:—This means you. If you are not a resident of this grand and glorious Northwest, it means *you* very emphatically. Why? Well, this is as a land yet undiscovered; that is, its resources, rich in timber, coal, iron, gold, silver and agricultural products, that the man "back East" has no conception of. Washington, the youngest and richest State in Uncle Sam's domain, demands and is attracting the attention of the world. Tacoma, the "City of Destiny"—"The Gem of the Pacific Northwest"—whose marvelous growth astonishes all new comers, wants *you* for an investor and resident, and assures you rich returns. We have city and suburban property we can guarantee will advance from 50 to 200 per cent. the next year. *Buy in time.* We wish to see you. Respectfully, Frye & Mills.

Real Estate and Loan Brokers, Cor. 13th and Pacific Ave.

CHESTER F. GRIESEMER,

REAL ESTATE AND LOANS.

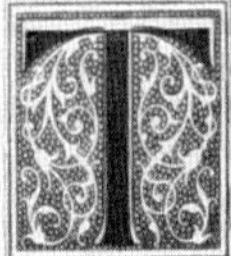

THE subject of this article, Mr. Chester F. Griesemer, although one of the comparatively recent comers to the "City of Destiny," has met with marked success, and occupies a standing in the front ranks of Tacoma's most distinguished citizens.

Mr. Griesemer first saw the light of day in the year 1850, at Philadelphia, and in his early days of manhood settled himself in that city in the jobbing business.

But for a business trip to the fair city of Tacoma, in the year 1888, he would probably have still been in the Quaker city; Mr. Griesemer, however, had been a great traveler, and having for a great many years traveled through the leading States of the Union from the Atlantic to the Pacific coast, he had by experience acquired a knowledge of the points of advantage held by one city over another in regard to location, surroundings, resources, terminal facilities and public spirit of its citizens as well as the *bona-fide* values of real estate; he was therefore characteristically quick to grasp the situation in Tacoma; he foresaw the vast field of success unfolding to a man of pluck and energy on Puget Sound; he noted the many advantages of Tacoma as the center of all the vast resources of this part of the country; he foresaw that from her advantageous site at the head of the Sound, and as the terminus of the Northern Pacific Railroad it was only a question of time when she must become not only a great manufacturing city, but a great foreign shipping point, a point of distribution for the surrounding country, and a great financial center.

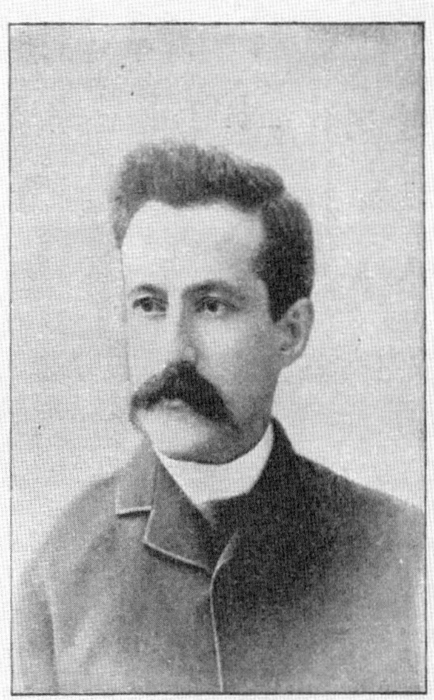

CHESTER F. GRIESEMER.

Naturally Mr. Griesemer's extensive acquaintance, reaching from the man of millions to the thrifty clerk and mechanic, gives him in his present vocation as real estate broker a great advantage over competitors many years older in the business, particularly from the fact that back of his own shrewd judgment he has the practical experience of one of the notable and well-nigh infallible retired real estate men of Tacoma.

Mr. Griesemer does not confine himself to his office desk, but keeps up with the times in looking around for advantageous locations; in this he shows great judgment by the investment in eligible locations of money intrusted to his care; he is especially cautious in the purchase of realty for absent patrons, and the value of his selections may be readily realized from the fact that very large amounts of money are constantly sent him from the East for investment as he thinks best. He has been quietly accumulating some valuable tracts of realty which will be put on the market in the near future at figures so reasonable that the man of even small means may find a way of doubling his investment in a very short period. This is aside from the fact of his having the sole agency of some very fine properties about being platted.

Thus it is that his predictions are being fulfilled even faster than his most sanguine expectations could have asked, and by his energy and tact he has accomplished more in the short space of time he has been a resident of Tacoma, and has built up a larger business than could have been expected in an Eastern city, in the space of ten or twenty years; but behind all this there are reasons for his success which are not confined alone to his energy and tact.

Our subject is in the first place a man of education, natural refinement and courtesy, three qualifications which are appreciated everywhere; then, again, he is full of ambition and loves his new home, and it is generally conceded that a man must enjoy his home to be successful in it. Last, but by no means least, he is in love with his work, and when a man combines other good qualifications with a thorough enjoyment of the business which employs his time, he is almost sure of success in the pursuit of his vocation; it never tires him, and he is able to give it the careful attention required to insure success anywhere in these days.

As a public-spirited citizen the subject of this sketch is by no means lacking. Appreciating the fact that it is the duty of every citizen to promote the welfare of his city, he does not forget those duties in his zeal for his business; knowing that his interests and those of Tacoma are identical, he is always willing to assist in all public enterprises, and forward everything that will combine to make his home fulfill all that her proud name, "the City of Destiny," implies.

In concluding our sketch of Mr. Griesemer it may not be out of place to refer briefly to this broad public-spirited policy. It seems to be a natural gift to Tacoma that so many of her citizens pursue such a liberal policy. Every stranger visiting the city and properly presenting himself, is shown the greatest courtesy by every one with whom he comes in contact, and nowhere, when the interests of the city are involved, is there any set of men who more untiringly devote their time and money to the cause of progress than do a certain number of men in Tacoma. Of course, this is to be found more or less in every city, but it has been the writer's experience that it is more far-reaching here than elsewhere.

CHARLES FOX.

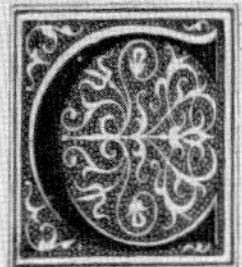

CHARLES FOX, the real estate broker, of 915½ Pacific Avenue, Tacoma, is well known as one of the most reliable business men in the city. Although he only appeared upon the scene in Tacoma in 1888, over $1,000,000 worth of property has already passed through his hands, and he has successfully put upon the market some of the largest additions to the city. He is the personification of business integrity, and promoters of wildcat schemes or those who seek to dispose of properties that have not solid, legitimate value, are very careful to avoid displaying their wares to his keen-eyed inspection.

By conducting his business in this perfectly straightforward and aboveboard manner, he has succeeded in gaining the entire confidence of the business community among which he transacts his affairs.

Very few men have had a more extended and diversified experience in the real estate field than the gentleman who is the subject of this article. He was born in the State of Ohio, and to escape being made a political office-holder - a contingency that early confronts all Ohioans—he made his escape from this place of his nativity when he was only eighteen, and settled in St. Louis, determining to let his feet grow among the Missourians. He remained in that city for ten years, when he made a new move, and settled in Wichita, Kan. He went extensively into real estate at that point, and became very widely known as an active and energetic business man. Later on we find him settled in Los Angeles, Cal., in the palmy days of that city. Here, again he made his mark, and added to his knowledge of real estate affairs on the Pacific coast. His last move was, as has already been stated, to come to Tacoma in 1888, his power of organization, grasp of detail and infinite fertility of resource, at once announcing to his wondering competitors that another Richmond was in the field. He deals mainly in the choicest sites for residence and business property, and intending purchasers seldom leave his office without being gratified to their heart's content. His extensive insurance interests also take up a share of his time and attention. He is the agent for several of the most reliable Eastern companies, and is valued by them as one of their most energetic deputies. Mr. Fox's social qualities are as varied and universal as his business abilities, and his friends, which term includes most all of his acquaintances, are as numberless as the sands of the seashore.

HANSEN BROTHERS & CO.

DEALERS IN DIAMONDS, WATCHES, JEWELRY, CLOCKS, SILVERWARE, ETC., 912 PACIFIC AVENUE.

The above firm is composed of Messrs. Theo. W. Hansen and Albert Hansen both of whom were formerly residents of California; their first venture in business in the Puget Sound country was at Seattle, where they opened in their present line of business some seven years ago, and where they to-day have the finest line of jewelry in the city; being alive to the importance of Tacoma as the terminus of the Northern Pacific Railroad, they opened a store July 1, 1888, iu this city, and met with immediate and unqualified success; another branch will soon be opened at Spokane Falls by this enterprising firm, so that they will then cover the three largest cities in Washington.

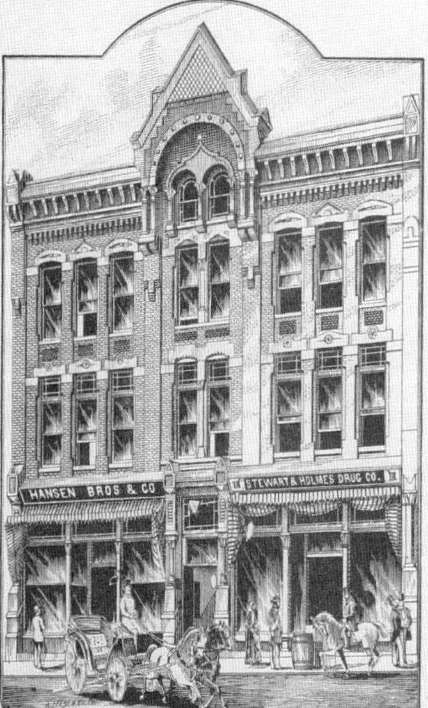

Although Hansen Bros. & Co. keep the finest lines of diamonds, watches and jewelry of all descriptions, they make a great specialty of optical goods and the fitting of all defects in eyesight; they are also the agents of the celebrated Steinway & Sons', and Knabe, as well as nearly all the celebrated makes of pianos, and organs.

THE TACOMA CRACKER COMPANY,

OF 938 C STREET, are manufacturers of all kinds of fancy biscuits, crackers, ship bread, etc., etc. This concern possess ample capital, and have equipped their large and commodious building with the latest improved machinery. Under the able direction of Mr. William Reid, who oversees the manufacturing department, a quality of goods is turned out that cannot be excelled anywhere. Mr. W. W. Sly, well known to the inhabitants of Tacoma, is the responsible manager, and Ed C. Morgan, treasurer.

The company has only been in existence a few months, but the enterprise is meeting with gratifying success, and bids fair in the future to become one of the most successful institutions of the city.

SMITH & TEMPLE,

REAL ESTATE AND FINANCIAL AGENTS, 916 PACIFIC AVE.

A well known and enterprising firm of Tacoma is the above, which is composed of Mr. Ward T. Smith, a native of Shelburne Falls, Mass., and Mr. W. S. Temple, formerly from Boston, Mass.; the former after having been some fifteen years a resident of St. Louis, came to Tacoma in February, 1888, while Mr. Temple has been in Tacoma less than a year.

Notwithstanding the short period which they have spent at Tacoma these gentlemen have been very successful, and their operations in real estate have been remarkably large; they have platted some very fine additions to Tacoma, and so improved them that they have met with ready sales, which have been profitable investments to the purchasers. They at present are the sole agents for the following named desirable properties: South Tacoma addition to Tacoma; Smith's addition to Tacoma; Clover Lea addition to Tacoma, and the Violet Meadow addition to Tacoma.

The latter addition is one of the grandest for sightliness and beauty yet offered to investors in Tacoma realty; it is due south from the center of the city on a high level prairie commanding fine views of the snow-capped Olympian range, and of Mount Tacoma. It is five blocks from Tacoma Avenue Extension, and four blocks from the Fern Hill Motor Line, now partially built and operated, and being constructed due south toward this addition as fast as men and money can do it.

The addition is a short distance only from the well-known $10,000 Fern Hill schoolhouse, already completed.

ARTHUR L. SMITH,

ARCHITECT,

has his offices at 1340 Pacific Avenue. Mr. Smith is well worthy of mention among the architects of Tacoma, as a gentleman not only of ability, but of long and varied experience in his profession. He was born in St. Louis, Mo., and was intended from his childhood for an architect, by his father, who was one of the prominent men in that profession, in St. Louis. Therefore, at an early age he put his son as apprentice, with one of the largest builders in the city, and wisely inculcated in him a practical knowledge of building, that has materially aided in giving him his present reputation. After he had thoroughly mastered the groundwork, young Smith went into his father's office, and perfected himself in architecture. Since then he has become a well-known man, and has designed many fine buildings, and superintended their construction, both in the East and the West.

The well-known California Block on Pacific Ave., owned by David Wilson, of which we present a cut, was erected by Mr. Smith. This building, which is of stone and pressed brick, speaks for itself, and the interior arrangements compare favorably with anything to be found in Chicago, or on the Eastern seaboard. The Gross Bros. block was also designed and built by Mr. Smith.

WALTERS & CO.

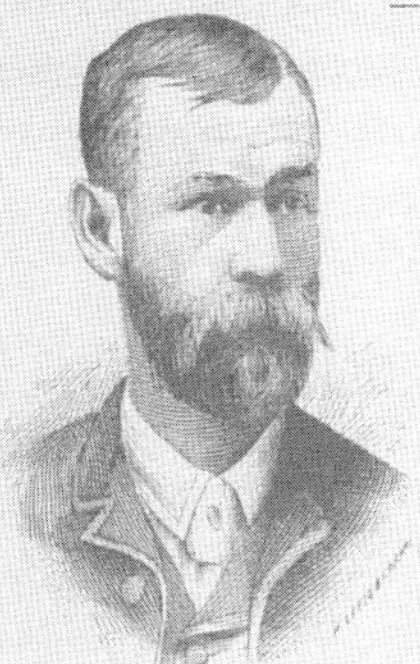

H. C. WALTERS.

Although one of the most recent firms in this line to establish themselves in the city of Tacoma, their commodious office on the corner of South Tenth and A streets immediately opposite the Tacoma Hotel, is already recognized as one of the leading centers for real estate transactions in the city.

Formerly Walters & Co.'s principal place of business was at Ellensburgh, the central city in the State of Washington, which is one hundred and twenty-seven miles east of Tacoma, where they were known as the pioneer and leading people of that town in real estate, mines and loans.

The particular line of business policy pursued by this firm, and the opinion entertained by them touching the real estate values of the Northwest, are very plainly set forth in the following interview had with Mr. Walters, the managing partner the firm.

To the writer, Mr. Walters said: "We established ourselves in Ellensburgh in advance of the construction of the Northern Pacific Railroad to that point. We saw in its local surroundings dormant value-yielding qualifications from the development of which the upbuilding of immense community interests must surely result." Around Ellensburgh are over 300 miles of productive farming lands; every staple agricultural product peculiar to the Middle and Northern States is here most successfully grown. Diversified farming and diversified live stock growing is also possible in a highly profitable degree. The climatic conditions are such that outdoor work may be carried on fully ten months of the year. Irrigation is necessary to secure the fullest possible yield per acre, but the contour of this agricultural area is such, that, once fairly established, the system is not only inexpensive, but is wonderfully remunerative, from the fact that a full yield is assured each year, and by this artificial aid, lands may be rendered fit for plowing, except when frozen, throughout the entire year. The principal crops grown for shipping to outside markets yield as follows: Wheat, 30 to 50 bushels per acre; barley, 40 to 55 bushels per acre; oats, 50 to 65 bushels per acre; potatoes, 350 to 600 bushels per acre; timothy hay from one and one-half to three tons per acre. The entire northern half of the county (Kittitas) of which Ellensburgh is the seat of government and commercial center, is a timbered mineral belt, in which most valuable coal, iron, copper and other mining interests have been developed. At the Roslyn coal mines thirty miles from Ellensburgh, some fifteen hundred tons of excellent bituminous coal are mined daily, and additional openings are being made. In and about the coal mining regions a population of some three thousand people has been established, contributing largely to the trade of Ellensburgh, and affording a very excellent market for the local agricultural productions.

The several varieties of commercial iron ores are found in abundance, and exploration of the iron mines is being actively pushed. A limited supply of lime and other valuable fluxes is to be found in the immediate vicinity. Timber is so plentiful and easy of access that the manufacture of charcoal iron may profitably be carried on for a great many years. Careful investigation has determined that pig iron may be made at Ellensburgh at not to exceed fifteen dollars per ton; as that staple commodity costs twenty-eight dollars and upward, net cash, per ton in the Pacific Coast markets, the establishment of at least one blast furnace immediately at Ellensburgh may confidently be expected. In the wake of a blast furnace will naturally follow the rolling mill, nail factories, foundries, boiler works and various other iron working domestic industries. This latter fact of itself will double Ellensburgh's present population of five thousand within one year from the date the blast furnace is started up; a proportionate increase in general values will naturally result.

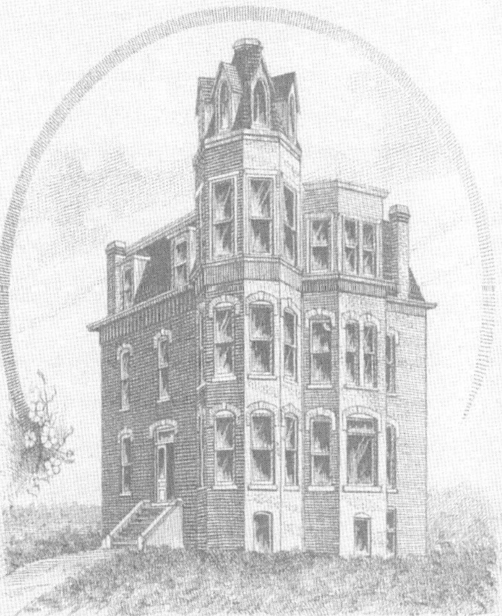

RESIDENCE ON CAPITOL HILL, ELLENSBURGH.

Gold mining has been successfully carried on within twenty-five miles of Ellensburgh during the past ten years. By the introduction of better methods, the amount of gold extracted, and profit per miner employed increases each year. From the placer mines some very handsome specimens are taken; only recently a nugget of native gold weighing some twenty-five ounces was found. The gold mining industry yields each year an increasing amount of business to Ellensburgh's commercial sum total.

North and east of Ellensburgh, extending clear up to the British line this mining area continues, being broken here and there by fertile agricultural valleys lying on every

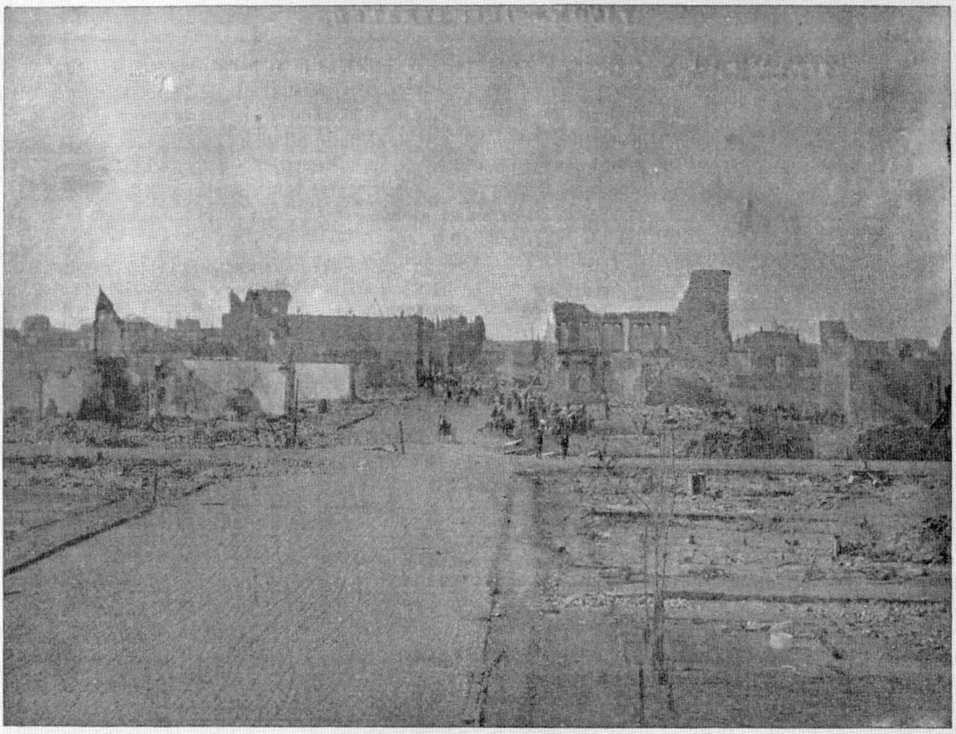

PEARL STREET LOOKING NORTH.

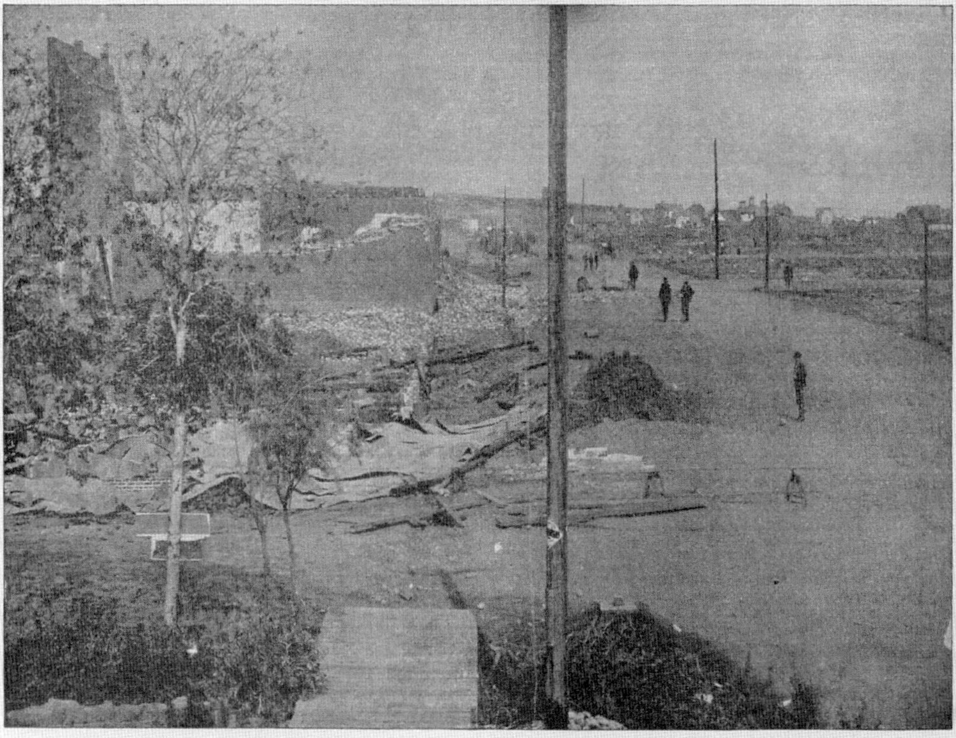

THIRD STREET.

ELLENSBURGH ON THE MORNING AFTER THE GREAT FIRE OF JULY

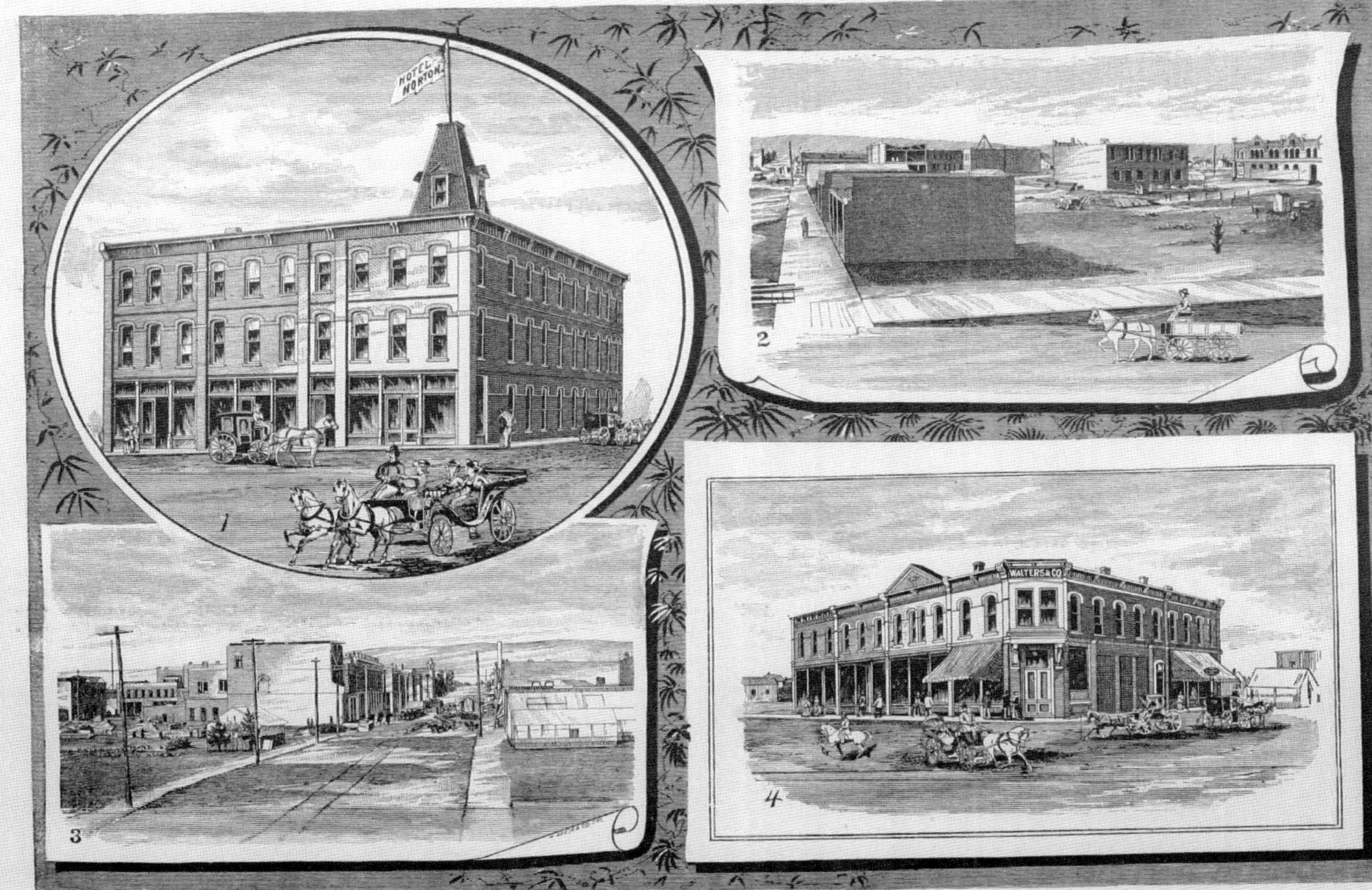

(2) REBUILDING IN SOLID BRICK AND STONE. (3) PEARL STREET LOOKING NORTH NOVEMBER 25, 1889. (4) HONOLULU BLOCK—OFFICE OF WALTERS & CO.

ELLENSBURGH BEING REBUILT.

side of the various mountain streams, and a continuous chain of settlements now exists along the entire eastern base of the Cascade Range. In Okanogan County, just south of the boundary line, two thousand men are engaged in the prospecting and development of what are known as the Conconnully silver mines. These mines having successfully passed through three years' exploration have an established reputation, and capital is being engaged in their equipment and development for extensive working. A line of steamboats owned by Tacoma capitalists, secures the principal trade of these mines to Ellensburgh, and the Ellensburgh & North Eastern Railway, ten miles of which is already built, will speedily be pushed into the mines, thus permanently securing the rapidly increasing traffic to Ellensburgh. The same railroad will next year form an intersection with the Washington Central and Seattle, Lake Shore and Eastern in the heart of the Big Bend wheat fields, thus enabling the Northern Pacific to shorten its route across the continent some ninety miles, and securing to Ellensburgh a large percentage of business from the country east of the Columbia. The local and adjacent trade possibilities of Ellensburgh are very greatly strengthened by the position of the city with reference to the trade centers of Puget Sound; being but one hundred and twenty-five miles from Tacoma, Ellensburgh's agricultural exports and commercial imports are naturally by way of that city.

The real growth of Ellensburgh dates from the completion of the Northern Pacific in 1886; then a hamlet of some six hundred inhabitants, it has now over five thousand population. The county acreage broken up, capital invested in various lines of business, and every natural factor in the community make-up, practically doubles each year. The character of the local population and confidence had by them in the city is clearly evident in the manner in which it is being rebuilt. The entire business quarter, comprising some twenty acres, was completely destroyed by fire on the evening of July 4th of this year. Over two million dollars' worth of property was destroyed. The work of rebuilding was immediately begun, fire limits were extended, the construction of anything but brick, iron or stone buildings was absolutely prohibited, and the most unshaken confidence in the future of the city was in every way displayed. Since Jul y 12th, over twelve million two hundred and forty thousand brick have been delivered from the local yards.

Third, Fourth, Fifth, Sixth, Main, Pearl and Pine streets are already practically rebuilt with first class two and three story bricks. Most remarkable of all attendant features, perhaps, is the fact that not a sheriff's sale or assignment followed the fire, and another important index to the estimate in which Ellensburgh values are held is evidencd by the fact that building loans were readily secured from Eastern companies at lowest rates of interest and upon the highest percentage of valuation ever allowed in a city of like size. No useful or ornamental metropolitan feature was considered too good for Ellensburgh by her enterprising citizens. A splendid electric light system and fine waterworks have already been established; the principal streets are macadamized, and an excellent system of sewerage is being constructed. A street railway system will undoubtedly be introduced next year. The various religious denominations are well represented; by reason of its geographical position, Ellensburgh is very aptly called Washington's central city, and owing to its accessibility, more than three-fourths of the annual assemblages of the various political, religious and fraternal organizations are now held at that city. The same facts will lead to the location of the seat of government at Ellensburgh when removed from Olympia, and a forty acre park has been proffered to the State government as a gift for State capitol uses should the removal occur. Meanwhile, although perfectly willing to accept the capitolian honors, the citizens of Ellensburgh do not base any of their business estimates or undertakings upon any State capital possibilities. Splendid agricultural, mining, manufacturing and shipping possibilities are the corner stones upon which their prosperity is based. It is a common expression, that go where one may, they will not be able to find a more prosperous population of equal number to that of Kittitas County, taking into account what each person had to start with, the long distance from steam shipping (150 miles) prior to the completion of the railroad, and the fact that but two grain crops have yet been exported. Nothing like a real estate boom ever having occurred in the county, both city and county values are moderate, and a broad margin of profit is fully assured to the intelligent investor in either Ellensburgh or surrounding county property.

WALTERS & CO., IN TACOMA.

Touching Tacoma, Mr. Walters said: "Last year I spent some six weeks about the hotels in this city and went away without buying anything, my impression being that everything quoted was too high. I could not have shut my eyes and made a purchase offered without being able at this time to realize a profit of 75 to 100 per cent. What I think now is based upon somewhat more extended investigation. Fully aware that between the summit of the Cascade Range and the head of Commencement Bay there are diversified natural resources fully equal to the upbuilding of a greater city than the Tacoma of to-day, and having discovered that within thirty minutes' journey in any given direction from the city a practically undisturbed forest is reached, I am convinced that no adequate estimate of the actual worth of Tacoma realty can at this time be formed, and when the great wealth of natural resources of Central Washington naturally tributary to this city is taken into account in connection with her local and shipping advantages, I believe that for a great many years to come her statisticians with each succeeding year will feel called upon to apologize for their under-estimates of the last preceding."

In Tacoma as in Ellensburgh, Walters & Co. have made a leading feature of the purchase and subdivision of large acreage tracts immediately in the line of the greatest growth of the city. Long experience in this particular

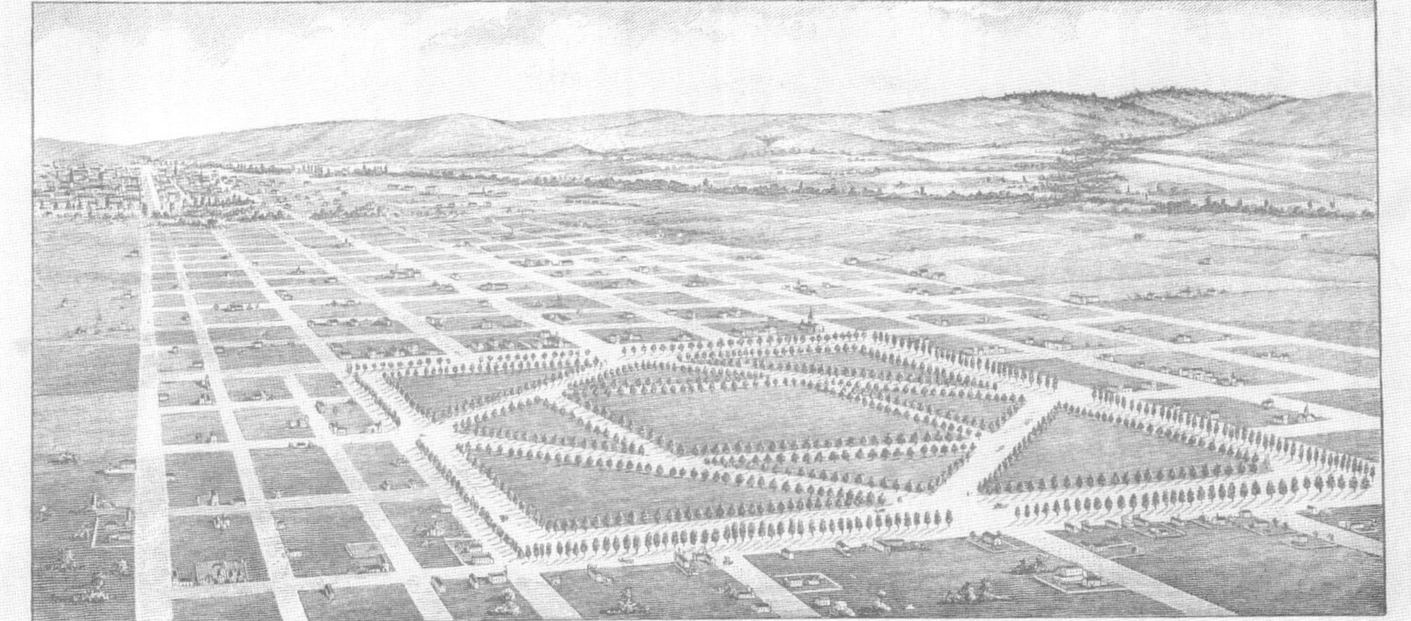

SOUTH WEST VIEW OF WASHINGTON STATE CAPITOL PARK AT ELLENSBURGH, WASHINGTON.

channel has enabled them to discern while values were merely nominal, the popular tendency of purchasers.

They have thus been enabled to secure themselves and their patrons against every possibility of loss, while the resultant profits have been very satisfactory. Business centers in these growing Western cities may for a certain time be diverted from one locality to another, but desirable acreage where the population not only of cities but of counties is doubled annually, is certain ultimately to be included within the magic circle.

To this firm belongs the undoubted honor of introducing to public attention, East Tacoma. Discovering that lands adjacent to the Puyallup Reservation immediately across the bay from this city were held at a less price per acre than were ordinary building lots an equal distance from the water front on this side of the bay, they proceeded to purchase and bond a large area of very favorably conditioned land overlooking in part the city, the Bay and the Sound, splendid views of both Mount Tacoma and the Coast Range being afforded. This property has been platted, and is now on sale. Public opinion having long conceded that upon the opening of the Reservation the entire east side would immediately be built up, Walters & Co. wisely anticipated this happening by taking the preliminary steps. That the movement is a popular one is evidenced by the fact that an entire addition of East Tacoma lots was sold from the plat before the ground could be subdivided. Immediately upon the beginning of this undertaking, contracts were immediately let by the Commencement Bay Improvement and other companies for the construction of large ocean docks and extensive milling and manufacturing establishments at the head of the bay and extending toward the east side as far as possible toward the Reservation, thus justifying the conclusions at which Walters & Co. had arrived, to the effect that the great manufacturing and shipping industries of Tacoma must ultimately surround the entire head and the eastern side of the bay, and cause East Tacoma property, even though a small strip of the Reservation might temporarily intervene, to advance rapidly in value, by reason of its convenience for the establishment of homes.

Purchasing this acreage at nominal figures, they are enabled to make popular prices. To use one of their trite advertising expressions, they believe an East Tacoma $33, $44 or $75 lot to have a $330, $440 or $750 future, and that with the splendid progress attained by Tacoma proper lying in full sight of East Tacoma as a guarantee of its future, an increase of fully one hundred per cent. per annum for several years to come, may safely be expected by purchasers of East Tacoma property at the nominal prices of to-day. Already an advance of 75 per cent. has taken place in acreage adjacent to the East Tacoma plats, and the occurrence of any one of several very probable happenings will send East Tacoma values up fully one thousand per cent. in a trice.

The West side water front being wholly occupied by the present railroads, the several transportation lines now building this way will be obliged to occupy the East Tacoma water front, either by purchase, lease or condemnation of that portion of the Reservation lands, and the moment

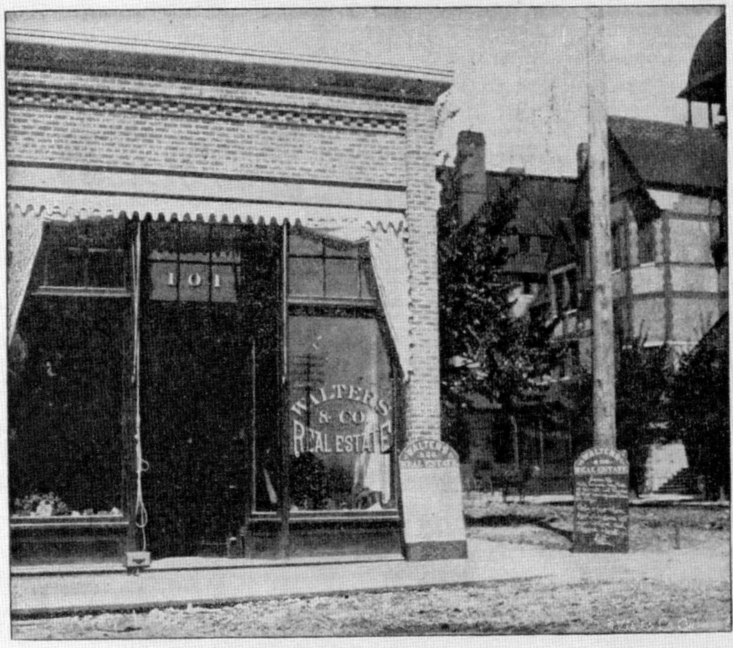

TACOMA OFFICE OF WALTERS & CO.

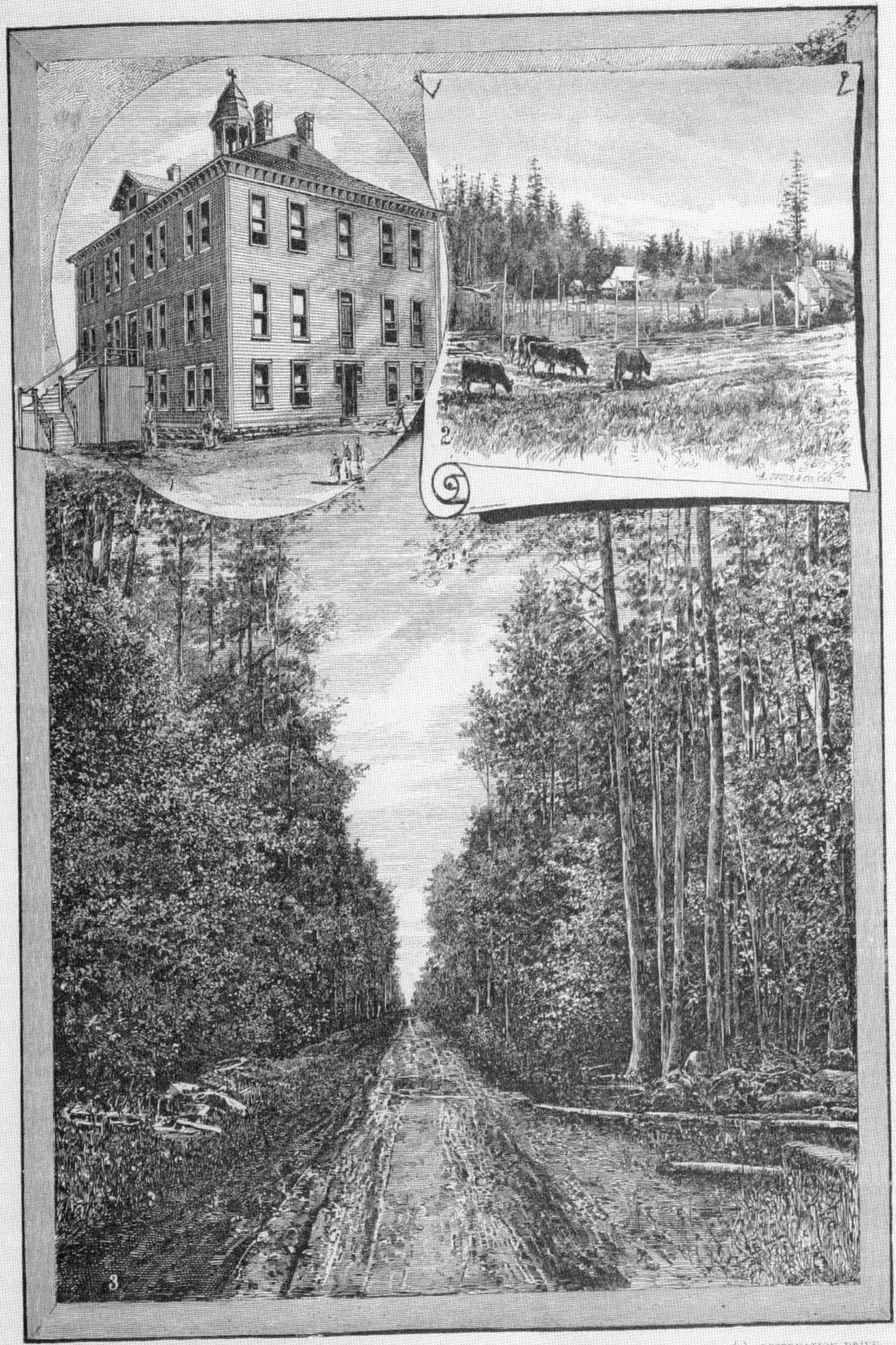

(1) ST. GEORGE INDUSTRIAL ACADEMY. ESTABLISHED 1888. (2) HOP FARM (3) RESERVATION DRIVE.

VIEWS AT AND NEAR EAST TACOMA.

that ground may be broken along the East shore, another of Walters & Co.'s expressive utterances to the effect that the greatest real estate advance that the world ever saw will one day occur in East Tacoma, will be practically realized.

That East Tacoma is not wholly an undeveloped region at this time may be gleaned from the several illustrations and particularly that of the St. George Industrial Academy, at which all branches of English language and various industrial arts are taught. Sister Helena from the Mother House at Glenn Riddle, Delaware County, Pa., is immediately in charge. The society owns 160 acres of valuable land, and will make this school a leading educational feature.

Maps, prices and any information desired touching real estate or loans will be promptly furnished by this firm.

In conclusion, we desire to say that Mr. Walters' statements have been made conservatively and in the case of both Ellensburgh and East Tacoma he has treated the subjects entirely without exaggeration; the visitor cannot fail to notice the grand location, transportation facilities and natural and as yet almost undeveloped resources of Ellensburgh. In linking the destinies of this city in certain ways to those of Tacoma, Mr. Walters has shown wisdom and foresightedness and his experience in real estate and mining matters is such that his opinion is greatly sought for and worth having.

There is no doubt as to the fulfillment of his predictions concerning East Tacoma; there is no question to-day in the mind of any one acquainted with the location of the reservation opposite Tacoma proper as to its being opened within a very short period; and when this is done, the map before us shows conclusively how it must affect East Tacoma, which is to-day progressing so fast on its own merits.

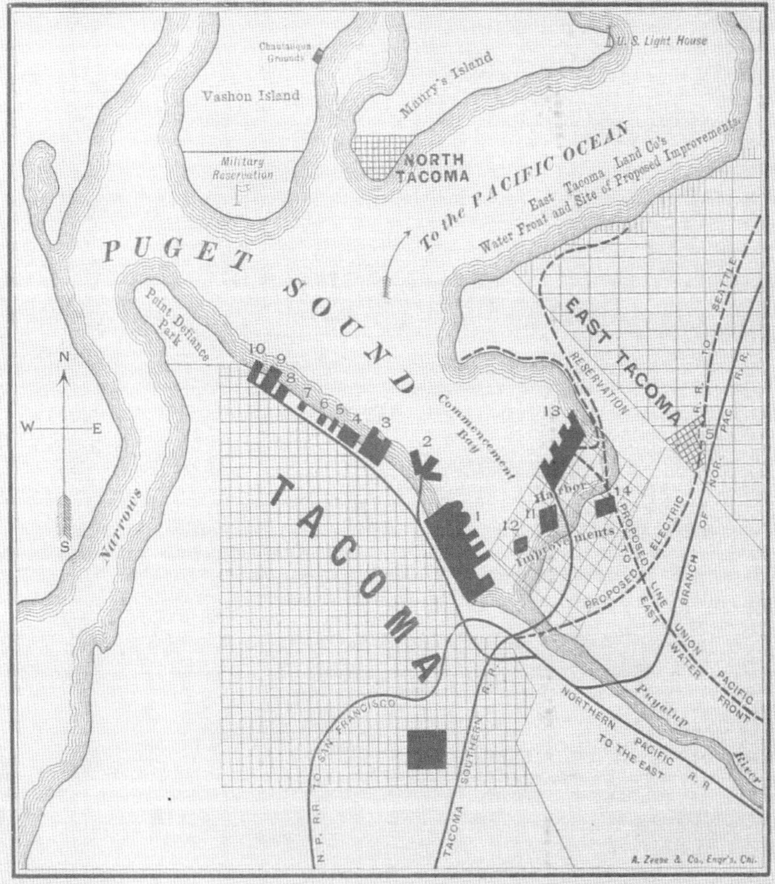

1. SOUND AND OCEAN DOCKS. 2. COAL BUNKERS. 3. WHEAT ELEVATORS. 4. GREAT TACOMA MILLS. 5. STEAMSHIP DRY DOCK. 6. FISH CANNERIES. 7. SHINGLE MILLS. 8. BRICK YARDS. 9. RYAN SMELTER. 10. GREAT PACIFIC MILLS. 11. ST. PAUL & TACOMA LUMBER CO.'S BIG MILLING PLANT. 12. WHEELER & OSGOOD'S SASH AND DOOR FACTORY. 13. COMMENCEMENT BAY IMPROVEMENT CO.'S GREAT OCEAN DOCKS, WAREHOUSING AND MANUFACTURING CENTER. 14. SITE OF HART BROS' BIG MILLS. 15. ORIGINAL PLAT OF EAST TACOMA.

MANGUM & WHEELER.

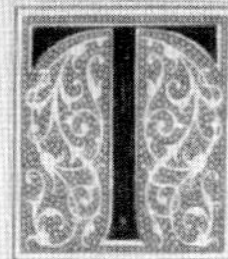

THIS firm does a very large general real estate business. Their comfortable offices are centrally located on A street, opposite the Tacoma Hotel. Their specialty is in buying and handling improved property for non-resident capital, and this field they have cultivated with such gratifying results as to make their reputation for accuracy and keenness of judgment stand very high in the community. Mr. Caraon L. Mangum is the active member of the firm, and a hustler when he starts out, while the other member, Mr. Willis Wheeler, is possessed of large landed interests in the vicinity of Tacoma. One of these gentlemen recently told the writer that he had sold a property to an Eastern man for $40,000 a few months ago, which, at the present time, was paying—independent of the rising value of the real estate—a profit of 30 per cent. on the investment. The National Bank of Commerce and Merchants National Bank of Tacoma both indorse Mangum & Wheeler, and a better firm to deal with by investing capitalists cannot be selected.

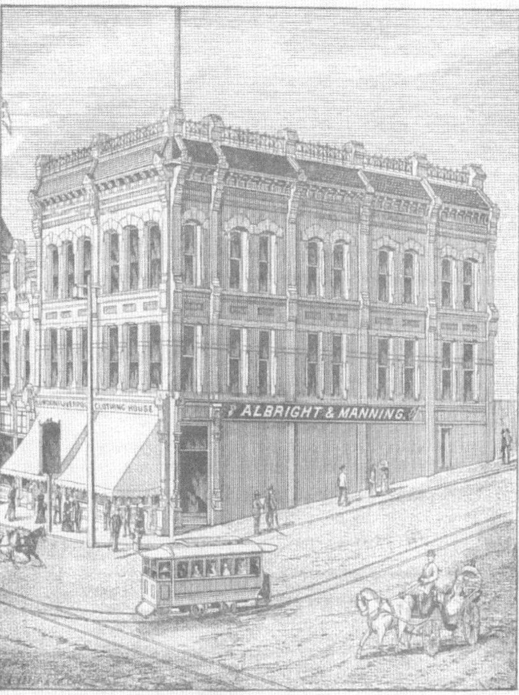

WRIGHT BLOCK.

ALBRIGHT & MANNING.

This firm of real estate dealers and brokers deals specially in investments for non-residents, also loan money at current rates. They have choice hop, hay, garden, farm and timber lands for sale. Their rooms are at 1 and 2, Wright Block.

Mr. Robert S. Albright, of this firm, was born in Madison, New Jersey. At an early age his parents removed to Cedar Rapids, Iowa, at which place he spent his childhood and youth. In 1878 he left the paternal roof, and removed to San Francisco. Being a man of keen observation, he closely watched the movements of the great railroads, and the tide of emigration, and foresaw that Western Washington, with her sheltered harbors, her inexhaustible supply of coal, iron, timber and the unlimited acreage of fertile lands was destined in a few years to surpass any other country in rapidity of development. With these facts in view, Mr. Albright left San Francisco and settled in Tacoma in 1881, engaging in the transportation business as chief clerk of the operating department of the Oregon Railway & Navigation Company, which position he retained until 1887, resigning his position to engage in the real estate and loan business in Tacoma.

Chas. T. Manning, the junior member of this firm, first saw the light of day in the little town of Abington, Wayne County, Indiana, where he resided with his parents until 1873, during which year his father removed with his family to Salem, Oregon. The rudiments of his education were completed in the Willamette University in that city. Young Manning early evinced an inclination for mathematics, and particularly for civil engineering, which eventually led him to join the engineering corps of the Northern Pacific Railroad Co., with which he remained until 1883. We next see Mr. Manning as chief accountant with the Carbon Hill Coal Company, and it was during this period that he formed the acquaintance of Mr. R. S. Albright, which finally led to the establishment of the firm of Albright & Manning in the fall of 1888. The firm launched forth under very favorable auspices. The irreproachable character of both members of the firm, the untiring energy, strict integrity and business ability, coupled with a constant effort to please their customers, with the unprecedented record of having never made a sale which has not netted a handsome profit to the buyer, both resident and non-resident, places this firm in a most enviable position. To an observant man the cause of this success is readily apparent, which is, that they have always refused (even when very flattering terms were offered) to handle anything which could be termed as "wild-cat" property.

The transferring of a piece of realty through this firm, whether it be a business lot or an acre tract, is a sufficient guarantee that it is what a Wall Street man would call a "purchase."

Parties seeking investment in realty in Tacoma or vicinity will subserve their interests by calling on or entering into correspondence with this firm. They refer to the National Bank of Commerce. This firm will take pleasure in furnishing any necessary information.

LAKE CITY LAND COMPANY AND LAKE CITY RAILWAY AND NAVIGATION COMPANIES.

WHEN the Lake City Land Company, and the Lake City Railway and Navigation Company were incorporated, and the news was given to the public, it was not fully understood that another gigantic enterprise was on foot for the building up of Tacoma, that is only equaled by the improvement made by the Tacoma Land Company. The organizing of these two companies meant the platting of a suburban city in one of the most picturesque portions of the country surrounding Tacoma, that would be eventually connected with the city by a substantial railroad.

In December, 1888, Messrs. F. C. Ross, C. A. E. Naubert, Fremont Campbell, J. D. Smith, L. T. Root, T. R. Jordan and R. B. Mullen, purchased 320 acres of land situated south of Tacoma some nine miles, and bordering on American Lake, the finest sheet of fresh water in Western Washington. The tract is an undulating prairie surrounded in the distance by magnificent forests of timber, such as can only be found in Washington. The scenery from this location is unsurpassed. The lake, with its irregular wooded shore line, lies to the south, while in the distance the Cascade Mountains loom up, and grand old Mount Tacoma stands forth conspicuously in all its rugged splendor. To the southwest for a considerable distance, the prairie stretches away until it is lost in the woodland in the far distance, forming a lovely panorama, unequaled anywhere.

American Lake with its placid surface dotted with wooded islands, its picturesque inlets and bays, has a shore line of about fifteen miles. Until a comparatively short time ago it was the undisturbed home of the eagle and wild ducks, but now the scene is changed to one of bustling activity. The shrill whistle of the steamboat is now heard, as the handsome steamer Lake City crosses the lake with a party of excursionists, and on a fine day sail and rowboats are seen on every side. These crafts were placed upon the lake by the Lake City Land Company, and have their headquarters at a handsome boathouse at the foot of Lake City Ave., one of the principal streets in the town site.

Soon after Lake City was platted, it was placed upon the market, and many at once invested largely, and still retain the land purchased, as lots have considerably increased in value. At present the town site has been withdrawn from the market, and no more property will be sold until the railroad between Lake City and Tacoma is finished, which will most probably be very speedily.

It may be safely said that there is not a better piece of engineering than the grade of the Lake City Railroad. Mr. R. B. Mullen, the assistant general manager, has devoted his entire lifetime to civil engineering, and it was under his personal supervision that the grade was established. The Tacoma terminus of the road forms a junction with the Tacoma Street Railway Company, the Allen C. Mason Electric Street Railway, and several other systems in the western part of the city, while the Lake City terminus is at the junction of Washington and Lake City Boulevards. The equipment of the line (which is a narrow gauge) consists of two Baldwin engines of 14 tons each, three coaches, one combination baggage and freight car, and eight flat cars.

The gentlemen enlisted in Lake City are among the most prominent in Tacoma, and are men who when they once start to do anything, always exert every effort to attain their object, regardless of money or time. Their intention in this case is to build a city in the vicinity of Tacoma that will be a beautiful pleasure resort as well as a location for the erection of reaidences for those who wish quiet and peaceful surroundings, and where the constant noise of the city is never heard, combined with an easy access to the business portion of Tacoma. Besides many large and costly residences that are to be built in Lake City, the company intends constructing a commodious hotel, bathhouses, laying out a public park, besides other attractions.

The real estate firms of Ross & Naubert, and Smith, Root & Jordan, are agents for Lake City, and will promptly give any information that may be applied for.

JOHN HUNTINGTON.

It is with pleasure that we introduce in the pages of "TACOMA ILLUSTRATED" the name of this well-known gentleman. it is to him, to a very great extent, that Tacoma owes its thanks for the substantial appearance for which it is so justly famous. Mr. Huntington has for many years been engaged in contracting, and more than one public work has been completed under his direction. When he first came to the Pacific coast, in 1867, he was engaged upon the construction of the State capital buildings at Sacramento, Cal., at which work he made a great success. In 1874, Mr. Huntington moved to Victoria, B. C., and between the years of 1874–'80 constructed, under contract, some of the excellent buildings in that city that were erected in that time. While engaged in business there, Mr. Huntington, with others, secured the contract for the construction of the Esquimaux dry docks at Victoria, but owing to intrigue on the part of the government officials, was unable to complete the work; thus Mr. Huntington suffered severely, losing considerable money. Shortly after this he came to Washington, engaging in contracting, with great success.

Beside contracting, Mr. Huntington owns one of the most valuable brick yards on Puget Sound, as it is situated only two miles from the center of the city. The yard has a capacity of 75,000 bricks per day.

In connection with Mr. J. D. Litle, Mr. Huntington constructed the present Chamber of Commerce building, as well as many of the finest brick blocks in Tacoma. The past season with these gentlemen has been one of great prosperity, and before the end of the year over $200,000 worth of work will be done by them. Some of the blocks now under construction are the Gross Block, which will be one of the finest edifices in the city; the Thompson, Baker, Exchange, Wolff, and others.

Mr. Huntington is a man still in the prime of life, genial, affable, and thoroughly conscientious in all his dealings.

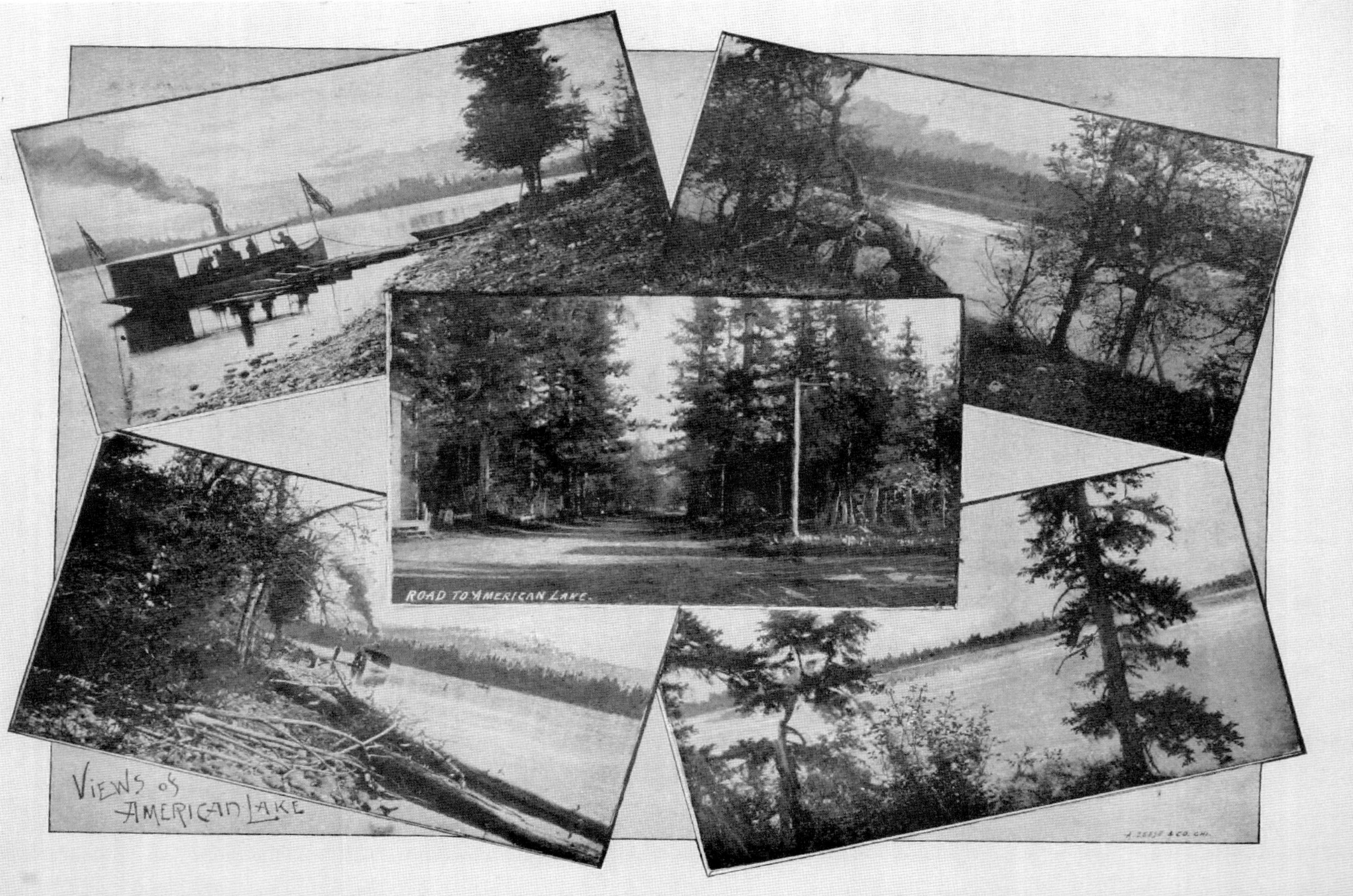
ROAD TO AMERICAN LAKE.
VIEWS OF AMERICAN LAKE
A. ZEESE & CO. CHI.

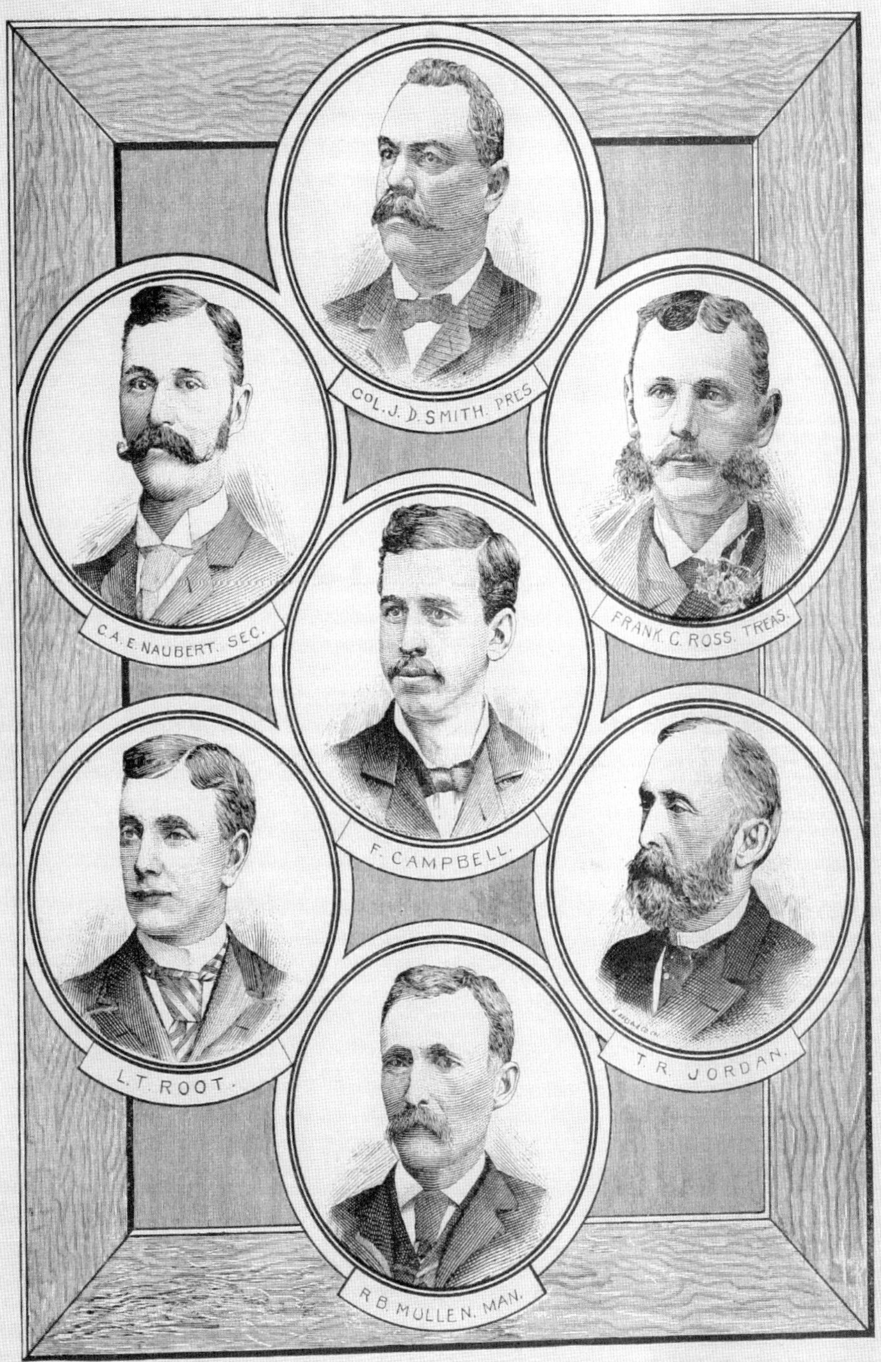

OFFICERS AND DIRECTORS OF THE LAKE CITY LAND COMPANY AND LAKE CITY RAILWAY AND NAVIGATION COMPANY.

HARRIS & COLLINS.

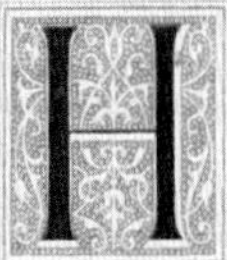

HARRIS BLOCK, on South Second street, in the First Ward, contains the offices of this firm, who deal extensively in real estate, besides carrying on a large insurance and legal business. As far as acting in the capacity of real estate agents is concerned, the firm has already gained a very wide reputation for the choice properties they have for sale as well as the extremely easy terms that they always succeed in giving all purchasers. Tacoma property owners rarely fail to list the property they have for sale, with Messrs. Harris & Collins, because the energy and push which so characterize these two gentlemen, insures a quick disposal of the land. Some of the best known fire, accident and marine insurance companies are represented by these gentlemen. The legal portion of the business is under the direct supervision of Mr. Harris, who as a counsellor and pleader has few equals. Mr. Collins is an ex-member of the city council, representing for some time the ward in which he lives, in a most patriotic manner. Both gentlemen are true Tacomans, and ever ready to promote the welfare of the City of Destiny.

HOTEL GANDOLFO.

This well known hostelry is owned and controlled by J. J. Gandolfo and R. J. McIntyre, and although not long established, is now looked upon by the traveling public as one of the best hotels in the city. This house is run upon the European plan, and both departments are looked after and superintended by the proprietors in such a manner as to give entire satisfaction to guests. The hotel has sixty-two rooms at present, but the owners intend adding another story to the present building, and hope to be able to accommodate double the number of guests. The restaurant connected with the hotel is a model one in all respects, and the very fact that it is under the supervision of Mr. Gandolfo is sufficient assurance that the cuisine of this house is excellent. Before coming to Tacoma Mr. Gandolfo was the proprietor of the famous and well-known Gandolfo Hotel of Wichita, Kan. Mr. R. J. McIntyre, previous to coming to Tacoma, held for nine years several important positions with the chief express companies of the Middle States. He is well calculated to cater to the people of the Pacific Coast.

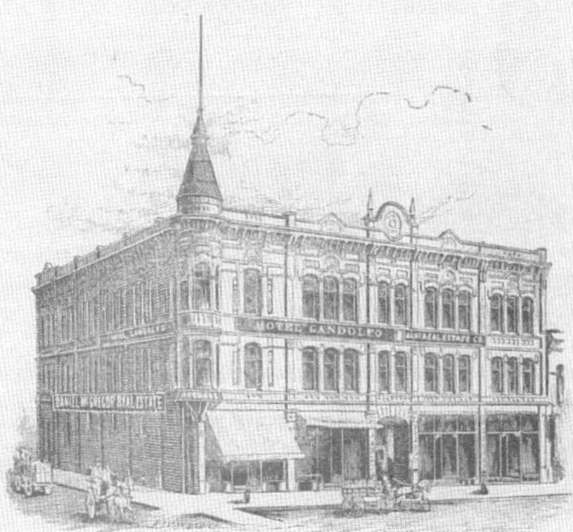

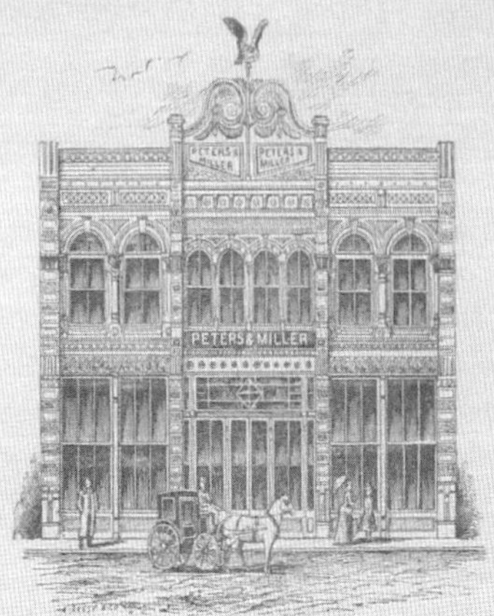

PETERS & MILLER.

This firm, whose offices are at 910 Railroad street, are quiet, conservative, unostentatious men, who create no fuss or feather, but accomplish a heap of effective work. Their galvanized iron cornices, skylights, metal roofing, fireproof doors and shutters, hot-air furnaces, grates and mantels challenge comparison with those of any other manufacturer, and may be seen on such edifices as the New Tacoma Asylum at Fort Steilacoom, and here in Tacoma on the new Opera House, the Episcopal church, and the Emerson School building. The accompanying cut represents a building which will be completed in January, in this city.

C. A. CAVENDER.

Four years ago this gentleman came here from St. Paul, Minn., and has been in the real estate business ever since. Soon after his arrival he made his mark among the struggling throng of business competitors, and shortly began to draw out of the crowd and leave the field far behind.

His opinion on real estate matters is looked for and accepted by leading men and old residents as being final. His efforts are and always have been for Tacoma, he being one of its ablest supporters in words and deeds. He is still a comparatively young man, but his reputation is such that he has become the Napoleon of real estate affairs in the City of Destiny. His keen insight and unerring business sagacity, united to the ample means placed in his hands by his clients, have furnished him opportunity to secure the cheapest sites in and about Tacoma, which he now holds, and from which he is reaping the present golden harvest. His strict attention to the interest of his clients, affability and personal popularity, all combine to make a visit to his office a pleasure to his patrons.

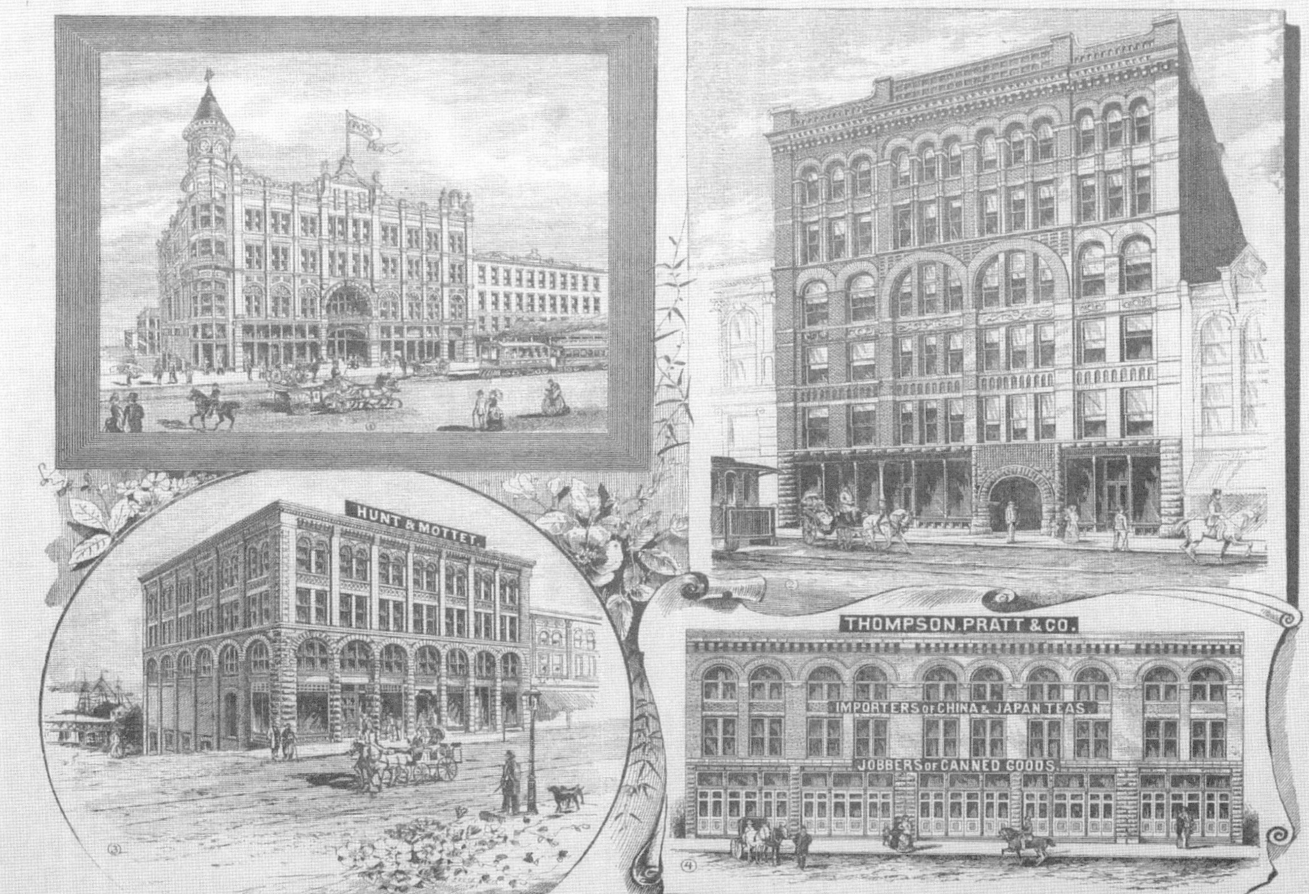

1. GROSS BROS. 2. NEW BARLOW-CATLIN BLOCK.

BUSINESS BLOCKS.

JOBBING INDUSTRIES.

THE WHOLESALE BUSINESS GROWING SO RAPIDLY THAT MORE HOUSES WILL BE WELCOME.

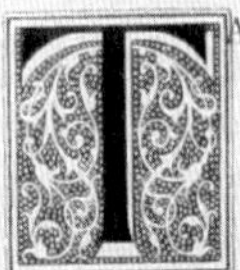

ACOMA'S enviable location far inland at the head of ocean navigation, with the advantages of the terminus of the Japan and China trade (she being 800 miles nearer Yokohama than San Francisco)—the terminus of the greatest transcontinental railroad in the United States, and various foreign and coastwise steamship and sailing vessel lines—coupled with her situation in the midst of a vast country highly favored by kind nature with a wealth of forest, mine and field, unsurpassed upon this continent, constitutes her the most natural, convenient and practical jobbing center of the great Pacific Northwest.

The jobbing business of Tacoma is yet in its infancy, the first exclusively wholesale establishment dating its advent into our commercial circles back only to February, 1888, but to-day there is scarcely an article needed in the general line of trade but that can be purchased in Tacoma, and at as reasonable a price as it can be purchased in any market on the west coast.

The exclusive wholesale houses doing business at present may be enumerated briefly as follows: One drygoods; three groceries; one tea, coffee and spice; two oils, paints and glass, and one paper house. The number of houses doing a mixed business—that is, selling at both wholesale and retail—are embraced in the following list: Three furniture; three hardware; one agricultural implements; two drugs and medicines; one wall paper; two crockery and glassware; one boot and shoe; one clothing and gents' furnishing goods; one carpet; two stationers and booksellers; two confectioners; one meat; one mantels, grates and fireplace goods; one barber supplies. There are about a dozen commission firms and brokers, who handle produce, provisions, butter, eggs, fruits, coal, lime, etc., in a jobbing way. In the manufacturing line: Two cracker factories; one starch factory; one trunk factory; two flouring mills; one oatmeal mill; one flavoring extracts and baking powder; one mattress factory; one harness factory; one watch factory; one broom factory; these sell their products to the trade only.

It is almost impossible at this writing to estimate the amount of business transacted annually. The development and growth of Tacoma's jobbing business has been phenomenal, and the record thus far for 1889 has been far in excess of the most sanguine expectations of our jobbers, and will aggregate for the year all that the greatest capacity of the various wholesale establishments and untiring efforts of our hard working merchants can make it. We can safely say, however, that the aggregate of merchandise sold at wholesale during the current year will approximate three and a half millions of dollars. Our jobbers are enterprising, progressive and ambitious, and are determined to make Tacoma the best market on the west coast in which to purchase stocks, and they are surely going to win if good goods, low prices, honest dealing and a broad and generous policy mean anything. They are full of enthusiasm regarding the development of our wholesale trade, and would welcome the advent of additional houses to help care for the crush of business which is coming to Tacoma. This seems almost incredible, but the wholesale business is so rapidly increasing that notwithstanding their every effort it is almost an impossibility for present concerns to keep up with orders.

THOMPSON, PRATT & CO.

WHOLESALE GROCERS, IMPORTERS OF CHINA AND JAPAN TEAS, SALT BATH BRICK AND SAL SODA, JOBBERS OF CANNED GOODS, FOURTEENTH AND A STREETS.

The pioneer wholesale and importing grocery house of Tacoma is that of Thompson, Pratt & Co., composed of Messrs. William J. Thompson, Willard N. Pratt and George Brand, and some idea of the enormous growth of Tacoma in the past few years can be gathered from the remarkable history of this, one of her leading houses.

At the time of the advent of this concern in Tacoma, in December, 1887, there was not a wholesale house of any description in Tacoma, and it was considered a matter of speculation as to whether such a business could be profitably conducted in the city. The three gentlemen comprising the firm came from Rochester, N. Y. Mr. Pratt came to Tacoma in December, 1887, and Mr. Thompson followed him four or five months later. They at once entered heavily into the interests involved, and began the direct importation of China and Japan teas. From Liverpool they imported by vessel both salt bath brick and sal soda, which they found they could land in Tacoma as cheaply as they could be gotten in New York. They began shipping by rail large quantities of teas to St. Paul, Chicago and New York. Their first year's business was a quarter of a million of dollars, and the past year shows the business to have been over half a million. One of the principal features of their business is the jobbing of canned goods of every description. A remarkable fact connected with this firm is that they have not found it necessary to employ any traveling men, the business increasing on its merits even faster than they could wish. Their quarters, although large, have proved too small for their increased business, and they will soon move to their new building, a beautiful structure of stone and brick, four stories in height, one hundred feet front, and one hundred and twenty feet deep. This building is located on the corner of Fourteenth and A Streets, and is one of the finest in point of artistic merit and durability to be found in the city. The gentlemen composing this firm have not forgotten the public interests of Tacoma, and have devoted themselves with much zeal and energy to the advancement of every interest which helps to make a great city. They are identified prominently with the public institutions of Tacoma, and are most keenly observant of her welfare. A cut of their new building will be found in our pages.

THE TACOMA GROCERY COMPANY.

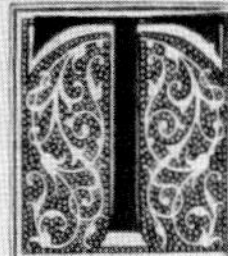

THE Tacoma Grocery Company is composed of Chas. E. Hale, President; Matthew M. Sloan, Vice-President; John G. Campbell, Secretary, and John S. Baker, Treasurer. The three first mentioned were formerly the Hale-Sloan Grocery Company, of Peoria, Ill., where they did a large and successful wholesale grocery business for several years, and sold their interest there only to come to Tacoma which was more adapted for health and profit. They have a capital paid in of one hundred thousand dollars here, and are doing a business of upward of one million per year with no traveling men on the road. Mr. Hale is managing partner, assisted by Mr. Sloan. Mr. Hale says he could do two millions as well as one if he had more room and more money; it is simply a question of these things only, as the territory tributary to this market is immense and doubling up every twelve months, and will continue to do so for years to come. The advantage of this market over most all others is the ease of jobbing houses doing their own importing. Mr. Hale has teas en route from China and Japan, and salt and many fancy groceries from London and Paris coming directly into the port of Tacoma by sailing vessels which take out a cargo of wheat or lumber for various ports of the known world. A fact worth mentioning, which may not be generally known, is that a ship has never yet sailed out of Puget Sound without a cargo. Can this be said of any other seaport in the world, and be it understood, this country is just beginning to be developed; what will it be in another ten years? Can any man estimate Tacoma's future? Mr. Hale says within that time those leaving here will be able to take steamship from Tacoma direct to New York via the Nicaragua Canal, and freight rates will be much lower than now from the Eastern markets. There can be no doubt that Tacoma offers actually the finest field for jobbing houses of all kinds of any city or locality in the world. Mr. Hale has secured for his company one hundred front feet on Pacific avenue, between Seventeenth and Nineteenth streets, upon which they expect to build a six-story building for their own use within the next two years. This property has the advantage of a side track from the Northern Pacific Railroad at the back, and this building, Mr. Hale says, will be as complete as money and experience can make it. It may be interesting to know that this one hundred feet spoken of, shows a profit of fifty thousand dollars to the Tacoma Grocery Company already, and Mr. Hale says it will show two hundred and fifty thousand by the time they are ready to build. This is, indeed, one of the advantages of doing business in such a city as Tacoma. The present quarters of the Tacoma Grocery Company, which are shown in our cut, contain 32,000 square feet of flooring, and cars are loaded and unloaded from the rear from several doors, giving them as complete facilities as are enjoyed by any wholesale grocery house on the Pacific coast.

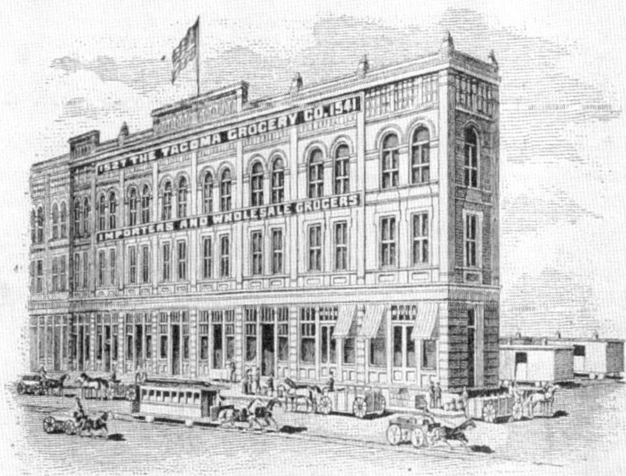

TACOMA GROCERY COMPANY'S STORES.

GROSS BROTHERS.

WHOLESALE AND RETAIL DRY GOODS.

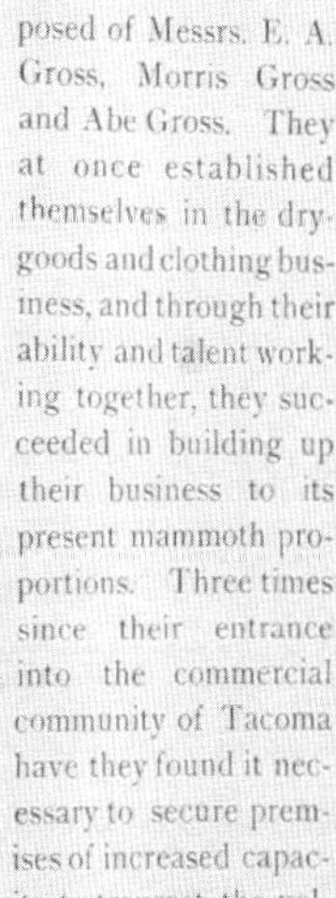

Just about twelve years ago, when the City of Destiny was only in embryonic cityhood, Messrs. Gross Bros. came to it, fully convinced of its great future. The firm is composed of Messrs. E. A. Gross, Morris Gross and Abe Gross. They at once established themselves in the drygoods and clothing business, and through their ability and talent working together, they succeeded in building up their business to its present mammoth proportions. Three times since their entrance into the commercial community of Tacoma have they found it necessary to secure premises of increased capacity to transact the volume of business, which became larger so rapidly that their various departments became handicapped for want of space. It was then decided by the firm to erect such a building for themselves as would in every way facilitate the handling of the large trade now being done by them, and on the 30th of May last, in the presence of thousands, among whom were the representative men of not only Tacoma, but of the various cities of the Pacific Northwest, the cornerstone of the finest drygoods store building north of San Francisco was laid. The frontage of the building on Railroad Avenue is one hundred and fifteen feet, on Ninth Street one hundred feet, and on C Street one hundred and fifteen feet. It will be four stories high, and cost about one hundred and fifty thousand dollars, and is situated near the main thoroughfare.

Messrs. Gross Bros., whose foresightedness and energy have brought them to this prominence in business circles, have now the largest retail trade in drygoods, boots and shoes, etc., on the Pacific coast outside of San Francisco, and their large corps of intelligent and courteous assistants are doing much toward adding to its growth.

HUNT & MOTTET,

Wholesale Heavy Hardware.

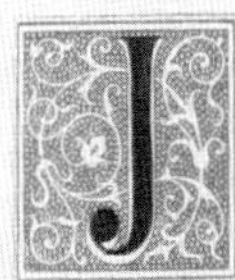

JANUARY, 1885, this house was founded by Mr. E. M. Hunt, senior member of the present firm, and Mr. S. A. Wheelwright, now mayor of Tacoma, under the firm name of Wheelwright & Hunt. During the year 1885, business was generally very much depressed throughout the entire Northwest, and it seemed an unpropitious time to establish a wholesale hardware business in a city of Tacoma's size, having at that time a population of less than 7,000, with a sparsely populated surrounding country. Having, however, faith in Tacoma's future and believing it wise to be early in the field, they faced the dull times and uncertain results with courage and energy, and their efforts at the close of that year had been rewarded with small profits and increasing trade that continued steadily to improve during the next eighteen months, at which time Mr. Wheelwright retired.

June 1st, 1887, Mr. Frederick Mottet associated himself with Mr. Hunt under the firm name of Hunt & Mottet. The business has rapidly grown in magnitude until at present they do the largest business of that kind in the city of Tacoma, and probably the largest even in the Sound country; though they recently doubled their store capacity they find their facilities far too limited to accommodate their fast growing trade, and to overcome this difficulty they have leased what will undoubtedly prove to be the best located block in the city for their business. This building, which is located on the corner of Pacific avenue and Fifteenth street, is under construction, being built of stone and pressed brick; it is 60x100 feet, four stories and basement, and will be one of the handsomest buildings in the city; a cut of the building will be found in our pages. In these new quarters Hunt & Mottet will be most advantageously situated, and will be able to handle their large stock at a minimum expense.

At the rear of this building will be a Northern Pacific side track, and all carloads can be unloaded directly into the store. The basement will be used for iron and iron pipe; a steam elevator will carry other goods above.

The firm carry a large stock of heavy hardware, mill, logging, railroad and ship supplies, and also are manufacturers' agents, having many valuable agencies. Besides the convenient railroad connections, their new quarters are only a stone's throw to the principal city wharves, enabling them to promptly and at the minimum of expense, deliver goods to all the Sound steamers. The merited success of this firm has been accomplished by increasing energy and honorable dealings with all. Both Messrs. Hunt & Mottet are gentlemen of strict integrity, high social standing, refined and courteous manners, and are very popular citizens of Tacoma.

THE PUGET SOUND IRON WORKS

are situated on the corner of Twenty-first and A Streets. They are extensive manufacturing machinists, millwrights and iron founders. The business was brought here from Albany, Oregon, where it had been run for the past fourteen years under the name of the Albany Iron Works, and conducted by Messrs. Cherry and Parkes. It was moved to the "City of Destiny" last January, and Mr. C. O. Bosse of San Francisco taken into the firm. They are manufacturers of steam engines, boilers, water wheels, pulleys, hangers and house-fronts, and they also make a specialty of grist and saw milling machinery and marine work. During the past summer they have had a season of great business prosperity; among other work they have furnished the machinery for the Tacoma Manufacturing Company, the Fairhaven Lumber Company, the Kent Mill Company, and W. B. Martin's mill at Sehome, which last is the largest mill in this part of Puget Sound.

Messrs. Cherry, Parkes & Bosse have lately put in the latest improved machinery, enabling them to turn out the best work of all kinds in their line that can be procured north of San Francisco. The stock of sawmill patterns which they have accumulated in the last fourteen years enables them to distance all competitors in supplying goods of this description, and the reputation of their headblocks is growing to be such that scarcely anybody else attempts to enter the field against them. Some idea of the magnitude of the business these gentlemen have built up since their advent in Tacoma, can be gathered from the fact that they employ over seventy hands, and their running expenses are from $600 to $700 per day.

Mr. C. C. Cherry of this company, whose portrait we present in the work, is a native of North Carolina, and is one of the best known practical machinists on the Pacific; outside of the above business he is a man of considerable means.

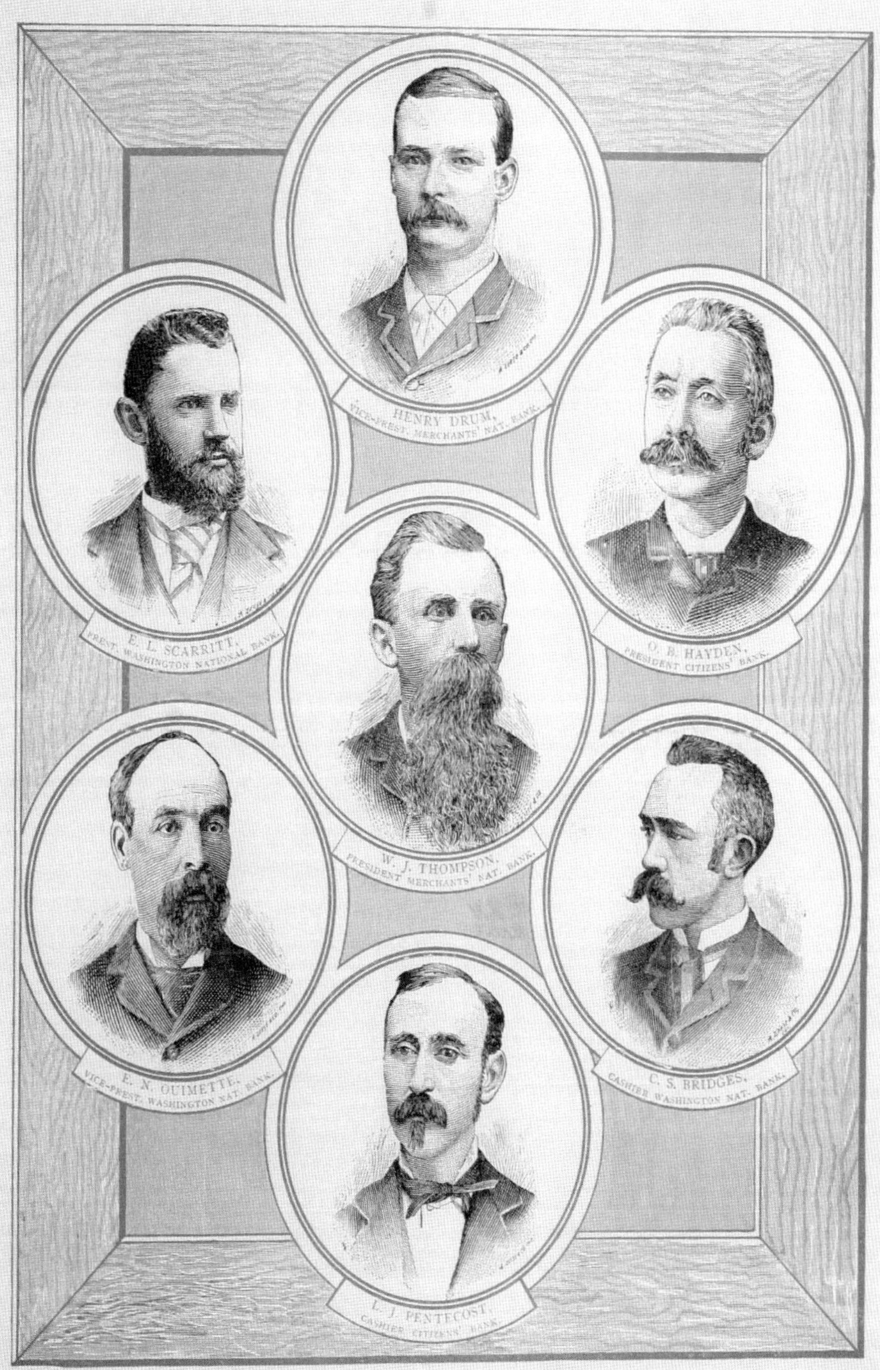

SOME PROMINENT BANKERS OF TACOMA.

TACOMA TRUNK MANUFACTURING COMPANY.

A MOST useful industry, having its factory on the corner of Twenty-fifth and Adams streets. This concern manufactures and deals exclusively in trunks, and is established on an extremely firm as well as substantial basis.

It was started in February with a paid up capital stock of $15,000, with Lake D. Wolford as president, S. M. Clark secretary, W. H. Shiling treasurer and general manager. The demand for the wares turned out of the factory has increased so rapidly that Mr. Shiling is now working a force night and day in order to fill orders. The company owns the ground on which the factory is situated, and will soon erect supplementary buildings and ground will be broken early in the spring.

Mr. Wolford was born on the Pacific Coast, and is thoroughly alive to the needs of the Western country. S. M. Clark the secretary, is a wealthy gentleman largely in manufacturing enterprises, notably the Fox Island Clay Works. Mr. Shiling, the manager, and practical man of the concern, was formerly engaged with his father in Indianapolis in the management of a trunk factory. At present the factory employs seven experienced workmen, and can turn out ten dozen trunks per week. With the new buildings the capacity will naturally considerably exceed this output, and the demand is so large that there will be no danger of taxing the capacity.

JOHN MACREADY & CO.

This firm have their spacious headquarters at 928 Pacific avenue, and are the oldest hardware establishment in Tacoma. They carry a large and varied stock of shelf and heavy hardware, and are also agents for the Giant Powder Co., Judson Blasting and Sporting Powder, Hall's Lock and Safe Co., Howe Scales, and Sargent & Co.'s Locks.

Mr. John Macready is known far and wide on Puget Sound as a man of indefatigable energy and determination. He is of that tough Scotch breed which has succeeded in getting on top of the heap wherever it had the ghost of a show, all over the world, and was born on the Eastern seaboard. His father, however, like a sensible man, came West when the subject of our sketch was only three years old. They settled at first in Kentucky, but finally settled in Sioux City. John Macready was brought up in the hardware business, and has a thorough practical acquaintance with every detail of it. He came to Tacoma in 1883, and started in business. In 1884 he was burned out and lost everything he had. Another man might have lost heart, for it was apparently a knockout blow. He buckled his belt tighter, clenched his teeth with grim determination, and went to work again. He is now one of the foremost merchants of Tacoma, a member of the executive committee of the Chamber of Commerce, a man of large capital and great public spirit, and one who is looked up to and honored on all sides, by every one.

ELVINS & PURCELL.

The above well known firm are dealers in groceries, provisions and general family produce. Mr. W. H. Elvins and W. M. Purcell associated themselves in business in July last, and since that period have built up one of the finest paying businesses in Tacoma. This firm makes a specialty not only of supplying private families with all the necessaries of life, but particularly furnishing hotels and restaurants with all kinds of the choicest food products. Mr. Elvins is a native of Bellevue, Ontario, and was formerly connected with his father in a large wholesale and retail grocery business in that town. He came to Tacoma last November, and after looking the Sound country over, decided to locate here permanently. W. M. Purcell is also an old-timer in the grocery business, and comes originally from Rochester, N. Y. During his residence here, his genial disposition and engaging manners, have combined to make him one of the most popular men about town.

S. J. HOLLAND & CO.

This firm have their wholesale store on Railroad street, near Thirteenth. They do a very large business in liquors, and are besides, the agents for a leading brand of Cincinnati beer, "Belle of the West." The Bourbon whiskey which they make a specialty is known fâr and wide, and extensively drank upon this coast.

One of their latest enterprises was the opening of the Milwaukee saloon on Pacific avenue. This is undoubtedly the most sumptuously fitted up place of the kind on the Sound, and would be a credit to San Francisco. The plate glass mirror behind the bar is the largest ever shipped, and is valued at $1,800. The saloon occupies the whole three story building, the first floor containing the bar and restaurant, while the upper floors are devoted to billiards and pool. The restaurant is one of the finest in town, and is rapidly gaining a large patronage.

MUSSUSOIT HOTEL.

This hotel is on the corner of Seventeenth and C streets. It is only one square from the depot and has 80 rooms. It has only been opened a year, but has already gained the reputation of being not only a good transient but the best family hotel in town.

The table is always kept up to the best standard and careful and attentive service by exclusively white labor is guaranteed to the guests. The whole building including the annex of the new three-story brick block containing three stories and forty-five rooms, is lighted with electric and the rooms furnished with electric bells.

In addition, it may be said that the Mussusoit is run on both the American and the European plans, and is the only first class hotel in town that runs a free 'bus, which is a rather remarkable departure in the western country, and is not only a great convenience, but is fully appreciated by all travelers.

NUHN & WHEELER.

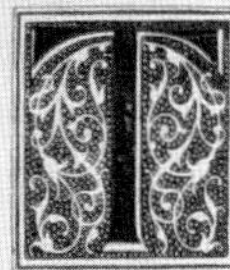

THIS firm is the principal wholesale and retail book and stationery house in Tacoma, and its business reaches out all over this State, Oregon, Idaho and British Columbia.

Their store and warerooms, situated at 930 Pacific avenue, a cut of which will be found in this book, contains everything appertaining to the business to which Messrs. Nuhn & Wheeler profess to belong. The firm is also the general agency in Tacoma and the State for all newspapers and periodicals published in the Western States, as well as for foreign publications. Although the business is now only in the third year of its existence, it has grown to such an extent that it is now considered one of the greatest and most important business houses in Tacoma.

Mr. Oscar Nuhn is a native of Brooklyn, New York, came to Tacoma about five years ago, and it was not until carefully looking over the towns in the Northwest that he decided on Tacoma as the only one destined to become the metropolis of the Pacific Northwest, and therefore established, with Mr. G. H. Wheeler, the above business.

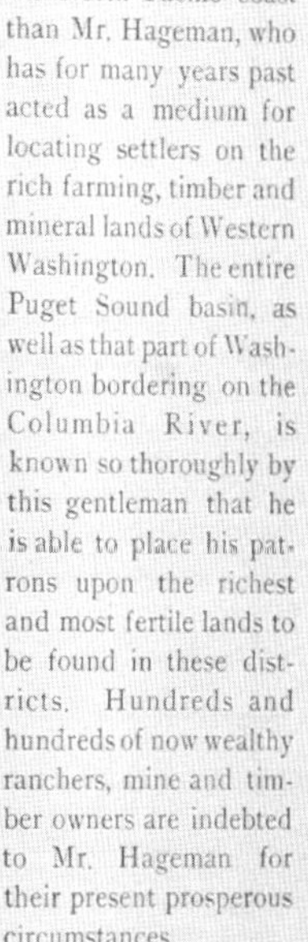

Mr. G. H Wheeler, the other member of this firm, is a native of the town of Wheeler, State of New York, and until his association with Mr. Oscar Nuhn in the above business, was manager of the *Tacoma Daily and Weekly Ledger*. Both Messrs. Oscar Nuhn and G. H. Wheeler are thoroughly capable and shrewd business men, as the flourishing condition of their business well testifies.

H. L. RICH & CO.

of 1317 Pacific avenue, are the flourishing proprietors of one of the largest and most successful harness emporiums on the Pacific coast. The business has been established for over three years, and Messrs. Rich & Co. claim with pardonable pride to keep in stock the largest varieties of saddles, harness, whips and robes, of any shop in their line of business north of San Francisco. They also do what very few dealers in saddlery ware do on this coast, *i. e.*, manufacture all their own stock of harness and saddles, thus enabling them to guarantee with perfect knowledge of its reliability every article of the kind that goes out of their shop, and giving them an immense advantage over competitors who deal in cheap and frequently auction-made stuff, coming from the Eastern seaboard, that is often bought for little, and worthless.

Mr. T. O. Butts, the company of the concern, is connected with Mr. Rich by family ties, and is really the practical manager of the emporium. He is an energetic and enterprising business man, and has trebled the value of the business since it first started, three years ago.

B. F. HAGEMAN.

GOVERNMENT LAND LOCATOR AND SURVEYOR, 108 SOUTH TWELFTH STREET.

No one is better known along the North Pacific coast than Mr. Hageman, who has for many years past acted as a medium for locating settlers on the rich farming, timber and mineral lands of Western Washington. The entire Puget Sound basin, as well as that part of Washington bordering on the Columbia River, is known so thoroughly by this gentleman that he is able to place his patrons upon the richest and most fertile lands to be found in these districts. Hundreds and hundreds of now wealthy ranchers, mine and timber owners are indebted to Mr. Hageman for their present prosperous circumstances.

Since the advent of the Northern Pacific Railroad and other transportation facilities, Mr. Hageman has been compelled to employ numerous assistants to supply the wants ofthe hundreds of land-seekers that are continually arriving from the East. The fame of the richness of Washington has gone abroad to such an extent that, although confident of its future greatness, Mr. Hageman's business has increased far beyond his expectations. But still millions of acres of the finest lands remain untouched, only waiting for the plow, the axe, or the pick, to yield up their abundance of wealth. Mr. Hageman has sought out the best of these tracts, and proffers his valuable services for locating immigrants.

To those, therefore, who are leaving the East to locate in such manner, we would say that Mr. Hageman is a man of thorough reliability and knowledge of the country, and they will consult their best interests by corresponding with, or seeing him personally.

DICKSON BROS.

CLOTHING AND GENTS' FURNISHING GOODS, 1120 PACIFIC AVENUE.

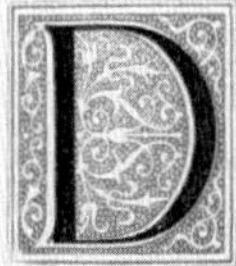

ICKSON BROS., a well-known and very popular firm, was founded in the spring of 1883, by Geo. L. and William H. Dickson, who opened for public inspection a well-selected, though small, stock of such goods as are usually found in clothing houses. Their first storeroom over which they hung the now famous U. S. store sign, was no larger than a big dry goods box, or about 10x12 feet. *Industry, hard work, courage, in* "Tacoma's darkest days," and a belief that the people would indorse honest efforts, and appreciate their endeavors to give them the most for their money, soon won for them a host of that most desirable class known as *cash customers.* Two years later a younger brother, Mr. Warren P. Dickson, became a member of the firm, bringing with him a lifelong experience from one of the largest drygoods concerns in the United States, thus adding additional strength to what is now acknowledged one of the most flourishing public-spirited—though keen sighted—concerns on the Pacific coast. It was reserved for Dickson Bros. to introduce into Tacoma rules of business, which have made popular all the leading houses of Eastern cities, viz.: Absolutely *one price to all;* strictly cash *sales,* with the lowest possible per centage of profit added to each article; also to prove that the golden rule could be applied to commercial as well as social affairs. Perhaps it would not be amiss just here to mention that this firm carry clothing, gents' furnishing goods, hats and caps, boots and shoes, and the many smaller items that accompany these staple lines.

The people seem to appreciate the additional fact that Dickson Bros. have guarded against the average merchant's stumbling block—high rent. Owning their own store building they gain a decided advantage, and that the Tacoma citizens are aware of it, is evident by the constant throng which passes in and out of the U. S. Store.

A. F. HOSKA.

The gentleman whose name forms the caption of this article, is well known to most people dwelling in Washington, as a man of business capacity and integrity. His present place of business is located at 1720 E street, where he conducts a large wholesale business in harness and saddlery. Mr. Hoska formerly had a prominent shop on Pacific Ave., where he was engaged in the same business in a retail way. Foreseeing, with shrewd business sagacity, the future business possibilities of the City of Destiny, he started his wholesale business, and is now one of the largest manufacturers of saddlery ware, north of San Francisco.

He carries a full stock of goods, and a purchaser never needs go further after he has examined his stock, but, from Mr. Hoska's enviable reputation and large experience, may rely upon the goods he buys being exactly what they are represented to be.

REED & CO.

A prominent firm of commission merchants in grain and hops, have offices at Tacoma and Walla Walla, managed respectively by Alexander Reed and W. H. Reed, his son. Their present business has been established about a year and a half. Mr. Reed Sr., was engaged eight years in the grain trade at Toledo, O., of which city he was twice the postmaster. He has held other responsible public positions, including those of auditor of Lucas Co., O., supervising agent of the U. S. Treasury, and receiver of public moneys at Walla Walla.

W. H. Reed was for many years cashier of the Toledo Savings Bank & Trust Co. He owns and conducts a farm of 600 acres close to the city of Walla Walla, and has other considerable interests in the eastern part of the State. Both members of the firm have been residents of Washington about eleven years. Their extensive acquaintance, prompt and careful attention to the interests of their customers, and reputation for integrity, have brought them a large clientage.

In addition to their commission business, Reed & Co. are agents for the product of the Eureka Flour Mills of Walla Walla—principal brands "White Rose" and "Dement's Best"—in which they have a very large trade on the Sound.

Their Tacoma office is at 923 Pacific avenue, over the Tacoma National Bank.

THE FOX ISLAND CLAY WORKS,

MANUFACTURERS OF SEWER AND CULVERT PIPE, DRAIN TILE, TERRA COTTA CHIMNEY PIPE, ETC.

The offices of this firm are at the Junction of Dock and Fifteenth Streets, at the head of Commencement Bay, a most convenient place for the receiving of products of the works situated on Fox Island, about sixteen miles from Tacoma, and there is also every facility for reshipment to outside points, as the North Pacific Railroad tracks run through the company's yards almost to the water's edge.

The Fox Island Clay Co. was established in August, 1888, and the plant was then owned by the Fox Island Brick Company. As soon as the company was incorporated, the yards at Fox Island, which are second to none on the Pacific coast for the finest deposits of various clays, were fitted with the very best machinery obtainable for the manufacturing of sewer and culvert pipe, drain tile, terra cotta chimney pipe, etc. All piping used by the city government, is manufactured by this company, and all the Sound cities, as well as numerous points throughout Washington and Oregon. Fifty men are employed to supply the constant demand.

The officers and directors are as follows: W. S. Bowen, president and general manager; J. M. Steele, vice-president; A. R. Zabriskie, secretary, and S. F. Sahm, J. M. Steele, I. W. Anderson, W. S. Bowen, and S. M. Clark, directors.

As we have mentioned in other parts of this work, the fine deposits of almost every kind of clay which are found in sections of this country are destined to play a great part in the future of our manufacturing industries.

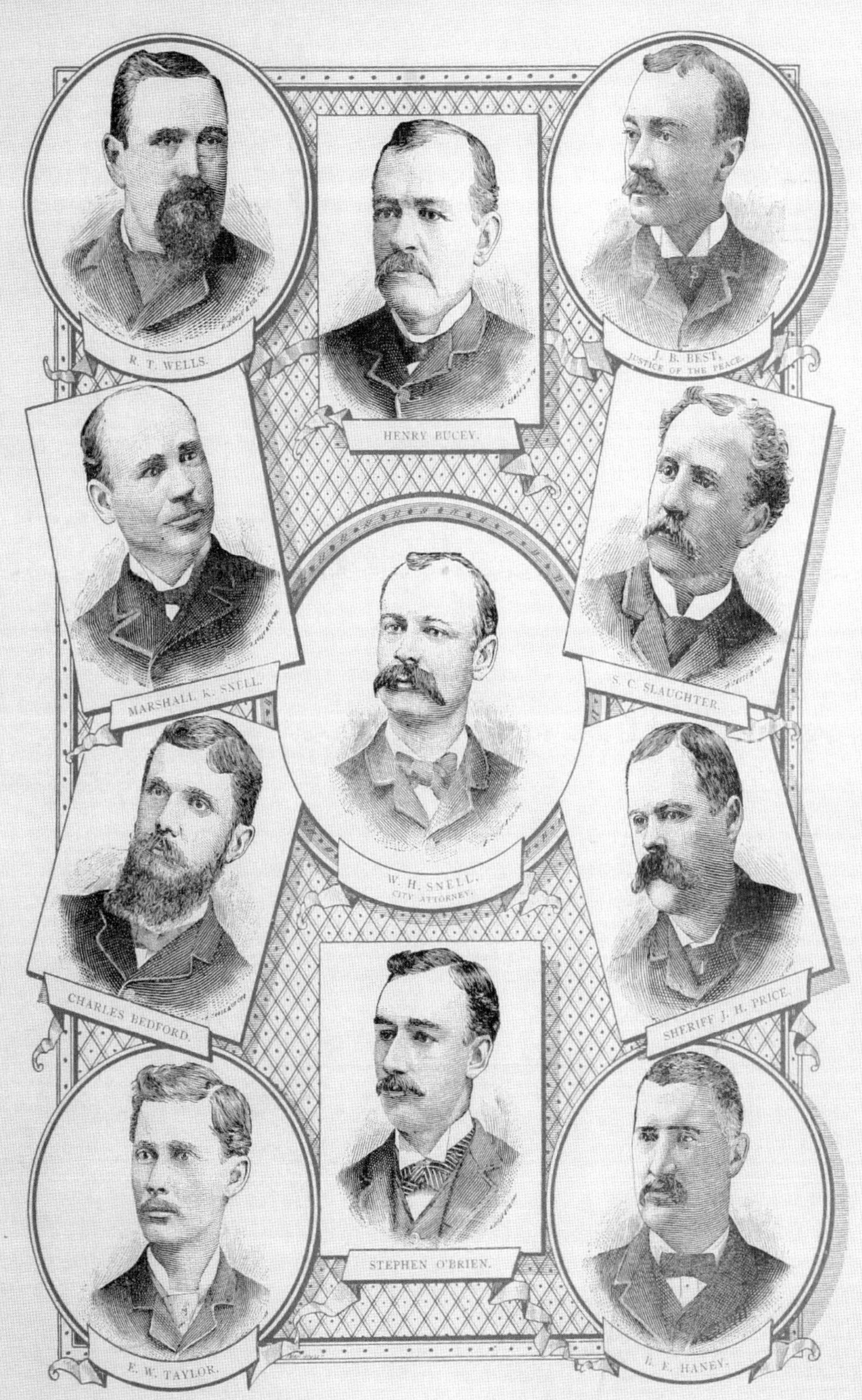

PROMINENT MEN OF TACOMA.

HIRSCH & FRANK.

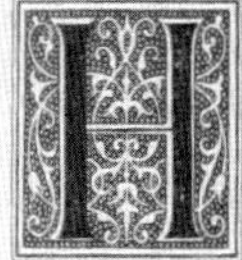IRSCH & FRANK, Merchant Tailors and Gents' Furnishers, are to be found at No. 1007 Pacific avenue. Although not long established, it is now recognized as the leading house of its kind in Tacoma. Their location in the Dougan Block, a handsome four story edifice in the center of the business portion of the city, and the energetic manner in which they have made known to the public their thorough capability for supplying gentlemen with every article of dress, has given them a reputation that is second to none in the State of Washington. Both Mr. Hirsch and Mr. Frank are young men. The former gentleman comes from Des Moines, Ia., where he was engaged in a similar business for upward of fifteen years, but the bright prospects of Tacoma attracted him, and he became a resident of this city about a year ago. Mr. H. C. Frank may almost be termed an old timer in Tacoma. For the past six years he has made the City of Destiny his home, and it is safe to say that he has made himself an extremely popular man, with the hundreds of people whom he has met. For a considerable time Mr. Frank was associated with the well-known furniture house of F. S. Harmon & Co. of Tacoma, but seeing the admirable opportunity to establish a gents' furnishing house on a first-class basis here, he joined Mr. Hirsch in his present business. For a well-fitting suit of clothes of the best material, one could not go to a better place than Messrs. Hirsch & Frank. They employ the best cutters obtainable, who spare no pains, and, in fact, take the greatest pride in turning out a suit that is faultless in make and design. The furnishing and hat department is equally well looked after, and is almost daily enlarged with the latest novelties of fashion.

JAMES H. PRICE.

James H. Price, the sheriff of Pierce County, styles himself an Oregon boy, and is proud of the fact. Previous to his nomination on the Republican ticket for sheriff of this county a year ago, Mr. Price had acted in the capacity of inspector of customs, and later as deputy collector of customs on Puget Sound of the port of Tacoma, for upward of fourteen years, and only quit the customs house to accept his present position, which was almost forced upon him. During those fourteen years, Mr. Price proved himself a faithful and efficient public servant. As sheriff of Pierce County he has acquitted himself most creditably. Owing to the constant and heavy stream of immigration many crooks, thugs and plug-uglies, driven by the police of Eastern cities to seek other quarters, have, owing to the prosperity of Tacoma, come here with the intention of practicing their calling; but the prompt action of Mr. Price and his deputies has prevented any violent acts of lawlessness, and to-day there is no county and city that is more free from crime and the criminal element, than Pierce County, and the city of Tacoma.

ROBERT A. TRIPPLE.

The largest shoe store in the city of Tacoma is at 1340 Pacific Avenue. Mr. Tripple is a shrewd, energetic business man, and although he has been established here but a year, is already doing a very large and flourishing trade. Mr. Tripple's business may fairly be called a representative one, as he sells to all grades in the social scale, and gives satisfaction, to quote from his trademark, "All the year round." The store contains a thoroughly well-selected stock of goods, and everybody, from the most fastidious purchaser to the laborer who wants a pair of high-lows, will find what he needs on his shelves. It may be mentioned in this connection that Mr. Tripple's show-windows are the most tastefully arranged, and display the largest variety of goods of any similar concern in town.

Mr. Tripple is a thorough believer in advertising, and his judgment in this department of business has been chiefly the cause to which he attributes the present flourishing state of his affairs, a just tribute to advertising methods.

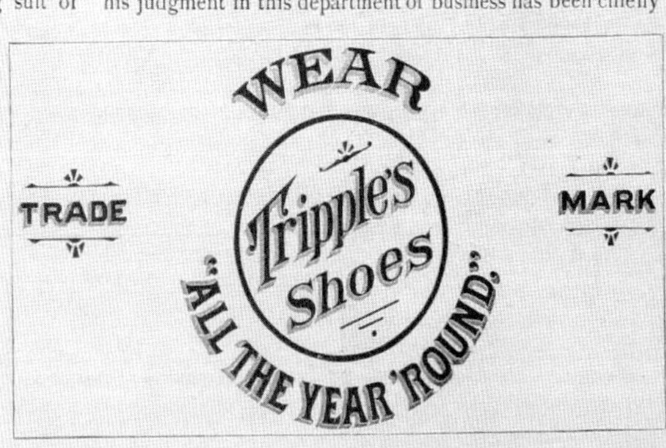

One of the chief claims of this new city is the resolve which seems to animate all of its business men, to commence right, and supply the best that any of the older emporiums of trade offer, thus building up business which will vie with the older cities of the East.

"HOTEL ROCHESTER."

AN ELEGANT HOTEL—SPLENDID BATHS AND FINE HAIR DRESSING ROOMS.

ON a triangular piece of ground overlooking the bay and the Sound, commanding the entire range of the Cascades and the magnificence of Mount Tacoma, has recently been erected the handsomest and most substantial structure in Tacoma or the Sound region, known as "The Rochester." The building has a massive stone foundation, the upper part is pressed brick, three stories and basement with bay windows to each floor, and on three sides. The Rochester is more of an elegant and select family than transient hotel, although the proprietor expects to accommodate some transients in the new wing which is now under construction. It has at present forty-two rooms, and is lighted throughout by incandescent electric lights.

The entire woodwork in the finish of the house is of the finest seasoned oak, and cedar of Eastern manufacture giving the tone and appearance of a princely residence suggestive of antiquity and elegance.

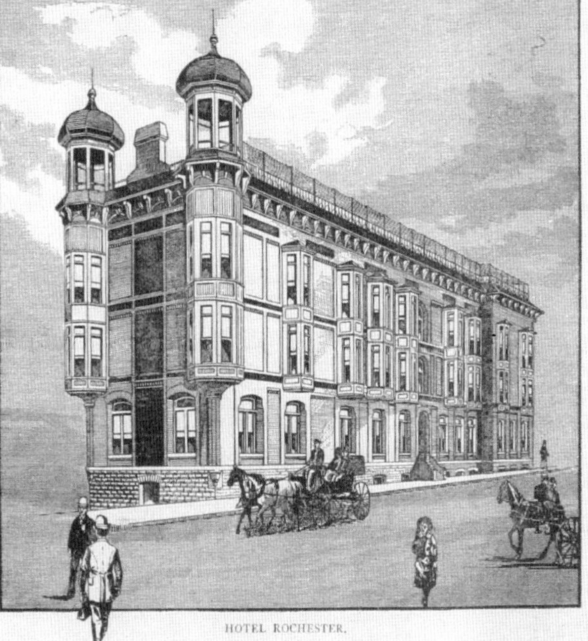

HOTEL ROCHESTER.

A fine dining-room elegantly furnished, along with the handsome parlors and reception-rooms, are among the most important features in connection with the hotel. A barber shop and ladies hair-dressing parlors, with Russian, Turkish shower plunge, also vapor, medicated and electric bathrooms (twenty-one in number), are in the basement of the hotel, conducted by Prof. Napoleon Le Blanc. A stairway leads to the roof where a promenade is securely arranged, which affords beautiful and entrancing views of land and water, forests and mountains.

The "Rochester" is located at the junction of Tacoma Ave. and D street. The neighborhood is the most select in Tacoma, with fine residences and lawns, and adjacent to the Annie Wright Seminary.

Mr. A. C. Smith, the proprietor of the hotel and the ground upon which it is built, is one of the most influential citizens of Tacoma, as well as one of the wealthiest. Mr. Smith is always ready and willing with his influence and money to promote the welfare of Tacoma. He is a member of the executive committee of the Chamber of Commerce, and it is with pleasure that the compilers of the work produce his photograph with the rest of the executive committee, as well as a cut of the Hotel Rochester.

TACOMA WAREHOUSE & ELEVATOR CO.

This prosperous concern is one of the largest business enterprises in Tacoma. It is located on the deep water front, with tracks of the Northern Pacific Railroad in front of the warehouse for delivery to the lower floor and at an elevation of sixty feet in the rear for delivery on that side, with piers running a depth of water sufficient to accommodate the largest vessel at low tide.

The warehouse is the largest and most capacious on the Pacific Coast, being 514 feet in length, 114 wide, and three and one-half stories high. Endless chain conveyors are also put in for the delivery of grain for shipment. The building has been built with special view as to danger from fire, and the torredo guarded against by the fact that the foundation of piles is encased in a solid gravel foundation. The trustees are William Dunn and A. J. Marble of Chicago, and A. M. Ingersoll, C. J. Kershaw, C. H. Marble of Tacoma. As references, the Tacoma & Elevator Company are permitted to use the following well known names: T. F. Oakes, president N. P. R. R., St. Paul., C. H. Prescott, 2nd vice-president N. P. R. R., Tacoma, Paul Schultze, General Land Agent N. P. R. R., Tacoma, National Bank of Commerce, Tacoma, Tacoma National Bank, Tacoma, Pacific National Bank, Tacoma, Traders Bank, Tacoma, and Miles C. Moore of Walla Walla, the ex-Governor of the Territory.

The business of the company is exclusively storage and they are prepared to receive in store all kinds of grain, wool, hops, or any commodity for long or short time.

They intend also to soon make a portion of the building a bounded warehouse, and be in a position to receive and store goods in bond.

PUGET SOUND BREWERY.

WHEN Messrs. Scholl & Huth established the Puget Sound Brewery just a year ago, they proved themselves enterprising and energetic business men. Previous to that time Tacoma was sadly in need of a first-class brewery that would be able to supply beer of a superior quality and in sufficient quantity to supply the ever increasing demand for this popular beverage. At the cost of many thousand dollars these gentlemen constructed a four-story building, 80x80 feet, at the junction of Jefferson avenue and 25th street, and later a wing has been added on the southeast corner that is of the same height, and 40x40 feet. The building erected, Messrs. Scholl & Huth spared no expense in fitting it up with machinery which is of the most approved pattern, and of the very best material. Two Corliss engines, one of ninety, and the other of sixty horse power, furnish the necessary propelling power, and they are in constant operation. A beer boiler, heated by steam, with a capacity of 4,300 gallons, is connected with a patent mashing machine that holds 6,500 gallons. The brewery also has an apparatus for the manufacture of their own ice for cooling the beer. With this machinery Messrs. Scholl & Huth are enabled to produce 260 barrels of beer per day. The Puget Sound Brewery has gained an enviable reputation for the manufacturing of their "Walhalla" and "Der Goetten Trank" beers, which are, as the name of the last implies, drink that is suitable for the gods. Before this brewery was started considerable beer was shipped to Tacoma from the largest and most popular breweries in the East, but now saloonkeepers are rapidly withdrawing their patronage from these Eastern houses, and supply the public with an excellent beverage made from Washington hops by a process that insures a drink equally as good, in fact, superior owing to its freshness and purity. The distance of the transportation of Eastern beer is said to have had a decidedly bad effect upon those drinking it; however that may be, those who have drank the beer of this brewery enthusiastically concede its good effects.

Under the supervision of Mr. P. A. Kalenborn, who at one time owned a large brewery in Kansas, and who thoroughly understands his business, the Puget Sound Brewery is now one of the best paying and most prosperous business institutions in Tacoma.

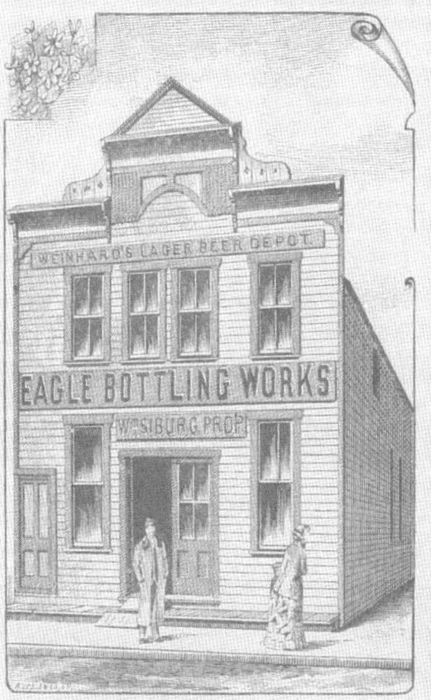

WILLIAM SIBURG.

This gentleman's main office is on the corner of Pacific avenue and Eighth street; he is one of the prominent German-American residents of Tacoma. He was originally a native of the Duchy of Brunswick, but became dissatisfied with his native city when the Prussian war engulfed all the smaller principalities and made a United Germany, and finally came to the land of freedom like so many of his countrymen. With the industry and economy which is the heirloom of every German, he went to work and labored gallantly in Brooklyn until he had accumulated sufficient money to go into business on his own account.

He is now the head of a completely organized beer-bottling establishment in this town, has a large amount of money invested here, and bids fair in the future to be able to go back, and buy up with fairly earned American gold, the little kingdom in which he first saw the light.

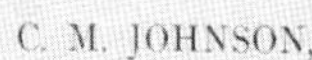

C. M. JOHNSON,

MANUFACTURER AND DEALER IN SASH, DOORS, BLINDS, MOULDINGS, WINDOW AND DOOR FRAMES, 2120 TO 2132 EAST D STREET.

There is not a more live and energetic business man in Tacoma than the subject of this sketch, who has built up for himself a business that is not only large in its production but a most important acquisition to the city of Tacoma. Mr. Johnson's plant is most advantageously situated at the head of Commencement Bay, and in close proximity to the side tracks of the railroad company. He came to Tacoma from the town of Walla Walla in Eastern Washington six years ago, and immediately started his sash and door factory. The rapid growth of the city made Mr. Johnson's business a flourishing and prosperous one, and he considered himself on the highway to fortune, but after two years' hard work, in June, 1885, the factory was swept away by fire to such an extent that nothing remained. Undaunted by this catastrophe, Mr. Johnson immediately rebuilt on a much larger scale, adding everything that goes to make a first class factory. To-day eighty-five men find employment in the various departments of this institution, manufacturing sash, doors, blinds, mouldings, and window and door frames of all descriptions. Mr. Johnson is a typical Tacoma man, public spirited, and one who has the interests of the city at heart so thoroughly that he is ever ready to exert himself in its behalf.

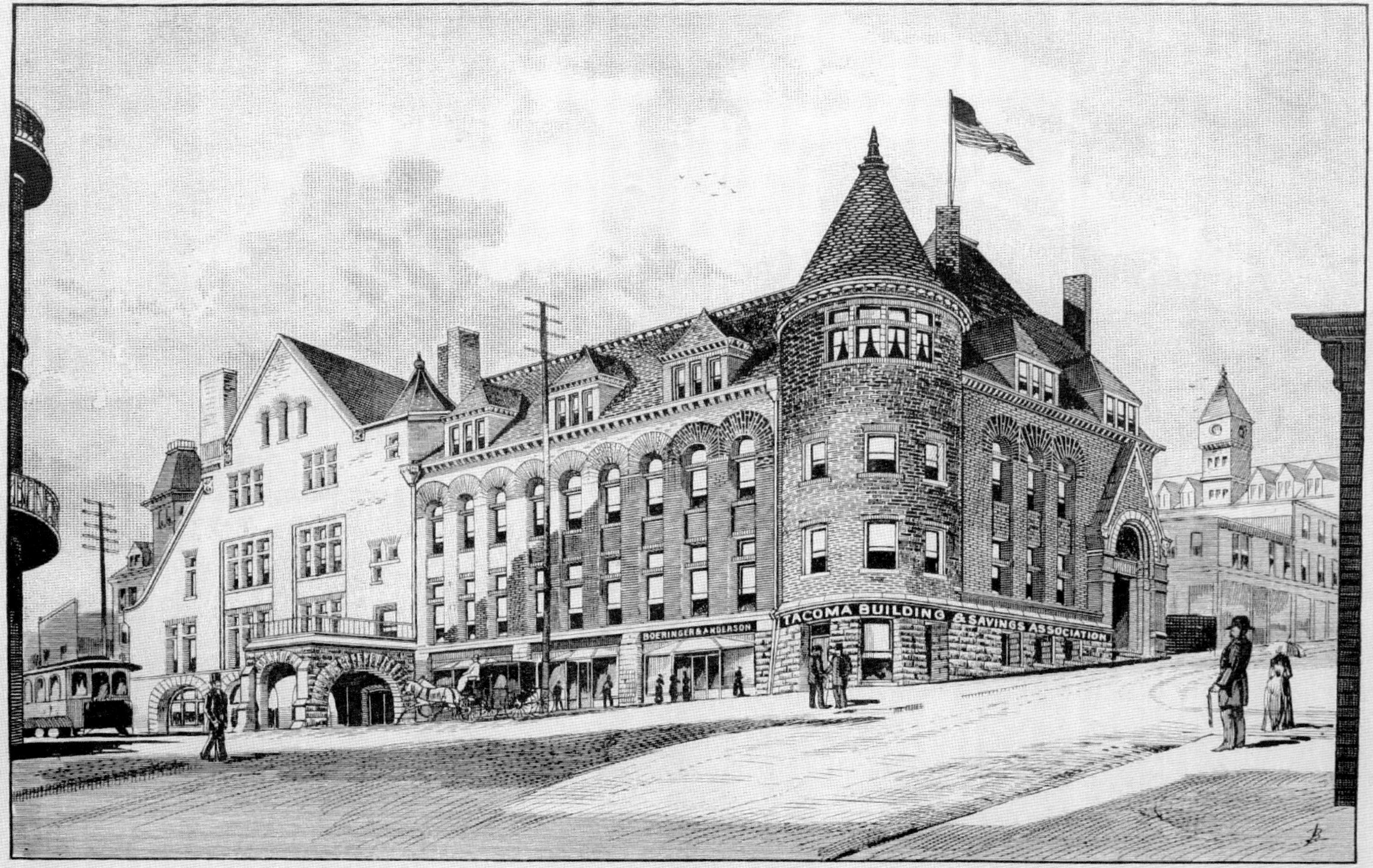

THE NEW TACOMA OPERA HOUSE.

MARSHALL K. SNELL,

ATTORNEY AT LAW.

NO lawyer in Tacoma, or in fact throughout the State of Washington, is better known than Marshall K. Snell. The great distinction which Mr. Snell has attained as a lawyer is well merited, for during his two years' practice in the courts of this State, he has in many instances proved himself a careful and well read counselor, and an eloquent and able pleader. As a criminal lawyer, Mr Snell has few equals anywhere, and there is perhaps not another man who would have made such a clever legal fight as he did recently in the case of the United States vs. B. F. Hageman, and one hundred and thirty-one others for alleged fraudulent location of government land. Mr. Snell's remarkably able handling of the case, is universally conceded a very great legal triumph.

Another case equally interesting, and reflecting great credit on Mr. Snell, is that of the Territory vs. Alfred Fostrom, for murder in the first degree; and although everything pointed to the worst for the accused man, Mr. Snell obtained his acquittal in comparatively short order. Marshall K. Snell is the son of John Marshall King, Sr., of Ottumwa, Ia., who as a physician and surgeon served with the Eleventh Iowa Volunteers during the War of the Rebellion. Having acquitted himself creditably and been dangerously wounded, Dr. King near the close of the war, returned to his wife and family on Nov. 1st, 1864, and died three days afterward. A few days later the terrible disease of smallpox broke out in Ottumwa, and the entire King family, with the exception of Marshall, died before the end of the month. During the excitement that prevailed at the time, Marshall was sent to the pest house and afterward to the State Orphans' Home, where he remained until seven years old, when he was adopted by William J. Snell, and his name was changed from Marshall King to Marshall K. Snell.

Mr. Snell's boyhood was spent on a farm, but he eventually acted as clerk to the legal firm of Button Bros. of Trempealeau, Wis., and soon afterward read law with Judge Alfred A. Newman of the Sixth Judicial District of Wisconsin. Mr. Snell graduated from the Wisconsin State University in 1881, and was admitted to the bar the same year. He settled in the town of Seymour, Wis., and there first began to practice his profession, acting as city attorney for three years and as a member of the board of county supervisors for two years during the five years of his residence in the town.

CHARLES T. UHLMAN.

Charles T. Uhlman, whose wonderful prosperity during his residence in the City of Destiny, stamps him at once as a true representative of the community in which he lives, came originally from Washington, D. C. in 1881. The first employment he secured was with Barlow Bros. A market was purchased by S. Coulter & Co., and Mr. Uhlman continued with them until he opened a little meat market on C street. After a short time he bought from Coulter & Co., the Ranier Market, where only a short time before he had worked on small salary. The city was growing then just as rapidly as it is to-day, and the business at the Ranier Market increased proportionally. Mr. Uhlman continued to conduct the business successfully, first supplying one or two smaller markets with meat and later on introducing a general wholesale department. In the fall of 1888 he constructed a handsome brick block on Pacific Avenue opposite Tenth street but last summer he conceived the idea of fitting up a meat market that in every detail would be the finest on the Pacific Coast. The Market Block was then built on the corner of Ninth and A streets. Half of the ground floor was arranged for a butcher-shop which was fitted up at a cost of over $6,000. The subject of this sketch has just completed the organization of the Puget Sound Pressed Beef and Packing Co., with a capital stock of $150,000, and he will be president of the company.

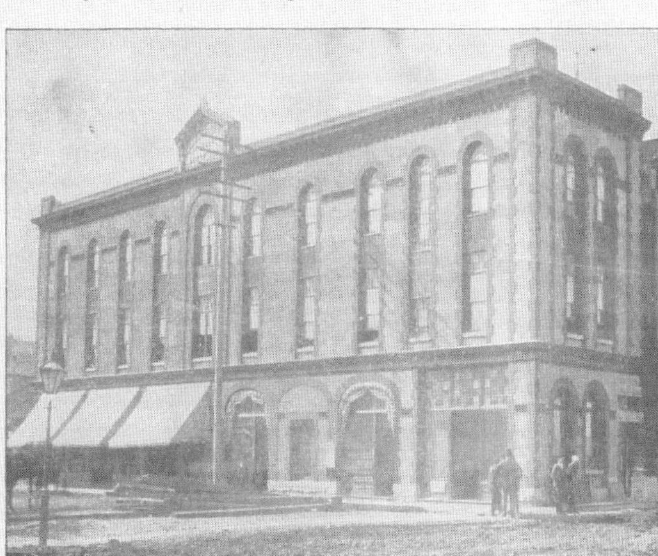

UHLMAN'S BUILDING.

Mr. Uhlman is also a stockholder in Brown's Wharf & Navigation Co., in which corporation he holds the office of secretary, and he is a leading member of the city council.

TACOMA LEATHER AND BELTING CO.

CLIFFORD & TOUSEY, PROPRIETORS. DEALERS IN BELTING, HOSE, PACKING AND LEATHER AND FINDINGS, 1527 PACIFIC AVENUE (SPRAGUE BUILDING.)

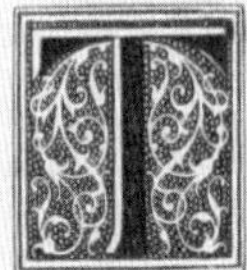

THIS firm, which is the pioneer of its kind in Tacoma, and in the State as well, is composed of Benj. F. Clifford and Albemarle C. Tousey, and is leading and representative in all respects. They occupy one story and a basement, each 20x100 feet in dimensions. This firm make a point to carry the very best goods that mechanical skill can produce, and in pursuance of this policy they have taken the State agency for Revere Rubber Co.'s unrivaled goods, consisting of their "Giant" Stitched and Seamless Rubber Belting, and "Granite" Seamless Belting, also "Granite" and Shawmut Hose, and "Granite" Steam Packing, and last but not least, their celebrated "Four Ace" and "Giant" Steam Fire Engine Hose.

They are manufacturer's agents for Hide, Leather and Belting Co.'s Pure Oak Tanned Short Lap Leather Belting, and carry a large and complete stock of all sizes, both single and double. This belting is the very best that can be pro-

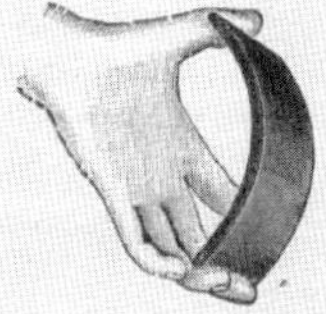

NEW STYLE "SEAMLESS."

"GRANITE" "SEAMLESS" BELTING.

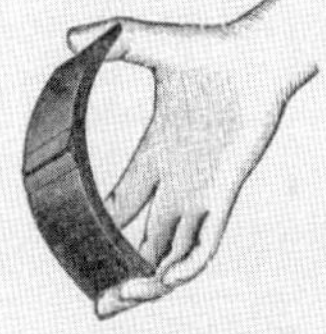

OLD STYLE SEAM.

duced by skilled workmen, using selected chestnut oak tanned leather, and is guaranteed to be second to none.

In each of their respective lines, belting and leather and findings, this firm carry the largest and most complete stock in the Pacific Northwest, and their large and rapidly growing trade attests their customers' appreciation of their motto, "Best quality goods only." In the management of their business, they bring to their aid a complete knowledge of the goods in their line, Mr. Clifford having been connected with a large Eastern firm in the same line from his boyhood up to the time they began business in Tacoma, some thirteen years, during which time he mastered the business in all its details, as bookkeeper, house salesman, traveling salesman, and for the last three years as manager and buyer of the firm with which he was connected. Mr. Tousey also brings to his aid a thorough knowledge of the goods he handles, having been connected with the same firm that Mr. Clifford was for a number of years, as bookkeeper, house salesman and road salesman, thus making him complete master of the situation.

Taking in connection the complete stock of *best* quality goods which they carry, and their comprehensive knowledge of the goods they handle, and the needs of their customers, we can safely pronounce this firm one of the best equipped for a successful business career of any in the rapidly growing "City of Destiny."

TACOMA STOVE COMPANY.

BRANSCHEID & YOUNG.

It is gratifying to the eye and business sense to note a thoroughly complete and well appointed commercial establishment, and one that more thoroughly realizes that sense of fitness than the one owned by Messrs. Branscheid & Young, located at 905 Pacific avenue, is not to be found in Tacoma. The premises are spacious necessarily for the purpose of carrying their large and varied stock, yet everything is so neatly and tastefully arranged that intending purchasers can examine goods and make selections with half the trouble endured in less systematically organized establishments. The concern does a large jobbing as well as retail trade, and besides dealing in everything pertaining to the kitchen, attend to repairing, plumbing and fitting ir the most efficient manner.

The Tacoma Stove Company claims to be, and is, the oldest house in its line in the City of Destiny, and has been

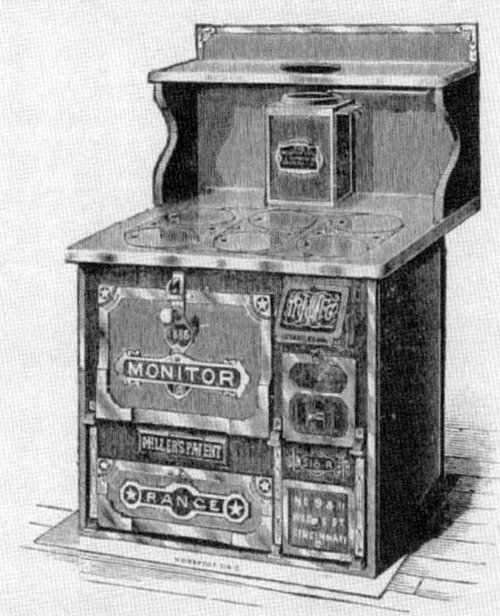

in existence over ten years—a period commensurate with thrice the time in a more slow-going and humdrum community. It was founded by Thomas B. Brown, who was bought out by Harvey & Young, the latter being the present partner, and later Mr. Branscheid bought out Harvey, on which event the business was enlarged and extended to its present position, which is that of being second to no other mercantile enterprise in the city.

They aim to handle only the very best goods, and a glance at the names of the following concerns that intrust them with their interests in this part of the world, will quickly convince any one that their claim is entirely justified by the facts of the case. They are: The Bridge & Beech Manufacturing Company, of St. Louis, Stoves; Redway & Burton, of Cincinnati, Ohio, Stoves; William Resor & Co., of Cincinnati, Ohio, Stoves; The William Miller Range and Furnace Company, The Monitor Steel Range Company, of Cincinnati, Ohio; John J. Ils & Co., of San Francisco, Hotel Ranges; The Boynton Company, of Chicago, Furnaces; The Minnesota Refrigerator Company, of St. Paul, and many others.

O. H. HARLAN.

ONE of the most complete establishments engaged in the somber industry of undertaking on the Pacific coast is that belonging to the above named gentleman, and situated at 1151 C street, Tacoma. Robes, shrouds, coffins and caskets are here displayed in such lavish abundance that one might well believe that Mr. Harlan was prepared to bury the whole city of Tacoma. At any rate, it may readily be understood that his claim of carrying the largest stock of goods of any concern in his line in this city, is founded on fact.

Mr. Harlan's personality and demeanor are by no means suggestive of his occupation. He is a slender, scholarly looking gentleman on the sunny side of fifty, and though polite and courteous in manner, has an expression about the mouth that announces to the student of character that it would be unsafe to "stir him up" too much. He has been engaged in the undertaking business in all its branches ever since he was a boy of thirteen, a period of time extending over thirty-six years. The writer has heard him tell with infinite gusto and many chuckles, his early experiences when an apprentice in the then frontier State of Indiana. How he frequently had to construct coffins from the very slab; how, the coffin made, he would have to harness the team to the old-fashioned box hearse and drive it over a "blazed" road through dismal forests, with the wolves and panthers snarling at him from the thicket, until he reached the farmhouse where the corpse lay, perhaps twenty miles distant.

Mr. Harlan handled the first metallic burial case ever shipped. It was long and oval in shape, and technically called the "Mummy Casket." This was when he was working for Westlow, Thayer & Co., of Peru, Ind. Shortly afterward he became interested in the science of embalming, and followed up the study with indefatigable ardor. He traveled in Europe, Asia and Africa—that is Egypt—in pursuing his investigations, and became one of the most expert embalmers of modern times.

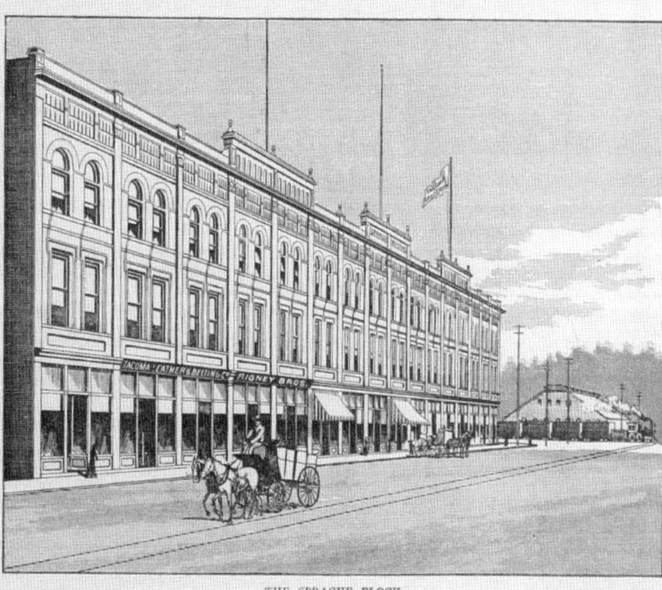

THE SPRAGUE BLOCK.

THE TACOMA BUSINESS COLLEGE.

This college, at 938 Pacific Avenue, is "a school that gives a practical education," and it is not for a moment to be doubted that a business education, such as can be acquired here, does sharpen and develop the reasoning and perceptive faculties, and fit one for the active duties of life.

Prof. John W. Tait is the principal of the college, and is assisted by a corps of capable teachers. He is prepared to ground pupils thoroughly in single and double entry bookkeeping, plain penmanship, commercial law, business arithmetic, practical grammar, letter writing, spelling, actual business and office practice, exchange, partnership settlements, business forms, Algebra, Geometry, Trigonometry, Statics and Hydrostatics, Greek, Latin, French, and German.

The college occupies upper floor of 938, and is already full to overflowing, so that increased quarters will soon be needed to accommodate all its pupils. Mr. Tait was born in Canada, and has been engaged in teaching for over twenty-eight years. He is not only thoroughly experienced in his profession, but is a man of very considerable ability, and is endowed with an excellent education.

RIGNEY BROTHERS.

This well-known firm is located in the Sprague Block, on Pacific Avenue, near 17th street. The firm name was originally Rigney & Foy. They deal in general produce, and more especially in hay, grain and feed, in which latter articles they do a very heavy business. The concern utilizes the services of six employes, and requires two teams to handle its increasing business. The Messrs. Rigney, John R. Jr., and J. W. R. respectively, were both born on this coast at no great distance from Tacoma. One of them in his earlier years held a responsible position in the employ of the Hudson Bay Company, which in those days monopolized about all the business of the Northwest. Before engaging in the commission business the Rigney Brothers were engaged in ranching on an extensive scale. The ranch is at Lakeview, and still in their possession. It comprises about 1,600 acres.

THE STEWART & HOLMES DRUG COMPANY.

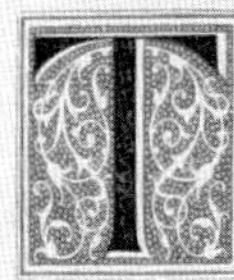

TWO bright young men a few years ago came from the province of Ontario, Canada, to establish on Puget Sound a first class drug-store. They opened an establishment in Seattle, which speedily became the leading pharmacy of that city, and afterward opened a branch store in the rising city of Tacoma. This branch store was established several years ago, and the business has continued to grow in proportion with the growth of Tacoma, and what was once the branch store in Tacoma, is now the headquarters of the company which has been formed with the addition of the large business of Mr. H. E. Holmes, a prominent druggist of Walla Walla, a growing city in Eastern Washington. These two young men were brothers, A. B. and A. M. Stewart, both graduates of the best pharmaceutical colleges on the Continent. The store of the company at 910 Pacific avenue, is very handsomely and tastefully fitted up. The company has opened accounts only with those houses that supply the purest and best drugs and chemicals. Those at the head of the company are men of more than ordinary ability as practical chemists, and they have special medicines prepared by themselves that received the indorsement of the best physicians in the State of Washington. When the company was organized, there was a demand for a wholesale drug house in the Territory. The company has filled this want, and now has three jobbing houses, one in Seattle, one in Walla Walla, and the third in Tacoma, and are constantly extending their business. The outlook for conducting the most extensive drug business in the State is very hopeful. The officers of the company are A. B. Stewart, president; A. M. Stewart, secretary, and H. E. Holmes, treasurer, all most energetic and capable men.

E. W. TAYLOR

has his offices on the corner of Pacific avenue and Thirteenth street. Mr. Taylor is a scholarly-looking man with lines of determination and energy on his face. He is a native of Ottawa, but came to the Pacific coast when a child. He graduated at the Santa Rosa College in California before he reached his majority, and then he managed a large farm in that State. After this he taught school, became interested in mining, and finally studied law. He was admitted to the bar in Nevada, and it is characteristic of Mr. Taylor that there were five applicants for admission at the time, and he was the only one who successfully passed. He was afterward County Attorney for Esmeralda County, Nevada. He finally came to Washington, settling in Tacoma.

THE TACOMA PASSENGER AND BAGGAGE TRANSFER COMPANY.

Since the old stage coach was abolished and fast through trains have been made to carry passengers from one side of the continent to the other, travel has increased to an enormous extent, and the general public have demanded better facilities for reaching the hotels from the depots, and for the care of the baggage and movable property. These facilities are supplied by the transfer companies in the various cities, and no city in the United States has a more complete system than that supplied by the Tacoma Passenger and Baggage Transfer Company, under the management of Mr. J. R. Patton.

The company has recently completed one of the finest carriage houses with barns and stables for horses, to be found anywhere. The methods of handling baggage have been reduced by Mr. Patton to perfection. Baggage is checked at the house of the owner, the checks handed over to him and his railway ticket is furnished him by the company without the necessity of his doing more than call up the transfer office by telephone; all the trouble incident to travel is thus removed from his shoulders by the system now in vogue, and his journey is rendered more pleasant because he is relieved of all worry. The company furnishes all of the buses for the leading hotels, and has a large number of handsome carriages and hacks.

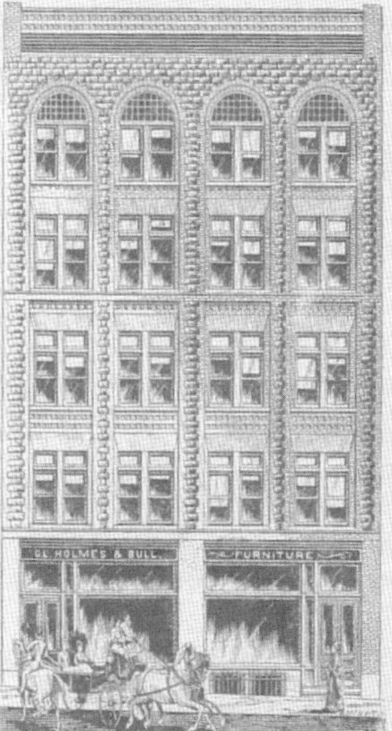

HOLMES & BULL'S NEW BUILDING.

G. L. HOLMES & BULL.

The above concern at this time of writing are located at 716 and 720 Pacific avenue, but expect to be able to occupy their new and spacious building, now in the process of erection on the east side of C street, between Ninth and Tenth streets before the new year comes in. The business is only a year old, but it has grown and flourished and increased with that amazing rapidity which seems to be characteristic of the City of Destiny. Messrs. Holmes & Bull claim—and with acknowledged justice—to carry a larger line of fine furniture than any firm doing business on the coast north of San Francisco. They also do a large jobbing trade in cheap furniture as well as a wholesale and retail trade in upholstering and carpets.

Mr. G. L. Holmes has been engaged in the manufacture of furniture all his life, and his knowledge of the business includes the smallest details. A. E. Bull, the second partner, is a Bostonian, who was so impressed with the advantages possessed by this coast from a business point of view, that he has come to permanently cast his lot among us. His energy and shrewdness have had much to do with building up the business to its present proportions.

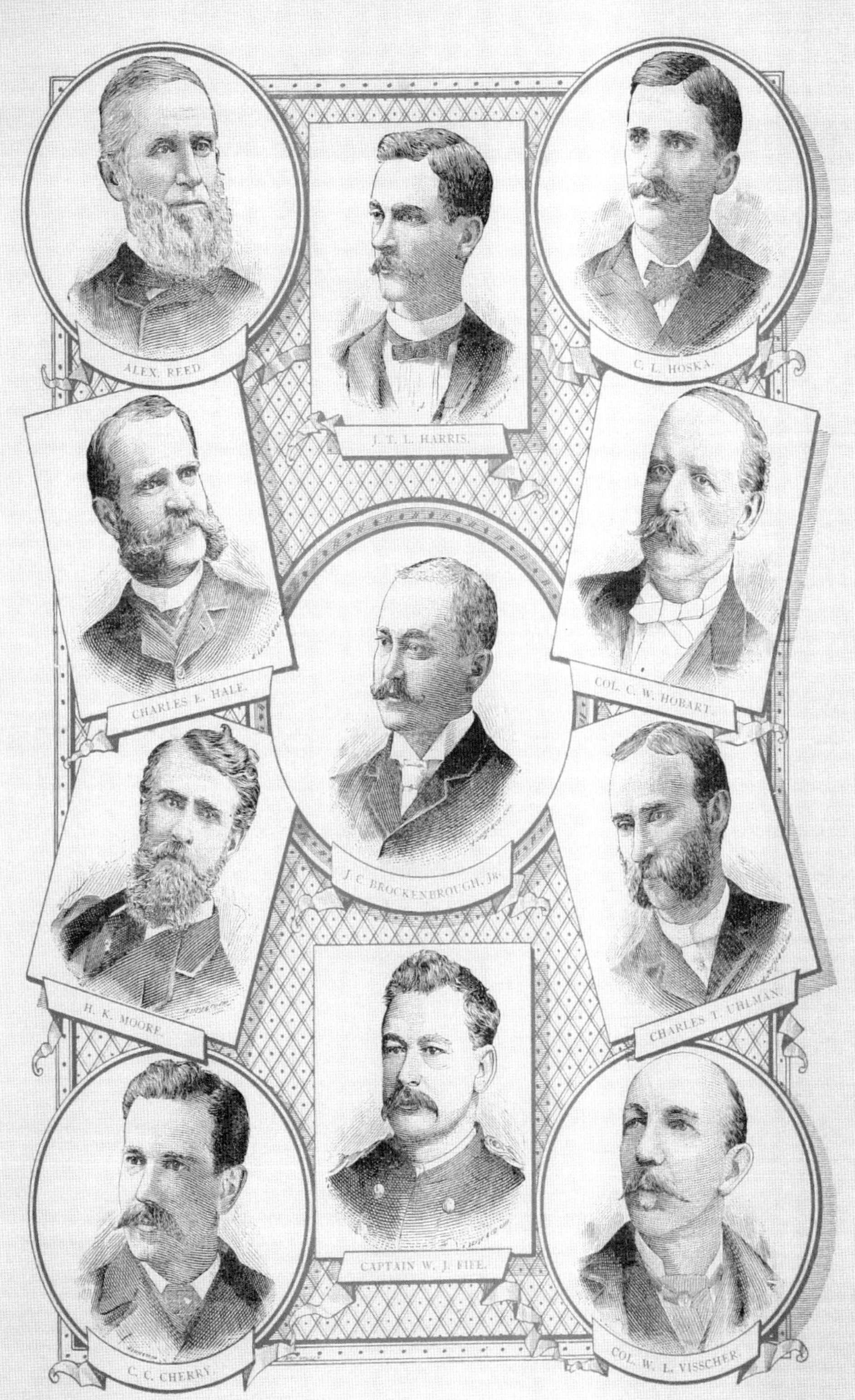

PROMINENT MEN OF TACOMA.

PUGET SOUND PRINTING COMPANY.

AMONG the many remarkably thriving institutions of this wonderfully progressive city, is the Puget Sound Printing Company, the interior of whose office is made the subject of one of our illustrations. This company was organized about a year and a half ago, and was formed by the consolidation of two small job offices, having nothing larger than a quarter medium press, and with a capital stock of $10,000. The company at once purchased the *Ledger* job office, leased the rooms in the *Ledger* building for one year, and took hold of the new business with a determination to build up a job-printing business that should keep pace with the growth of the city, and with an energy that meant success. Before the end of the year the business of the company had so much increased that it was compelled to remove to more commodious quarters. The capital stock of the company was also increased to $25,000, and a purchase was made of the plant of the *Tacoma World*, including an engine as well as three presses, and the company secured one-half of the upper floor of the Davis Block, where it has now the largest and best equipped book and job printing establishment in the State of Washington, and is doing a very extensive business. Thus the power of the press asserts itself in new countries at the very start, nor waits for their growth. The present board of directors of the company are, F. F. Hopkins, president and manager; E. L. Jones, secretary; Geo. A. Tuesley, treasurer; Geo. F. Orchard and Geo. P. Eaton. In addition to their general job printing business, which extends to all parts of the State, it publishes a full line of real estate and legal blanks, a line which, with the growing transactions in real estate and kindred business, will call for a large supply, and which can be found at their establishment, as they have secured a large wholesale trade, which they are amply able to make a permanent and profitable one.

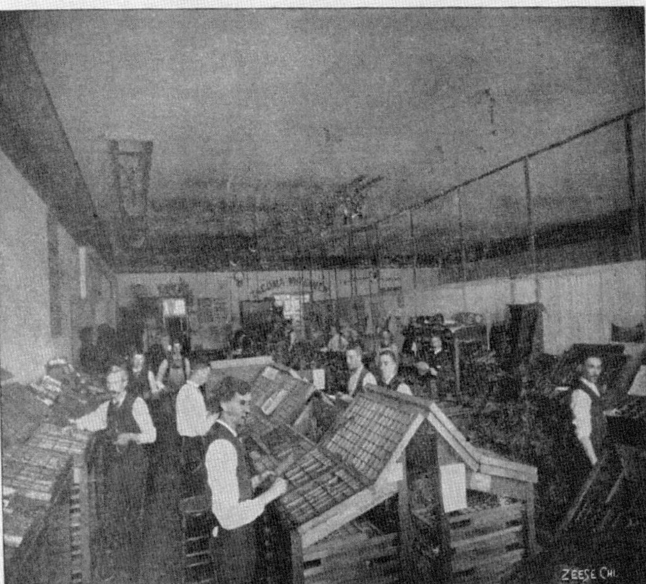

PUGET SOUND PRINTING COMPANY'S OFFICE.

EFFINGER & ABBOTT.

This firm on Pacific Ave., opposite Tenth, may be described as belonging to the class of men we would wish to be thoroughly representative of Tacoma. Mr. Effinger was born and brought up in the State of Virginia, and is a warm-hearted, chivalrous, impulsive Southerner. His forte is criminal and admiralty law, and in that line he is reputed to be exceptionally brilliant and signally successful. Mr. T. O. Abbott is a considerably younger man than his partner, with whom he, in fact, studied. He was born in Illinois, but his father came across the "great divide" with a wagon train when our subject was only three years of age, and settled in Portland, Oregon. Here Mr. Abbott grew to manhood. His father being extensively engaged as a publisher, the son naturally embraced newspaper work as a profession, and when he reached his majority he was already the proprietor as well as editor of a most flourishing journal at Dayton, W. T.

About this period he began to study law, and was finally admitted to the bar in Salem. He is thoroughly posted on realty law, and attends to that portion of the firm's large and rapidly increasing business with earnestness and ability.

Tacoma is rapidly taking rank among the well built cities of the new Northwest. Her public edifices are substantial and handsome. One of the finest brick blocks in the city has recently been erected by Mr. Abbott on C street, and the postal department at Washington has seen fit to locate the postoffice in the building. The block was erected at the cost of many thousands of dollars, and the owner can congratulate himself that there is not another building in the city that is more substantial, or of more elegant finish. A cut of this edifice is given in this book among the public buildings of Tacoma, with which our work is so profusely ornamented, and affords still another undeniable proof of the excellent taste and liberality of spirit which so strongly characterized Tacoma's founders, and which to-day stands as a monument to its future greatness.

SMITH, ROOT & JORDAN.

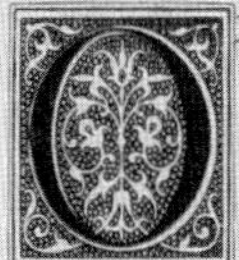

ONE of the most successful real estate firms in Tacoma is that composed of Col. J. D. Smith, L. T. Root and T. R. Jordan. Their partnership has been in existence a comparatively short time, but it has proved very lucrative. Messrs. Smith & Root were first associated together, Mr. Jordan becoming a member at a later date. Besides being owners of and agents for large properties in the most eligible locations of Tacoma, they are building fine residences here and there, and thus beautifying and improving their property.

They are associated with Messrs. Ross & Naubert and others in the Lake City Land and Railway and Navigation Companies, and these assuredly successful ventures will no doubt bring them handsome and substantial returns for the capital which they have invested so wisely.

The publishers of this work are indebted to the gentlemen of this concern for such courtesies as can hardly be repaid, and desire herewith to express their thanks. While all three members of the firm kindly placed their office at the disposal of the publishers, Col. Smith extended many social kindnesses which will always be fondly cherished. Col. Smith is a Southern gentleman, and is in every way a typical Mississippian, being whole-souled and generous to very near a fault; he spent much of his valuable time in showing to the compiler of this book the principal features of Tacoma, and which are destined to make it a great city.

Col. Smith owns a fine residence in the city and proposes next year building a fine Southern home on the Tacoma Land Co.'s site

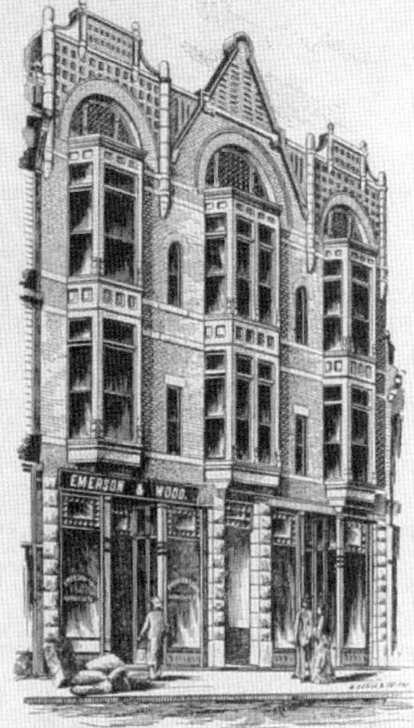

OFFICES OF EMERSON & WOOD.

EMERSON & WOOD.

This firm of well known commission merchants, situated at 936 C street, started in business here in August, 1889, in a new handsome brick block just completed.

Mr. S. H. Emerson is lately from St. Paul, Minn., where he is well known and bears a most favorable reputation as a careful financier and business manager. He was quite recently with Mr. Morgan in the commission business in Tacoma. Mr. W. H. Wood, the second member of the firm, hails from San Jose, Cal., in which place he was connected in a responsible capacity with the First National Bank. He is now largely interested in the Washington National Bank of Tacoma.

Emerson & Wood handle a full line of fruits, vegetables, farm produce, etc. Butter and eggs they make a specialty. They are working up a fine country trade, and buy goods from Oregon, Washington, Minnesota and California. Having ample capital to work with, they intend doing a large business, such as will be a credit to the City of Destiny.

ISAAC W. ANDERSON.

It is with regret that the absence of Mr. Anderson has prevented us from obtaining his photograph for insertion among the representative men of the city of Tacoma. Mr. Anderson is the general manager of the Tacoma Land Co., and his affable manner as well as honorable dealings, alike with rich and poor, have not only done much for the upbuilding of the city's manufacturing interests, by the Land Company, but have gained for him the confidence, regard and respect of all classes.

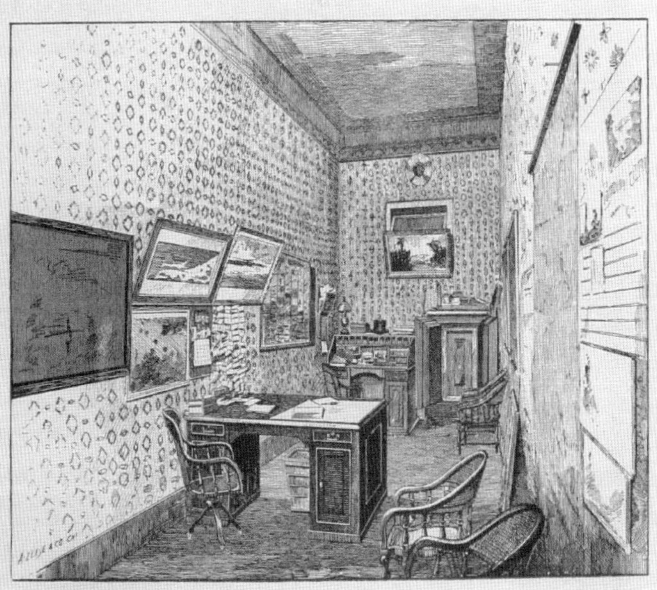

OFFICES OF SMITH, ROOT & JORDAN.

E. C. VAUGHAN & CO.,

WHOLESALE AND RETAIL DEALERS IN BOOKS, STATIONERY, OFFICE AND SCHOOL SUPPLIES, 1102 PACIFIC AVE.

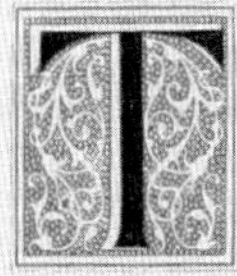

HIS firm is an old established one in Tacoma. It is six years since Mr. Vaughan and his associates first opened their present business in Tacoma. To residents in the East, six years is not considered a very long period, but of those who have spent that time in Tacoma, there are hundreds who have made handsome fortunes. During this time Messrs. Vaughan & Co.'s business has grown with the City of Destiny until it equals any of the prominent business houses in the city. This firm is the exclusive agents for United States coast survey charts, for Andrews' school and office supplies, and the Globe filing company. Attention is especially drawn to this firm's assortment of draughtsmen's and architects' supplies, which is complete and unrivaled by any other firm in the city. The firm consists of Messrs. E. C. Vaughan, C. W. Morrell, and T. J. Thompson; these gentlemen also own a half interest in the Tacoma Picture Frame Company, which establishment is located in the rear end of the store.

CONRAD L. HOSKA.

This well-known undertaker has his office on the corner of Pacific avenue and Thirteenth street. He is well known as the leading man in his line in Tacoma, and is probably the best funeral conductor north of San Francisco. He always keeps on hand a full line of burial goods of every description and variety, and is ready to meet any demand that may be made on him in his business with promptness and dispatch. He is still a young man, and possessed of much shrewdness and business energy which enables him to distance all competitors. He is also a public spirited citizen, and largely concerned in many of the important enterprises that have tended to make Tacoma the City of Destiny.

WALKER H. TISDALE.

This gentleman has been identified with the fortunes of Tacoma for the last seven years. At that time he came here from Detroit, Michigan, and recognizing the immense future possibilities of the City of Destiny, threw himself into the field, and bought property wherever he thought he was justified in the purchase. As a consequence he is now the possessor of some of the choicest business and residence sites in the city, which are rapidly becoming very valuable. Mr. Tisdale is one of the most undaunted believers in the future of Tacoma, and if the city, as we all hope, ever becomes the New York of the Pacific coast, will reap the harvest of his faith by being one of the richest and most popular men upon this coast.

SAUL & AVERY.

These prominent and well-known merchants have three stores for the sale of groceries and food products in Tacoma. The head and principal is in their commodious building on the corner of Ninth and E streets, while the others are located respectively at 1916 Jefferson, and 1919 D streets. Their telephone call is No. 159.

Both partners are thorough grocers, and they do business in a business-like manner. Their stock is well selected and complete, and the system and order, and attention to detail, with which they conduct their business is simply unrivaled. Their knowledge and judgment as to quality of goods, gives them a decided advantage over their competitors, and thus enables them to assert with truth that they carry the very best stock of staple and fancy groceries on Puget Sound. The fact that they do such a large trade, gives them another decided advautage over business rivals, as it enables them to buy in large quantities—purchasing proportionately cheaper—and consequently able to undersell others in their line, and give their patrons the benefit of the transaction in superior quality at the same price. Messrs. Saul & Avery are agents for the following line of goods, to which they would call especial attention, as being of the very finest quality:

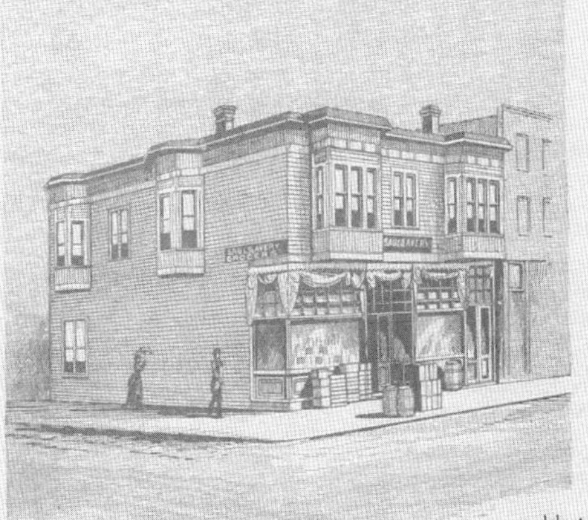

SAUL & AVERY'S STORE.

Silver Spray Flour.

Fleischman & Co.'s Compressed Yeast.

Huntley & Palmer's Crackers, Confections, and Fruit Cakes.

Rountree's Chocolates, Cocoas and Elect. Cocoa Extract.

Knorr's Soup Tablets.

Wurzen Salt and Sugar Wafers.

Kennedy's Biscuits.

Bent's Water Crackers.

American Business Co. Crackers, Wafers, etc.

German and French canned and bottled meats and patties.

Cross & Blackwell's pickles, jams, jellies, etc.

Gordon & Dillworth, Snider, Haas (Wiesbaden), etc., preserves, jellies, jams, etc.

DR. WILLIS E. EVERETTE.

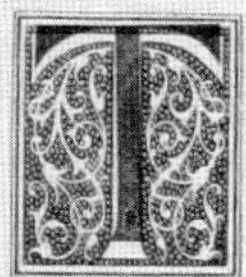

THIS gentleman, to whom we are indebted for valuable information in our article on minerals, is one of the best known mining geologists and experts on the Pacific slope; he has made the minerals of Washington, Idaho, British Columbia and Alaska, a study for years, and there are few men so competent as he to give information on this particular subject. Dr. Everette has made tests of every conceivable description, and the results of these tests will certainly be of great value to the industries relating to their subjects; he has on exhibition at his mining office, No. 1318 E street, Tacoma, some four thousand samples of ores, minerals, coals, clays, etc., of the Pacific Northwest, and he has expressed his willingness to show them to any accredited persons and give honest and trustworthy information relative thereto; he will also send, on application, a price list for all kinds of mining, engineering, assay and analysis work. In connection with his office, Dr. Everette has a fine chemical laboratory where most of his tests are made.

Those who wish information relative to the keramic industries and possibilities of the Puget Sound basin, would do well to confer with him as he has lately made a collection of the many various kinds of clay found here, and is now subjecting them to a practical test. Already he has secured kaolin clays which will make beautiful porcelain ware, fire clays which have stood over 3300° Fahrenheit, and tile and brick clay which will make a beautiful yellow red tile or bright red pressed brick.

These heats may be relied upon, as Dr. Everette uses the best imported "Pyrometers" direct from the Prussian government factory of the Royal Berlin Porcelain works at Charlottensburg, Prussia.

To those, therefore, who take an interest in the mineral properties of Washington, a visit to Dr. Everette's office will be a great treat, and will give them thoughts on these subjects which will not only afford great enlightenment, but would be difficult and on some points actually impossible to obtain elsewhere.

F. S. HARMON & CO.

This furniture house has its headquarters at 926 Pacific avenue, and is the oldest established house in Tacoma in this line; the firm probably do the most extensive business of any furniture house on Puget Sound. They handle everything in the way of furniture, and it is so arranged on their different floors as to present as handsome showrooms as can be found in the city. They have also a large warehouse situated close to the tracks of the Northern Pacific railroad, making it accessible.

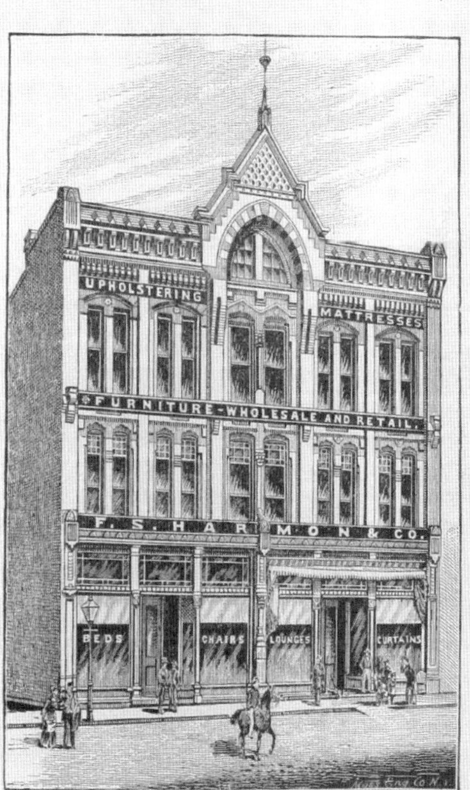

Mr. F. S. Harmon is a young man and has met with great success in the City of Destiny. Some years ago he came to Tacoma, in company with John Macready, the hardware merchant, and the success of both has been phenomenal. Mr. Harmon, soon after establishing his business, took up a claim of government land adjoining the city, and retains this property to the present day; its value can hardly be estimated, as it is now eligible for residence sites, and from that holding alone Mr. Harmon could realize a handsome fortune. But his business in itself has yielded immense profits, and it is due to him to say that it was built up by his energy alone; he has a shrewd intellect and keen perceptions, courteous demeanor, and great determination, and is also a prominent man in public affairs.

WILLIAM S. TAYLOR.

William S. Taylor was born in Lawrence County, Pennsylvania, Oct. 5, 1840. His father, Col. Joseph W. Taylor, with his family, moved to Iowa in 1845, and the subject of this sketch was raised in Iowa, near Keokuk; but in 1861 returned to Pennsylvania, remaining there until 1868, when he was ordained to the ministry in the Free Will Baptist Church. As a pulpit orator he has few equals. He believes a business man should be a Christian, and while one of the most successful real estate brokers, he preaches and lectures constantly. He is a very kind and generous man, and has been honored in many ways by his fellow men. He represented the Nez Perces District in the Idaho Senate with ability and distinction in the session of 1883–84. He and his estimable wife and son, Orrin DeW. Taylor,

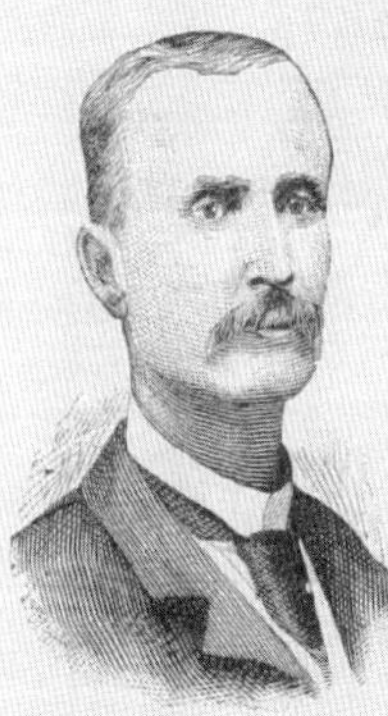

W. S. TAYLOR.

and his beloved mother, reside at Orting, in one of the loveliest spots on Puget Sound (Rivulet Park), Orting, W. T., and his gardens are the very finest in the Puyallup Valley.

A HOME ON PUGET SOUND.

No real estate broker on the Sound can offer better bargains than Mr. Taylor, owning as he does a large amount of propery in all parts of Orting and Tacoma, and throughout Pierce County, and no one who has invested through his office has ever failed so far to realize on it handsomely. He has the finest property in Orting and "Lake View," and offers great inducements to those seeking nice homes in these lovely villages, or in Tacoma, or in small farms on the Sound and wheat farms in Eastern Washington. He particularly recommends his five and ten acre tracts near the great City of Destiny. All inquiries made of him are promptly and reliably answered from his Orting office.

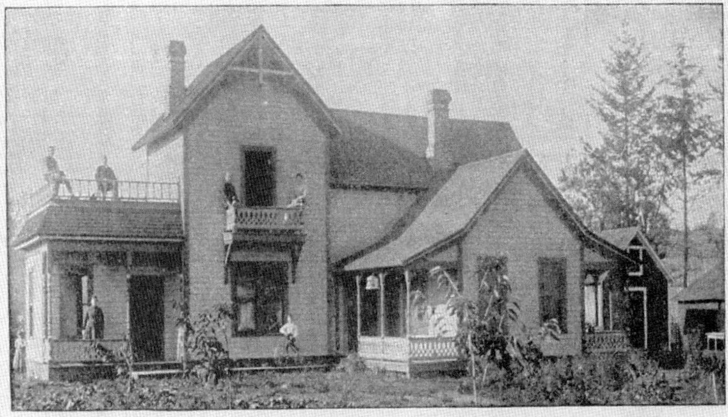

RESIDENCE OF W. S. TAYLOR AT ORTING, WASHINGTON.

E. STEINBACH,

Notary Public and Conveyancer.

This gentleman's offices are situated at 909 Pacific avenue. He does a large business in real estate, loans and mortgages, and is one of the busiest men in this busy city; his office is constantly thronged with visitors desirous of investing in some of the numerous real estate properties which he controls.

He started business in this city in 1886, and his resistless energies have done as much toward forwarding Tacoma's interests and advertising its merits to the world, as that of any other one man. He also stands sponsor for the well known "Swett's Addition," and handles besides, various other very choice acreage and addition property.

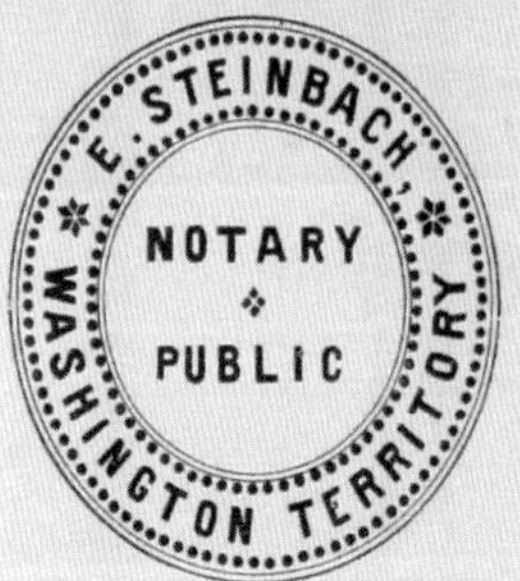

Mr. Steinbach has had a most valuable experience in his own line of business, and combines his natural bent for the business with strict integrity in all his transactions, thus building up a reputation for probity which will last as long as Tacoma does.

C. A. SNOWDEN & CO.

Real Estate, City Property and Timber Lands,

This firm has its offices at 918 A street, opposite the Tacoma, and, though one of the youngest, is one of the most active and enterprising in the city. Before coming to this Coast, Mr. Snowden was engaged in the newspaper business, to which he was educated by the late Wilbur F. Storey, the founder and famous editor of the *Chicago Times*. He began work as night reporter on that paper, after leaving college in 1872, and in less than three years was made city editor, a place which he held until 1880, when he was made managing editor, with full authority. Under his management the paper undertook and carried successfully some of the best known enterprises which made it famous, and gave it the largest circulation of any newspaper in the West. Among these was the publication of the revised edition of the New Testament entire, in its Sunday morning edition. Previous to this publication of the Testament, the *Times* had secured, through its special correspondent in London, extracts amounting to four thousand words which were cabled over and published nearly a month in advance of any publication elsewhere. This was probably the longest cable message ever sent to any single newspaper up to that time. When Mr. Storey began to be incapacitated for business in 1882, Mr. Snowden went to Washington and became manager of *The National Republican*, which he conducted successfully up to the end of President Arthur's administration. In the spring of 1885 he made his first visit to the Coast, and after about a month spent in California returned East with the firm determination to come back at some future time and remain here permanently. This determination he did not immediately carry out, however. Finding what he thought a promising opening in his old business he formed a company and purchased the *Chicago Mail* in June, 1885, and in three years built it up from a very unpromising beginning to be one of the most attractive evening papers in Chicago. In 1887 he got together the combination which ended the litigation over the Storey estate, by buying up the claims of all the heirs, not only to *The Times* but to all the rest of the property which the deceased editor had possessed. The negotiations which led up to the successful conclusion of this deal, involving over $600,000, were made possible by Mr. Snowden's former connection with the paper and his acquaintance with the parties, and they were carried out largely through his efforts. By this success he became the owner of a considerable block of *The Times* stock, and was made editor of that sheet, which position he filled until December, 1888, during which time the paper, which had suffered considerably during the long period of litigation following the death of Mr. Storey, was restored to its old time prosperity, its circulation increasing by 7,000 copies per day more than it ever had in its most successful days under its former proprietor.

During his management of *The Mail* Mr. Snowden organized and was prominent in the conduct of the "boodle" investigation in Cook County which resulted in sending five of the conspirators to the penitentiary for three years each, the sentence of two others to similar terms, which they escaped by a reversal of their case in the Supreme Court, and the conviction of three others, who paid fines.

Leaving the newspaper business in 1888, through a disagreement with the other stockholders, none of whom had ever had any previous experience in newspaper management, Mr. Snowden again came West and began at once to apply himself to his new business. He has been abundantly successful. He has made a careful study not only of the city but the resources of the State, particularly of its timber, about which he can perhaps furnish as much reliable information as even the oldest resident. While in control of *The Times* in 1881, he sent John F. Finerty, the famous war correspondent and explorer of that paper, over the line of the Northern Pacific railroad, then completed to Missoula. The series of letters furnished by that brilliant correspondent, and printed at the time, were widely read and commented on, and no doubt did much to swell the tide of immigration which has since set strongly toward the Puget Sound country. He now regards this enterprise as one of his principal journalistic successes. Mr. Snowden is an enthusiastic believer in Tacoma, and the new State of Washington.

C. E. CASE, M. D.

Dr. Case, a prominent and well known physician, is one of the representative men of Tacoma, and there are few citizens to whom we may point with more pride than we do to him. Dr. Case is not only representative, but he is the ideal type of Westerner who has made the Pacific coast the wonder of latter-day civilization by the audacity and immensity of her enterprises and the vigor and determination with which they are carried to a successful conclusion. Dr. Case is a large man physically as well as intellectually, and his magnificent growth of black beard renders his individuality still more striking. He was born in California, but studied medicine in St. Louis during his earlier manhood. He practiced medicine in that city during the years 1876, 1877, and 1878. Then he returned to San Francisco and took a course of study in the Medical College of the Pacific, which is now known as the Cooper College. He afterward attended the California Medical College, from which he graduated in 1880. He was then offered and accepted the chair of Professor of Surgical Anatomy in that institution. He filled it with great credit to himself and satisfaction to the faculty during the courses of 1881 and 1882. Shortly afterward he came to Tacoma and soon built up a large and flourishing practice in this city. Besides possessing the credentials to the confidence of the community already enumerated, the Doctor graduated from the College of Physicians and Surgeons of Chicago in 1886, from the New York Post Graduate Medical School and New York Polyclinic in 1888, and has certificates of private instruction from Prof. A. Reeves Jackson of Chicago, on surgical diseases of women; of John E. Harper, A. M., M. D., of Chicago, on the eye and ear and the use of the ophthalmoscope and otoscope, and correction of the errors of refraction. He has also a certificate from the New York Polyclinic for the satisfactory performance of operations in the Surgery Sessions of 1888 and 1889.

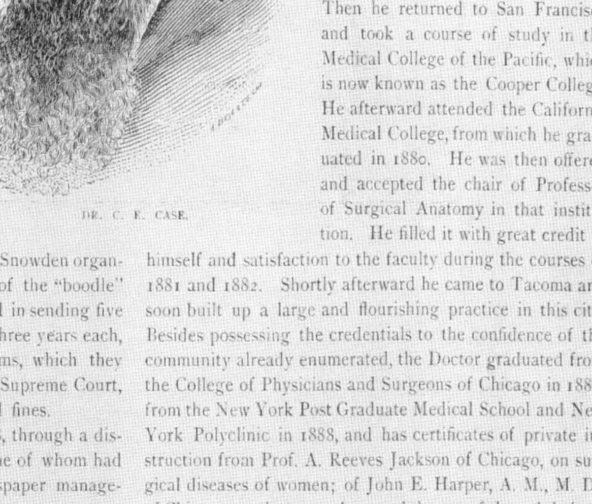

DR. C. E. CASE.

Since Dr. Case has been located in Tacoma, he has performed many remarkable and interesting operations. Among them, indeed, were some that have made his reputation almost world wide. Notably the case of Alfred Huntington, the son of John Huntington of the firm of Huntington & Little, was the eighth instance of successful abdominal operation for gunshot wound of the liver on record throughout the world. The boy was shot through the body by a 32-caliber pistol, the ball passing through the boy's liver. The abdominal cavity was opened its whole length, and the injured structures properly cared for. A great deal of blood was found in the abdominal cavity, which was thoroughly cleansed and all bleeding vessels secured preparatory to closing the abdominal walls by silver wire and catgut sutures. Since the operation the abdominal cavity has been washed out as often as the temperature indicated any danger of blood poisoning, a glass drainage tube being left in the abdominal cavity for that purpose. The strictest antiseptic precautions have been observed throughout the operation, and the subsequent treatment, and the boy may now with certainty be pronounced as out of danger.

An almost equally interesting case was that of Jesse Steele, a fifteen year old boy, who lately shot himself in the forearm in this city. Owing to the retraction the skin on the arm could not be brought together and then caught up by sutures, so Dr. Case grafted skin from the upper forearm on to the naked place, and the boy is now almost well. He has also performed several very difficult surgical operations within the past sixty days.

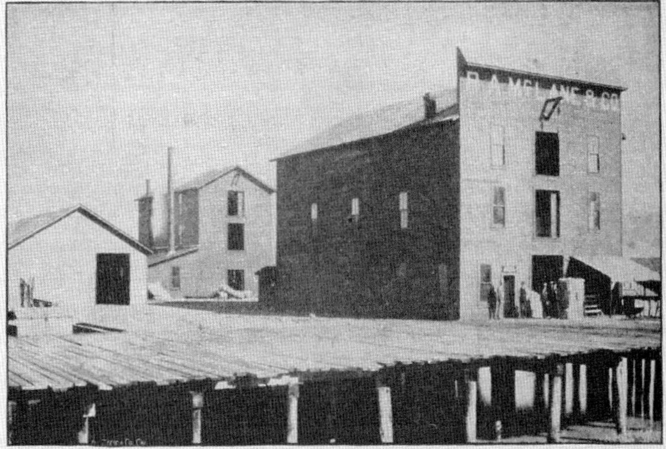

Dr. Case is as much in love with Tacoma as if it were his birthplace, and extols its virtues and advantages to every visitor he meets. He takes an active part in the welfare of the city, and there is seldom a movement on foot for the city's benefit which does not surely find him in some way identified with its promotion.

PUBLISHERS' NOTICE.

The publishers of this work cannot express too highly their appreciation of the encouragement given their work and the liberal handed policy pursued during its compilation by the citizens of Tacoma; our feelings in this regard may be understood when it is stated that Mr. C. A. Snowden was our first acquaintance in the city, and this gentleman did a world of good for the interests of the book; Mr. Isaac W. Anderson of the Tacoma Land Co., interested himself to a great extent and much of the compilation as well as embellishment of the book was due to his most timely suggestions.

Many other gentlemen of Tacoma whose names we have already mentioned did everything possible in its behalf but there is one who may be said to head the list and whose name has not yet found a place in our columns.. This is Mr. S. A. Wheelwright, the honored mayor of Tacoma, a man who is the embodiment of refinement, intellect, modesty, education, courtesy and love for, and pride in the city of Tacoma; there is no one in Tacoma whose friendship we can point to with more pride than that of Mayor Wheelwright, and we wish it were in our power to reciprocate his disinterested kindness; as this is not possible, we can only thank him and assure him of our heartfelt appreciation.

TACOMA ILLUSTRATED

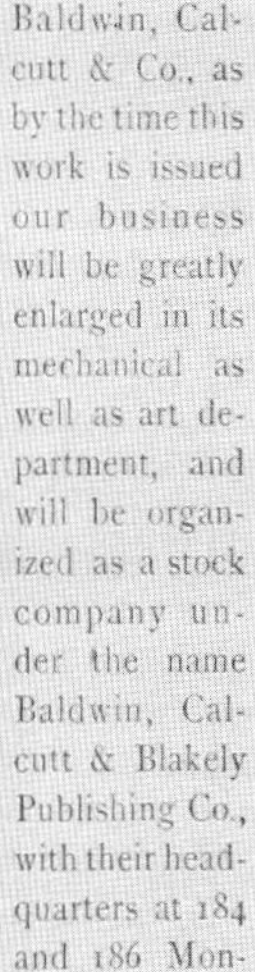

is the last book which will be published under the name of Baldwin, Calcutt & Co., as by the time this work is issued our business will be greatly enlarged in its mechanical as well as art department, and will be organized as a stock company under the name Baldwin, Calcutt & Blakely Publishing Co., with their headquarters at 184 and 186 Monroe street, Chicago; heretofore we have outside of Chicago and vicinity solicited little else than publishing contracts, but the new company will include not only general lines of publications, but in addition a general printing, binding, engraving and lithographing business; our departments include the largest composition rooms in Chicago, our line of steam presses are of the largest and most improved patterns; the binding, engraving and lithographing departments are second to none, and our staff of artists includes some of the best known for portrait, map and scenic work to be found in the country. The variety of work produced may to a limited extent be seen in this volume; we shall establish a branch in some city of Washington, and do business with all parts of the State as well as the Pacific Coast.

We would therefore be glad to give estimates for any description of composition, printing, binding, lithographing, and map, pen, wood, half-toned and zinc-etched engraving. BALDWIN, CALCUTT & CO.

New Company—

BALDWIN, CALCUTT & BLAKELY PUBLISHING CO.

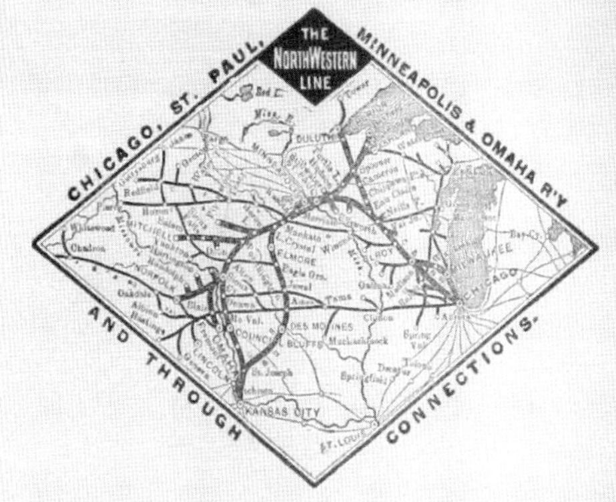

THE

"NORTHWESTERN LINE"

IS THE

GREAT SHORT LINE

Between Principal Points as shown on Map.

It was the first line in the Northwest to run Pullman Sleeping Cars.

It was the first line in the Northwest to run Dining Cars.

It was the first line in the Northwest to run Vestibuled Trains.

OTHER LINES MAY IMITATE BUT CANNOT SURPASS IT, EITHER IN EQUIPMENT OR TRAIN SERVICE, AND ALL TRAVELERS ADMIT THAT ITS MOTTO,

"A·L·W·A·Y·S ✦ O·N ✦ T·I·M·E"

IS AN ESTABLISHED FACT.

Be sure and ask for Tickets over "The Northwestern Line." Tickets can be secured at Offices of Connecting Roads.

THE FOLLOWING ARE PRINCIPAL OFFICES OF THE LINE:

ST. PAUL, 159 East Third St. MINNEAPOLIS, 13 Nicollet House Block. DULUTH, 332 Hotel St. Louis Block.
MILWAUKEE, 102 Wisconsin St. NEW YORK, 409 Broadway. OMAHA, 1401 Farnam St.
PORTLAND, ORE., 4 Washington St. CHICAGO, 208 South Clark St.

For Rates, or any desired Information, address,

E. W. WINTER,
General Manager.

F. B. CLARKE,
General Traffic Manager.

T. W. TEASDALE,
Gen. Passenger Agt., ST. PAUL.

CHICAGO, MILWAUKEE & ST. PAUL RY.

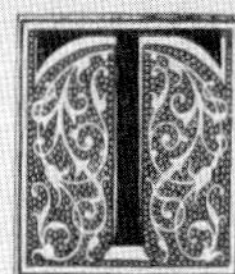

THE Chicago, Milwaukee & St. Paul Railway is the longest line owned by one company in the world, being 5,670 miles in length, and its tracks run through a never-ending panorama of all that is entrancing in the way of sublime scenery.

In Illinois it operates 316 miles of track; in Wisconsin, 1,304 miles; in Iowa, 1,572 miles; in Minnesota, 1,122 miles; in Dakota, 1,216 miles; in Missouri, 140 miles, and the end is not yet. It has terminals in such large cities as Chicago, Milwaukee, LaCrosse, St. Paul, Minneapolis, Fargo, Sioux City, Council Bluffs, Omaha, Kansas City, St. Joseph, and along its lines are hundreds of thriving cities, towns, villages and hamlets. From the management manufacturing interests receive encouragement, and all branches of trade are fostered. The railroad company has a just appreciation of the taste of its patrons, and demonstrates that appreciation in every possible way, and its magnificent earnings point conclusively to the fact that the good feeling which it has for the traveling and shipping public is fully and fervently reciprocated. The populariiy of the line with both classes of customers is fully attested by the fact that, notwithstanding the severest kind of competition, both from old and new lines, the company continues to do an immense and ever increasing business. In point of freight and passenger equipment it is not surpassed by any line in the United States. On all its through lines it operates the most perfectly equipped trains of sleeping, parlor and dining cars and day coaches known to the modern car builder.

The freight business of the road is simply enormous, shippers having confidence in its ability to send their goods through on quick time, owing to the company's stupendous equipment. Even in the busiest season of the year, the fall and winter months, the patrons of the road are never compelled to wait for cars.

In one point the C. M. & St. Paul excels all others, and that is in regard to summer resort business. For years it has been regarded as the summer resort road, all the best points in Wisconsin, Minnesota and Iowa at which to pass the heated term being either reached by its lines or a close connection formed for them.

When one reflects on the number of people who annually cross the water in search of pleasure, and remembers how little there is over there that can be compared to the beauties of America, it is strange that people evince such a desire to view the so-called wonders of the Continent without first seeing the glories of their own land.

A journey over the lines of the C. M. & St. P. alone would demonstrate to these seekers after the alleged glories of the Old World that there is more that is sublimely beautiful in Uncle Sam's domains than in all the lands ruled over by all the kings, queens and emperors of Europe. Between Milwaukee, St. Paul and Minneapolis, over the Hastings and Dakota Division to Aberdeen and Roscoe, from the Cream City west by two routes to Woonsocket on the one hand and Chamberlain, Dakota, on the other; from the Garden City of Chicago to Omaha, on the banks of the "Big Muddy," and from Marion, Iowa, to the "City on the Kaw," the country presents one never-ending panorama of beautiful scenes. Over a stone ballasted steel track, as level as a board, a flight of eighty-five miles as swift as that of a carrier pigeon, lands the traveler in Milwaukee, the first point of importance from Chicago, on the Northwestern route. This is the metropolis of the Badger State, than which no finer place can be found for location and settlement, presenting as it does, the benefits of a new, unopened country without its disadvantages, for the complete system of railroads opens up every portion of the State, bringing city and country closely together, each to work in the other's interest. From the bustling city, through the towns, villages and hamlets, to the unbroken forests and prairies, the immigrant can take his choice, selecting both locality and occupation, that seem to offer him the greatest pecuniary reward for the honest toil he is willing to give in return for it.

While the State has been vastly improved, and large cities built with the wealth accumulated by well directed energy in the past, there is still plenty of room for development. At no time have inducements to settle in Wisconsin been so great as at present, for the years through which the pioneers have labored, and the results which they have accomplished, have been of vast benefit to the immigrant himself.

From Milwaukee north, the road penetrates the broad prairies of the North Star State, Minnesota, which contains a greater amount of interior lake and river surface than any other State in the Union, except Florida.

From Minneapolis, in a southerly direction, or from Milwaukee west, it penetrates the great commonwealth of Iowa, which is pre-eminently an agricultural State, the true source of whose greatness lies in the capacity of her soil to supply those staples necessary for the sustenance of mankind.

South from Cedar Rapids, Ia., in a direct line, the road operates its own line into Kansas City, Mo., tapping the richest, because the most extreme northerly portion of the State.

West from Chicago a line runs through Northern Illinois, a distance of over 300 miles, the advantages of which, as a place of residence, are without number. Almost in a straight line the C. M. & St. P. runs out through Southern Iowa, and at Council Bluffs and Omaha forms connections which enable it to ticket passengers or land seekers into the heart of the broad prairies of Nebraska, to the vast mineral deposits of the Centennial State, to the ranch of the cowboy and the cattleman in Wyoming, and even to the Pacific laved sands of the Golden State itself. At Kansas City connection is had with lines of road that gridiron the State of Kansas in every direction, so that the amount of business done by the road can no longer be a matter for marvel.

In this way almost every city and town in the country can be readily reached over the line of the Chicago, Milwaukee and St. Paul.

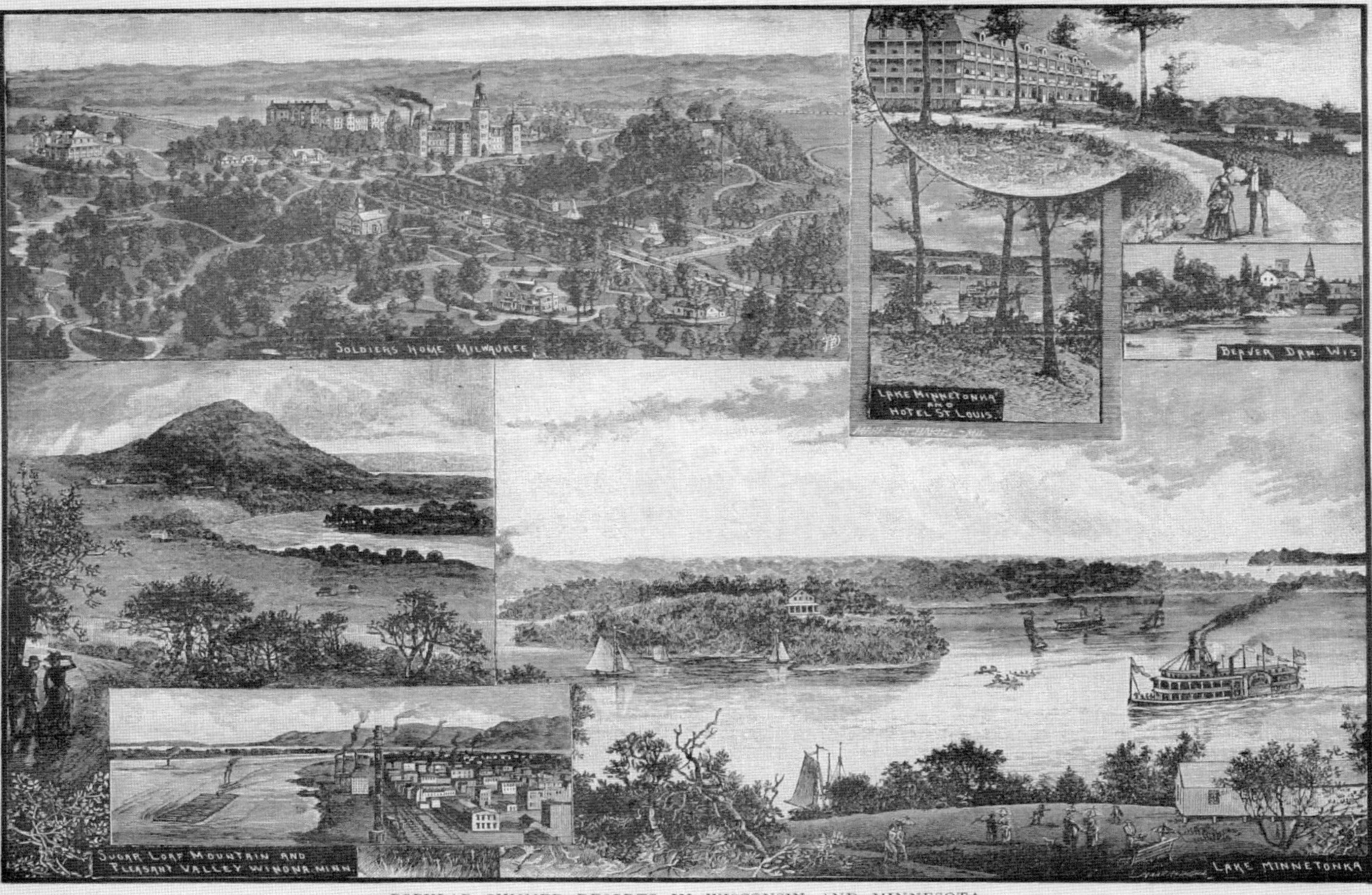

POPULAR SUMMER RESORTS IN WISCONSIN AND MINNESOTA.
ON THE LINE CHICAGO, MILWAUKEE & ST. PAUL RAILWAY.

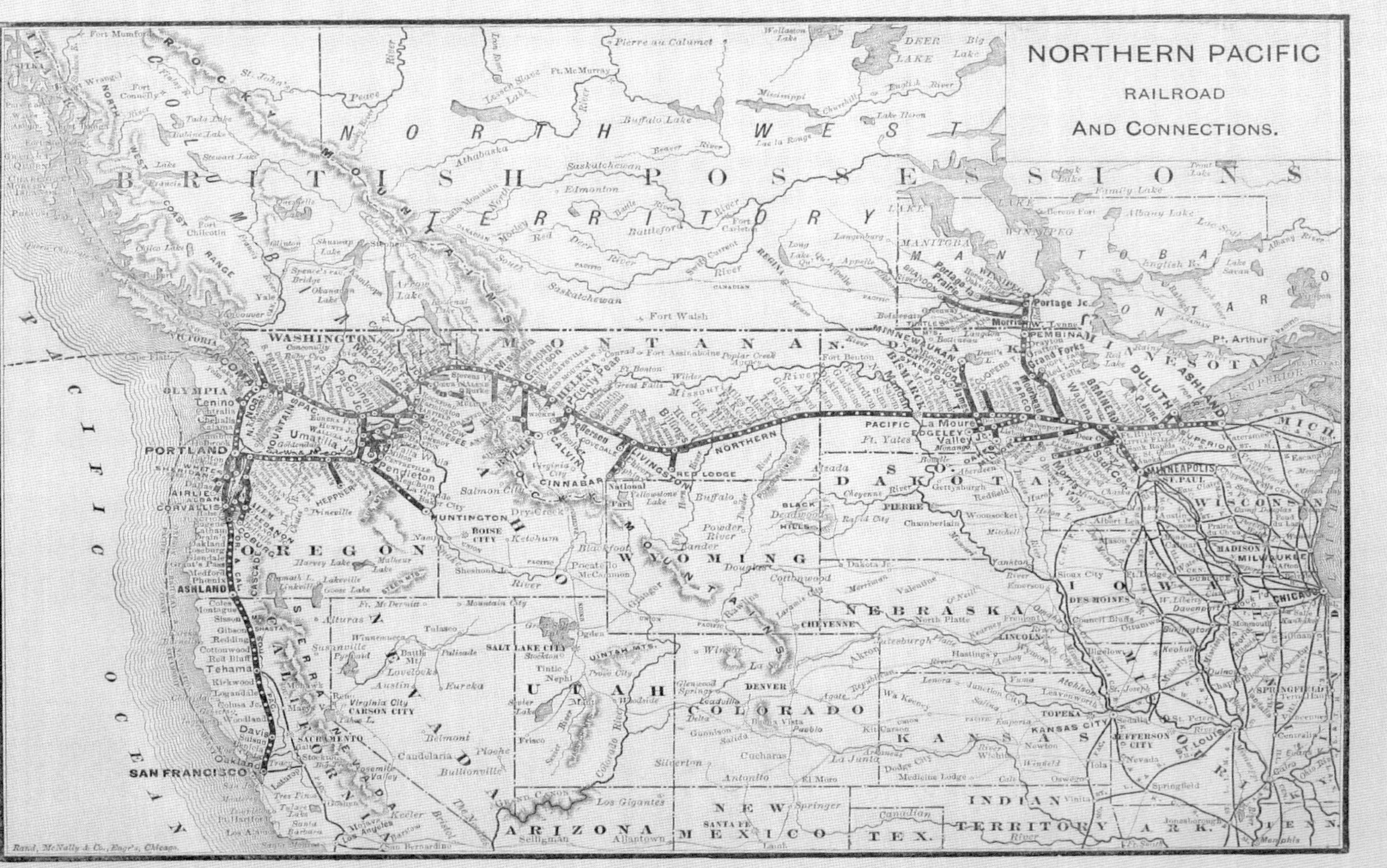
NORTHERN PACIFIC
RAILROAD
AND CONNECTIONS.
BRITISH POSSESSIONS
NORTH WEST TERRITORY
MANITOBA
ONTARIO
WASHINGTON
MONTANA
IDAHO
OREGON
WYOMING
DAKOTA
MINNESOTA
WISCONSIN
IOWA
NEBRASKA
NEVADA
UTAH
COLORADO
KANSAS
MISSOURI
CALIFORNIA
ARIZONA
NEW MEXICO
INDIAN TERRITORY
TEX.
ARK.
PACIFIC OCEAN
PORTLAND
TACOMA
OLYMPIA
SAN FRANCISCO
ASHLAND
HELENA
LIVINGSTON
BISMARCK
FARGO
BRAINERD
DULUTH
MINNEAPOLIS
ST. PAUL
CHICAGO
MILWAUKEE
Rand, McNally & Co., Engr's, Chicago.

THE NORTHERN PACIFIC.

The Only Through Line to Tacoma Direct from Chicago to the City of Destiny—Unsurpassed in Equipment by any other Transcontinental Line.

HAT is the Northern Pacific railroad to the "City of Destiny?" What is it not? Both questions can be answered at once; the Northern Pacific founded Tacoma, heralded her resources and advantages to the world, and is attracting vast capital to make her the greatest seaport, manufacturing and financial center of the Pacific coast, and is daily bringing capitalists, investors and merchants to build up the city, farmers to till the soil of Washington, miners and surveyors to uncover the immense mineral wealth of the surrounding country, and lumbermen to send her great timber in every conceivable form to all parts of the world. All this and more has been done by this road, and all the facts will be vividly brought to the reader by a thorough perusal of "Tacoma Illustrated."

THE ROAD'S EQUIPMENT

is surpassed by no road in the country, and equaled by few; it is safe to say that the Pacific Express which leaves St. Paul at 4:15 P. M. each day, takes with it as much comfort and enjoyment, gladdens the eye with more fascinating splendor of scenery, more interesting country, and causes more wonderment at the magic development of our Western country by the hand of man, than any other route to the Pacific coast.

The management of the road has added to its equipment all the modern improvements. Its trains are all vestibuled, and there is no convenience which experience could suggest that has not been provided. The sleeping cars of the company are models of what is possible to be done. The company recently received a number from the Pullman shops. They were on exhibition in St. Paul and were inspected by hundreds of people. It is not only the first-class passenger trade that the company is catering to, but the second class as well. The tourist cars, or as they are vulgarly called "emigrant sleeping cars," are in keeping with the Pullman sleepers. They contain everything needed for a pleasant and comfortable journey, and are so fitted up that the strictest privacy can be had. In this latter particular they are superior to any tourist car running west of the Mississippi or Missouri Rivers. The immense passenger travel the company is now having shows plainly how well its efforts to satisfy its patrons in this direction are appreciated. The freight equipment is in keeping with the passenger. Its cars contain the latest improved contrivances, and the danger of wrecks is reduced to a minimum.

THE SCENIC ROUTE WEST

on the Northern Pacific Railroad for varied, grand and peculiar scenery, far surpasses any road of equal length in the country. At the eastern end of this transcontinental highway is Lake Superior, the greatest lake in the world. At its western end is the Pacific, the greatest ocean in the world, Puget Sound, the most picturesque inland sea in the world, and the Columbia River, the finest scenic river in the world. No mountains in the Alps surpass in grandeur the gigantic, solitary snow peaks of the Cascade Range. In Northern Minnesota are hundreds of small lakes as lovely as those of Scotland and Ireland. In the Bad Lands of Dakota is a singular region, where subterranean fires are still burning, and where forests have been petrified and strata of blue clay converted into red scoriæ. The Yellowstone National Park, reached by rail only by way of the Northern Pacific, is the world's wonderland, attracting tourists from every part of the civilized globe to gaze upon its surpassing geysers, its boiling mud pools, its cliffs of shining black obsidian, its profound cañons, where the rocks have been painted by nature with rainbow colors, and its inspiring Rocky Mountain scenery. From Tacoma, the western terminus of the Northern Pacific, steamers make the round trip from Alaska in about two weeks, a distance of over 2,000 miles. This is beyond question the most superb marine excursion in the world, showing to the tourist the loftiest mountain peaks of the continent, glaciers, icebergs and beautiful land-locked bays, straits and estuaries. The route is entirely between islands and the mainland, so that, although the whole voyage is on salt water, there is no suffering from sea sickness.

The tide of immigration has increased immensely in the past year, which is evinced principally by the heavy passenger movement toward the North Pacific coast.

THE NATURAL RESOURCES

of Washington are so varied and extensive, and the climate so mild and healthful, that no falling off in the tide of immigration to that field is anticipated until the present population, about 250,000, shall be increased to at least 1,000,000.

The facts we furnish will convince even the most incredulous how far greater these resources are, than they can possibly be pictured. There are many parts of the country from which there has been an ebb tide of disgusted immigration; not so with those who leave the East to make their home in the prolific State of Washington; these find themselves imbued with wonderment at the vast fields of prosperity open to them, and with a corresponding love for their new home. Thrift and prosperity lead to happiness, and it is well nigh impossible to find any one settling in this grand country who is not thoronghly enthusiastic over his adopted home, and anxious to promote its prosperity.

Those who expect to land in a wilderness will find the march of civilization more pronounced here than in many of the Middle States, and in these days of traveling, equaling in comfort even one's own fireside, it is absurd to say that the journey to Washington is too tedious; neither is the expense one of great significance. New comers will find plenty of encouragement and plenty of substantial assistance in the pursuance of their vocation; they will find good institutions of religion and learning for their children, and the finest climate on the face of the earth.

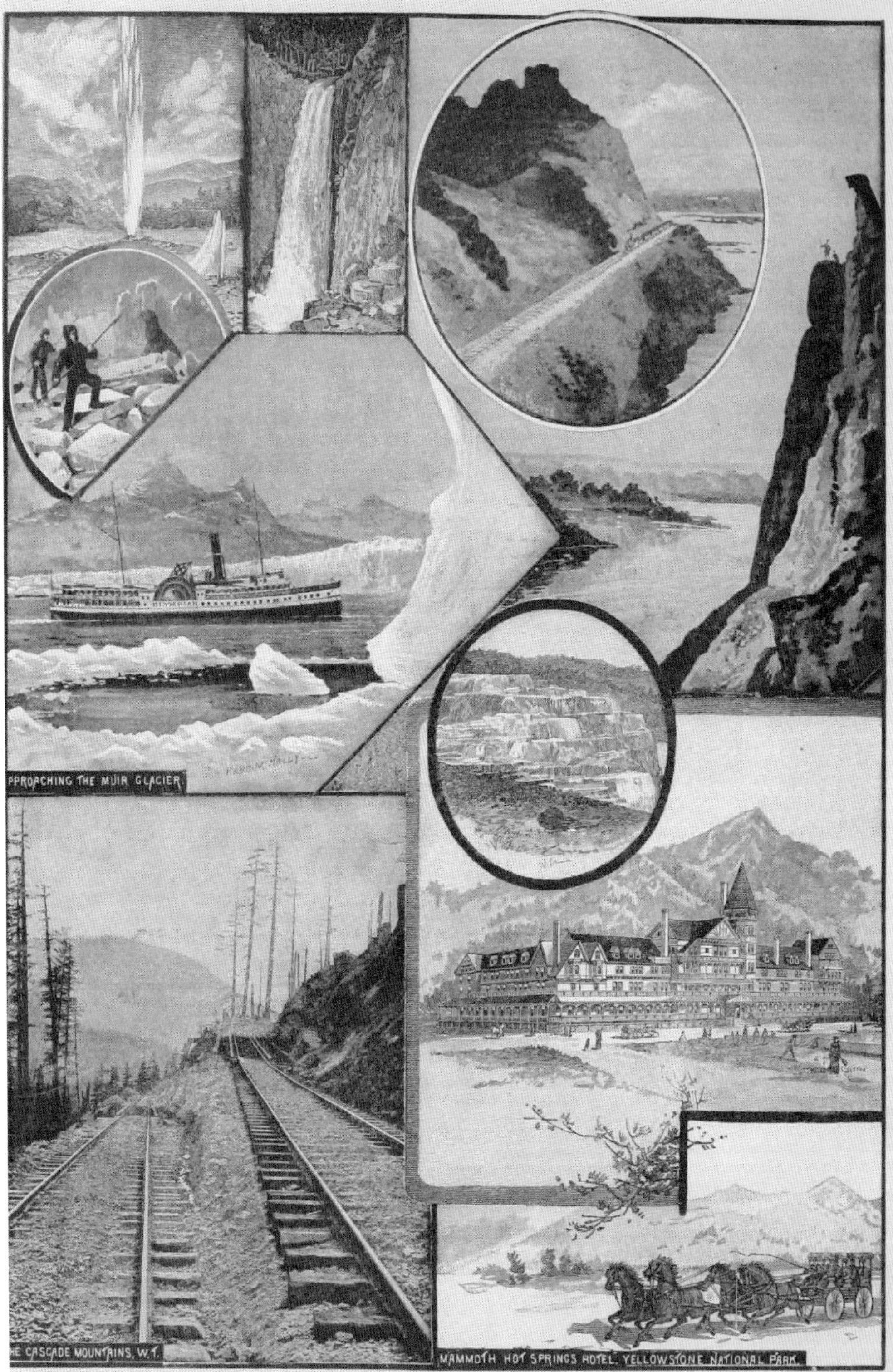

VIEWS ON LINE OF THE NORTHERN PACIFIC.